The Gender of Latinidad

The Gender of Latinidad

Uses and Abuses of Hybridity

Angharad N. Valdivia

Registered Offices
John Wiley & Sons, Inc., 111 River Street, Hoboken, NJ 07030, USA
John Wiley & Sons Ltd, The Atrium, Southern Gate, Chichester, West Sussex, PO19 8SQ, UK

Editorial Office
The Atrium, Southern Gate, Chichester, West Sussex, PO19 8SQ, UK

For details of our global editorial offices, customer services, and more information about Wiley products visit us at www.wiley.com.

Library of Congress Cataloging-in-Publication Data

Names: Valdivia, Angharad N., author.
Title: The gender of Latinidad : uses and abuses of hybridity / Angharad N. Valdivia.
Description: First Edition. | Hoboken : Wiley-Blackwell, 2019. | Includes
    bibliographical references and index.
Identifiers: LCCN 2019040140 (print) | LCCN 2019040141 (ebook) |
    ISBN 9781405163385 (Paperback) | ISBN 9781119574965 (adobe pdf) |
    ISBN 9781119574972 (epub)
Subjects: LCSH: Hispanic American women. | Women in popular culture–United States. |
    Hispanic Americans. | Mass media and minorities–United States. |
    Commodification–United States.
Classification: LCC E184.S75 V335 2019 (print) | LCC E184.S75 (ebook) |
    DDC 305.48/86872073–dc23
LC record available at https://lccn.loc.gov/2019040140
LC ebook record available at https://lccn.loc.gov/2019040141

Cover Design: Wiley
Cover Image: © Angharad N. Valdivia

Set in 10/12pt Warnock by SPi Global, Pondicherry, India
Printed and bound in Singapore by Markono Print Media Pte Ltd

10 9 8 7 6 5 4 3 2 1

Gracias a la vida que me ha dado tanto
Me ha dado el sonido y el abecedario
Con el las palabras que pienso y declaro
Madre, amigo, hermano y luz alumbrando
La ruta del alma del que estoy amando
Violeta Parra

I dedicate this book to ICR Nation, present, past, and (hopefully) future.

Contents

Contents

Acknowledgments

I began to write this book over a decade ago. I proposed it to Jayne Fargnoli, then my editor at Wiley-Blackwell, who sent it out for review and approved its publication. Meanwhile, a number of events delayed its progress, such as a 5-year period serving as administrator of two academic units, the Institute of Communications Research and the Department of Media and Cinema Studies; editorship of a major journal, *Communication Theory*; editorship of a seven-volume encyclopedia, *The International Encyclopedia of Media Studies*; injuries sustained after a major car accident; and continued attacks on my academic home, the Institute of Communications Research. The latter has been the most demoralizing and time-consuming. Being able to finish this book feels like resilient victory over natural, bureaucratic, and neoliberal elements. Of course, I could not have accomplished any of it without a circle of support.

Jayne Fargnoli, my first editor, supported and nourished this project and two others. I miss her gentle yet firm guidance. Unwittingly, the book process charts the turbulent waters of academic publishing, with its rapid rate of editorial staff turnover. I finish the book with Mohan Jayachandran as my Wiley editor. I know that none of our work as scholars could be accomplished without the unsung labor of press editors.

As a member of the faculty at the Institute of Communications Research, I have had the fortune of working with world-class research assistants and collaborating with faculty whose awesomeness truly amazes me. As I began the final push on this manuscript, Diana Leon-Boys functioned as my uber-research assistant, editor, and sounding board. I look forward to her scholarship and hope mine did not delay hers. Morten Kristensen Stinus, another world-class scholar in the making, provided additional excellent editorial assistance. Neither he nor I could figure out what happened to Salma Hayek's CVS Nuance product line, though we tried. I finished the book while writing with the Friday Afternoon Writing Retreat Group, composed of Meghan Grosse, Diana Leon-Boys, Andrea Ruehlicke, elizaBeth Simpson, and Alejandra Aguero. Scheduling this regular Friday writing retreat – which always ends with a champagne toast – is truly one of the most brilliant and effective ideas I have ever had!

I hope the other writers experienced as much productivity within such an enjoyable setting and group as I did.

Two semester leaves allowed me time to develop Chapters 2 and 3. In fall 2014, I spent a well-earned administrative leave in Madrid, Spain. In fall 2016, I divided my half-year sabbatical between Madrid and Solana Beach, California. I wish this for all of you: the opportunity to write in a wonderful global city and by the Pacific Ocean.

Some of the material in this book has been presented at conferences and talks, and some of it was published in earlier and less-developed versions. Kelly Gates invited me to present an early version of the Girl Disney and Spitfire chapters at UCSD, which allowed me to sharpen my arguments. I first elaborated on utopia and Latinidad at a film conference at Indiana University organized by John Nieto-Phillips. My first stab at a written version was previously published as "Implicit Utopias and Ambiguous Ethnics: Latinidad and the Representational Promised Land" in the *Routledge Companion to Latina/o Media Studies.* I especially want to thank Maria Elena Cepeda for her editing and help on that chapter, as well as for her unfailing valuation of my scholarship. I write with a little Maria Elena in my head, my Latina version of the Id. The Spitfire chapter received a well-deserved tightening as a result of a presentation at the Hispanic/Latinx Research & Creativity Symposium at Texas Tech University. Thanks, Kent Wilkinson, for the opportunity to share my research with your faculty and students.

Academic waters are turbulent, and having genuine friendly colleagues makes the neoliberal and postracial attack on public education somewhat bearable. Isabel Molina-Guzmán has been my colleague, friend, and fellow Critical Gender and Ethnic Studies traveling companion for decades. Despite an incredibly busy schedule, she took time to give me line-by-line advice on this manuscript. Without John Nerone's friendship and advice, as well as his revision and reorganization of the Utopia chapter, this book would have never been finished. Leslie Reagan always provides a listening ear and a way to navigate myself out of professional and intellectual turmoil. Her feminist historical research deserves every award it has earned, and many more that are yet to come. I draw on the wisdom, scholarship, and friendship of Sarah Projansky. I miss her daily since she left us for the University of Utah. We co-administered and ethically tried to defend a unit under fire. Her research on Girls Studies remains a model for me, especially in the Disney chapter. Mentors and fellow scholars Cliff Christians, Paula Treichler, and Norman Denzin provide me with models of academic excellence and integrity. I remain thankful to have worked in their company and belonged to what was once a functional unit full of integrity and a democratic vision. I have experienced working in a temporary academic utopia – I know it's possible.

I belong to circles of friendship and scholarship that nourish me. I met Sharon Mazzarella when we were both young and overwhelmed first-year doctoral students, and we've sustained our friendship and intellectual collaborations all of these years. Our parallel academic paths have now intersected through Girls Studies. Since the early days in Feminist Media Studies, Radha Hegde and I have connected on issues of gender and the global. I am an interloper and admirer of her sophisticated postcolonial analysis. I hired Safiya Noble to our faculty when I was head of department and realized that, though she was tenure-tracked, she'd be lured away within the year – and I was right. Her approach and commitment to social change through her scholarship inspire me. I am thankful that Lori Lopez had the brilliant idea to create the Race and Media conference so that senior and junior scholars could form a network of connections to grow a field. I've attended two of its four meetings and have found them to be temporary utopic spaces where a small group of scholars functions in community to listen to, support, and extend our work. I am so honored to just sit, listen, and learn from Ralina Joseph, Leilani Nishime, Roopali Mukherjee, and the many other brilliant scholars who regularly attend that conference. Fellow Latina feminists Maria Elena Cepeda, Jessica Retis, and Viviana Rojas compose a growing area of studies. In Spain, I count on the scholarly spirit and friendship of Paloma Diaz-Soloage and Amparo Porta Navarro, whose suggestion to lengthen the four chapters rather than composing a fifth, which I did not want to write, paved the way for the conclusion of this book.

My transnational feminist GNO has been life-saving – the founders, Manisha Desai, Faranak Miraftab, Zsuzsa Gille, Lisa Rosenthal, and Angelina Cotler, carved out a space of sociality and survival in what has become an increasingly hostile institution. Without Faranak Miraftab's constant insistence that I begin writing my book about my personal history, I would not have pushed myself to finish this one. Newer members of the GNO, Dede Ruggles, Terri Barnes, Helga Varden, Shelley Weinberg, and Elena Delgado, expand our group's areas of expertise as their presence contributes solidarity and mirth. Helga took a bunch of us hiking in the sub-Artic circle of Norway. Dede takes me through Spain with the sharp eye of a globally renown Islamic art expert. We all want Terri Barnes to run for president. The transnational feminist GNO does not forget that we are the winners of the second wave of US feminism: we got our degrees, were hired at Research 1 universities, were promoted, and if we haven't been fulled yet, we certainly will be. We will continue to pay it forward. We will not buckle down. The academy needs us, is lucky to have us, and we will keep at it.

Working at the Institute of Communications Research has meant that I have had the privilege of working with world-class students, who easily surpass me once they graduate. I read their dissertations and humbly return to my less sophisticated work in progress, ready to reference their work and sharpen my analysis. Within the period I wrote this book, I have learned from all of my former advisees: Carrie Rentschler, Boatema Boateng, Kelly Gates, Lori Reed, Diem-my Bui, Jillian Baez, Dennis Redmond, Christina Ceisel, Rich Potter,

Mei Bai, Michelle Rivera, Alicia Kozma, Arnau Roig Mora, Koeli Goel, Rico Chenyek, Stephanie Brown, and Meghan Grosse. My former RA Susan Harewood, on whose committee I participated, remains one of my heroes. It is taking me years to get over her departure (I am still working on it). My current advisees, Diana Leon-Boys, Morten Stinus Kristensen, elizaBeth Simpson, and Stephen Hocker, collectively promise to extend the boundaries of our interdisciplinary field. #BESTJOBEVER!!!

I am a family person with an extensive family network. Mom, sisters, brothers, in-laws, nephews and nieces, cousins, and grandchildren. I have been blessed by three children, two daughters and a son, who have grounded me, made me a better person, and revealed my faults and shortcomings. My daughters Ailín del Carmen and Rhiannon are sharp, beautiful, and brilliant beings. Any style or common sense I have acquired, I owe to them. Lucas = happiness, pure and simple. I am still waiting for Tobin to come home. Cameron remains my rock, my sage, my funny partner, my solid supporter, and my irrepressible and unstoppable traveling companion – through the world and through life. I live surrounded by love, and I wish this for everyone.

Gracias a la vida, que me ha dado tanto.

1

Continuities and Ruptures

The Gender of Latinidad

...the gendered subject of globalization, far from being self-evident or transparent as often assumed, has to be situated within shifting formations of power.

(Hegde 2011, p. 1)

When I started, I was labeled "exotic." That was it. It was like you had to be mysterious and sexual. Back in the day if you were Latina it was always a stereotype. They couldn't write you as a normal person in the world. [Director] Robert Rodriguez was kinda the first person who made Latinos commercial in his movies, like in the Spy Kids franchise. And then Jennifer Lopez and Salma Hayek [helped pave the way]. It was tough in the beginning.

(Jessica Alba, quoted by Brown 2018, p. 93)

In this millennial rewriting of Latina/o media history, Jessica Alba, a 37-year-old Latina mogul, takes us back to Robert Rodriguez's success story, begun in 1991, and Jennifer Lopez's *Fly Girl* days in 1992 – or perhaps to her major starring role in *Selena*, in 1997. Salma Hayek also crossed over to Hollywood from Mexico in 1991 but did not achieve a major role until she landed a part in Robert Rodriguez's *Desperado* (1995). Alba nails a historically significant period of Latina/o popular culture ascendance in which Latina/os functioned in particular roles but managed to rupture stereotypes and achieve lasting inclusion in the entertainment industry. All of those mentioned by Alba remain in the spotlight today: Robert Rodriguez, Jennifer Lopez, and Salma Hayek have not disappeared. Indeed, their careers are solid, their legacy secure. Jessica Alba herself continues to have success as a cover girl and neoliberal entrepreneur, creator and owner of the billion-dollar Honest Company, selling organic and environmentally sustainable baby and beauty products. All of these prominent popular culture Latina/os have a broad range of provenances and function in relation to one another and to other ethnicities within a national and global terrain of mainstream media. None of them are pure, nor do they resemble

The Gender of Latinidad: Uses and Abuses of Hybridity, First Edition. Angharad N. Valdivia.
© 2020 John Wiley & Sons Ltd. Published 2020 by John Wiley & Sons Ltd.

one another. Yet, they represent mainstream Latinidad. Their varied careers, geographical and professional roots, and visibility speak to the gender of Latinidad in contemporary mainstream media.

One undeniably enduring component of any politics of inclusion continues to be mainstream media – whether legacy, digital, or thoroughly converged – as this serves to circulate narratives with embedded ideologies to a wide swath of the population. So-called "minority" populations deserve presence, respect, and dignity in the mainstream because they/we are part of the mainstream, and expectations that apply to mainstream presence go to the core of citizenship issues (Amaya 2013; Casillas 2014). This book focuses on Latinidad as a broad multiplicitous and diverse category of ethnicity that is pan-national, multi-ethnic, intersectional, and transnational. Latinidad is a flexible and unstable hybrid construct whose mediated presence remains salient in the new millennium and indexes broader currents of population mixtures, resulting demands, and backlashes from and through the mainstream, which both construct and are constructed by the cultural struggle identified so long ago by Gramsci, amended by Bauman, and articulated to media by Shohat and Stam (1995).

Thoroughly grounded in a set of analytical frameworks derived from the intersection of Media and Cultural Studies, Gender Studies, and Latina/o Studies, as a form of Ethnic Studies, *The Gender of Latinidad* explores the tension between the politically necessary strategic essentialism that identity categories rely on to make demands upon the state and the impossibility or untenability of maintaining these categories as discrete and easily identifiable – the conundrum of authenticity. Moreover, *The Gender of Latinidad* explores this tension as it is played out through the bodies of and cultural forms signifying girls and women. Given the growing institutionalization of Latina/o Studies as a pan-ethnic construct, this project sets out to contribute to an extension of existing paradigms.[1] As a way to understand the increased acknowledgment of the heterogeneous complexity of Latina/o populations, industries, and cultural forms, *The Gender of Latinidad* draws extensively on hybridity and mixed race as essential, recurring, and unifying concepts for understanding the contemporary situation of ethnicity and the media. Given that the Latina/o population and Latina/o popular culture encompass a wide range of origins – perhaps running the gamut of origin possibilities – *The Gender of Latinidad* maintains a tension between identifying and acknowledging Latinidad, allowing or erasing its multiplicity, and identifying its spillage into other ethnic categories or markers. Ultimately, this book explores the tension between the top-down efforts by media industries to market ethnicity and the bottom-up pressures and efforts to gain employment, expand visibility, and transform the mainstream. What are some of the current degrees of freedom? Rules of engagement? Who benefits within Latinidad? The material conditions that segregate racialized communities and generate bottom-up community pride formation, as well as strategies for inclusion in the body politic and in mainstream culture, coexist with efforts to exploit newly created niche audiences for the purposes of increasing profit. Latina/os draw on symbolic resources to maintain an identity and draw from a shared history even as their massive mobility and mixture generate a hybrid culture. Mainstream media industries draw on an archive and an overflow of talent and creativity from ethnicized populations to pick and choose what fits best with their vision of "multiculturalism." Latina/os must disrupt and provide their vision, which itself is contested due to their heterogeneity.

The year is 2019. In the past 5 years, Latina/os have been highly visible in a range of mainstream television programs, post-network digital offerings, and feature-length films, such as *Modern Family* (ABC, 2009–19), *Jane the Virgin* (CW, 2014–19), *Narcos* (Netflix, 2015–), *East Los High* (Hulu, 2013–17), *Coco* (Disney, 2017), *One Day at a Time* (Netflix, 2017–19), and *Beatriz at Dinner* (Killer Films/Bron Studios, 2017). Latina/os are present on the screen, behind the screen, and as audiences. As we explore and analyze visibility through presence, production, and interpretation, we need to consider the demands for visibility as a complex process and dynamic that encompasses the trifecta of media studies – production, content, and representation – in relation to issues of cultural citizenship, the inescapable hybridity that works against the fantasy of authenticity, and the implicit utopia that is both never articulated and always beyond the possible. As Latina/o Media Studies ascends into a field of its own, in relation to a number of interdisciplinary projects, it also experiences the limits and possibilities of expansion, dilution, and acknowledged hybridity. It was much easier for hegemonic forces to produce mainstream popular culture and proceed when a simplified purity and imposed homogeneity prevailed as dominant discourses. From a mostly white mainstream, to a Derridean juxtaposition of white and black bodies and narratives, to the inclusion of the homogenized bronze[2] race, to the suggestion of AfroLatinidad, the presence of Latina/os disrupts easy narratives of the US national imaginary. Moreover, because the United States has been an imperial power and thus US media conglomerates function across a global terrain, these narratives circulate transnationally. Thus, the visibility of US Latina/os has global implications, though these remain to be extensively researched.

Latina/os unsettle the US racial binary arrangement. Latina/o internal diversity poses many challenges to strategies for inclusion. We can no longer pretend that Latina/os are a pure group – the "bronze" race – nor that Latina/os remain within Latinidad, in terms of culture, reproduction, and geographic mobility. Latina/os fan out globally (both racially and geographically), sample and mix culture globally, and reproduce across ethnic, national, and cultural groups. In sum, Latina/os are inescapably hybrid, and any analysis of visibility or activism through media must take this mixture and hybridity into account. Latina/os lead hybrid lives, consume a hybrid diet of hybrid media, and deserve to be treated in relation to their hybridity. While this book focuses on gendered

Latinidad in contemporary mainstream media, a hybrid analysis can be made for all other ethno-racial groups (e.g. Washington, 2017b). Issues of mixed race and hybridity apply across the racial spectrum. Nonetheless, mixed-race studies and postracial studies still cohere around transnational feminist studies, which in many ways precede all of these areas in providing a bridge between nation and transnation, ethnicity and mixed race, and gender and transgender. The concept of hybridity connects Latina/o Studies to Feminist Media Studies, as it connects Media Studies to Ethnic Studies.

Whether we are looking at the academic location, salience, and influence of Latina Feminist Media Studies or at the media and public discourse inclusion of Latinidad as a gendered construct, with enduring narrative tropes assigned to a binary gendered terrain, there is undeniable presence. The objective of this book is to explore contemporary strategies for gendered visibility in a range of mainstream forms of popular culture. The prism of the female body, drawing on extensive gender scholarship, is chosen precisely because, historically, the female body has been used to carry out national identity struggles and struggles over the belonging of the ethnic subject. For example, López (1991) documents the Hollywood representation of Latin American women, and by extension US Latinas, as a double threat – sexual and racial – to the dominant popular culture and, by implication, the nation. The threat represented by Latinas is likely to be overrepresented across a range of discourses, from the oversignified freeway signs foregrounding the female gendered border crossers, discussed by Ruiz (2002) and now fronting a popular T-shirt in Southern California, to the development and wildly successful marketing of ambiguously ethnic doll brands such as Bratz and Flavas (Valdivia 2004a, 2005a, b, c).

Latina/os are part of the population, part of the electorate, part of business, part of media industries and representation, and part of the cultural fiber of the United States. Latina/o culture is a core component of the United States – whether in terms of food, as in the recent taco truck moment or the more dated salsa over ketchup historical marker; of music, with all the Latina/o-influenced genres that circulate and hybridize in the United States, such as samba, salsa, merengue, reggaeton, and hip hop; or of literature, with major authors such as Sandra Cisneros, Junot Diaz, and Isabel Allende and entire subgenres such as "chica lit." Musicians like Marc Anthony, Daddy Yankee, Juan Gabriel (recently deceased), Los Tigres del Norte, and Enrique Iglesias demonstrate the "hotness" of Latinidad. In fact, if we google "Top Latin Hits," Billboard rewards us with a website entitled "Hot Latin Songs." Rather differently, but still alluding to the hotness of Latinas, the cover of the *Latino Media Gap* has a spotlight on a faceless yet light-brown "cartel gunman #2," a dark-brown "Officer Martinez," and a light-brown "Latina with hot accent" (in a short yellow bodycon spaghetti-strap dress) (Negrón-Muntaner et al. 2014). All of these Latina/o icons reiterate the trope assigned to Latina/os and our culture: a dangerous masculinity and an exotic and sexualized female othering that continues unabated within the mainstream, and which scholars find in their research about Latina/os and the mainstream media.

In 2019, the presence, significance, and popularity of social and digital media is inescapable and undeniable. As with previous media, original "common wisdom" about Latina/o absence or indifference is not borne out by research. Whereas it was once thought that Latina/os did not read mainstream media, Selena's death news repeatedly selling out *People* magazine issues led to *People en Español* – a weird response, given that the issues Latina/os were purchasing were written in English. Research continues to deliver the findings that there are millions of Latina/os who consume English-language media (e.g. Chavez 2015). A report by Pew Research (Flores and Lopez 2018) reveals that for US Latina/os, the internet rivals legacy television as a source of news. That study reiterates that radio remains an important source of information for Latina/os. Latina/os appear in and consume media across the spectrum.

In presence and erasure, Latina/os stand in for the imagined nation. They/we track the interstices and struggles of the contemporary identity crisis that face the United States, which formerly thought of itself as homogenously white or binary in composition (i.e. black and white). The rather recent and reluctant public acknowledgment that Latina/os are a numerically and culturally significant part of the United States documents the fact that from its very beginning, the country was anything but homogeneous. Prior to the relentless settler colonialism enacted since the 17th century, native populations were numerous and heterogeneous. Involuntary waves of slaves and "voluntary"[3] waves of immigrants from every region of the globe have continued to expand the heterogeneity of the US population. Maintaining a predominantly white mainstream media has taken an enormous amount of exclusionary labor. Given that a huge chunk of the continental United States was Mexico until 1848, and that border crossings were not considered as such – that is, they were not named, articulated, and regulated – the flow of Latin Americans into and out of the US national space was fluid. The presence of what is now known as the US Latina/o[4] dates back to the birth of the US nation, and even before. Waves of slaves and migrants from Africa and the other continents further complicated the homogeneous fiction assiduously circulated by the mainstream – a fiction that had to be sustained, as all political fictions do, through unequal power arrangements. Present and culturally productive US Latina/os have been excluded – an active process. Resistance to demands, refusal to employ, insistence on rehashing old genres and tropes, all form part of the conscious labor of exclusion – that is, the active construction of a fictitious homogeneity.

The institutional level of analysis rests above the organizational layer, wherein, at the site of production of media, decisions and routines serve to perpetuate existing arrangements. In a capitalist economy – or, rather, in a capitalist global system – the search for profits reigns supreme. From an industrial perspective, the inexorable search for increased profits must include an effort to discover new audiences, beyond the mass audiences that had previously been conceptualized as white. Looking for audience niches involves the tricky task of not alienating the dominant white audience. The search for new audiences in the 21st century reaches out to previously ignored segments such as women, working-class people, nonheteronormative people, and people of color. The tension between identifying these "niches" to begin with and moving to the realization that niches are not mutually exclusive, within or without Latinidad, is a rather big lesson for an industry that remains mired in whiteness or with a binary black and white representational terrain and audience conceptualization. Latinas are part of all these targeted audiences, and their/our hybridity makes us as desirable as we are slippery, in terms of being difficult to peg down concerning our presence, predilections, affect, and attention. Moreover, our belonging within multiple Latinidades (Báez 2007) and across ethnicities and races further muddles efforts to track us, to include us, certainly to coopt us, and totally to market to us.

The complexity of Latinidad derives from and informs the global circulation of mainstream media. Narratives and situations must be produced with acknowledgment of global flows and diversity. This is not an altruistic enterprise. Rather, from an industrial perspective, a global sensitivity potentially increases audiences, and therefore profits. If done well, frontloading the global possibilities can pay abundant dividends, not only for a particular media vehicle, but also for many more products in a franchise, for a particular company, genre, or actor (Meehan 2005). Indeed, given the synergy deployed by the major media conglomerates, initial global attention is the crack in the door through which massive investments will hopefully yield consistent, long-term returns. Economic figures support this global move. Traditionally, in the network era, US mainstream producers of television shows recouped a large portion of their production costs with the large US audience. Global circulation of these media vehicles, leading to multiple syndications, was merely the icing on the cake of a very profitable national distribution model. In the contemporary post-network era, when conglomerates release their films simultaneously across a range of countries, or parse out releases to coincide with national holidays, the global is no longer the afterthought but the very core of a distribution strategy. In fact, film production has experienced a flip of its 80/20 budget model – that is, whereas through the 1980s, Hollywood film planned to recoup 80% of its investment with domestic audiences, nowadays the aim is for 80% to come from global audiences. Another facet of media industry expansion alongside Latina/o exclusions is that mergers of Latina/o-targeting media do not include Latina/os in the process. No apparent upward mobility from entry-level to executive ranks in the merged top brass exists for Latina/os working in Latina/o-targeted media industries. Workers from the Latina/o or Spanish-language side do not move to the merged English company. Negrón-Muntaner and Abbas (2016) found that Latina/o media underemployment is actually accelerated by media market consolidation.

The large sums that it takes to greenlight a Hollywood blockbuster, such as the now ubiquitous superhero movie, apparently have caused Latina/os nearly to disappear from our screens when such movies are shown. This generates an internal contradiction, in that big-budget movies apparently prefer a racialized binary, but these movies are supposed to appeal to a global population whose composition is much more complex than black and white. Indeed, the global majority is "brown," even as Hollywood film remains either uninformed or resistant to this fact (Silva 2016). Music, digital gaming, advertising campaigns, and pornography all include Latina/o production and representation, but the continuities are far greater than the ruptures. Today's US Latina/os continue to appear in the mainstream mostly according to stereotype, and more often in sidekick or background roles than as protagonists. However, we cannot pretend that nothing has changed. Indeed, numerical analyses show both gains and losses that run counter to linear hopes of incremental improvement (e.g. Negrón-Muntaner et al. 2014; Negrón-Muntaner and Abbas 2016).

Some of the most promising theoretical and conceptual developments for an exploration of Latinidad in mainstream media are the inclusion of hybridity (Lowe 1991; Kraidy 2006), multiracial studies (e.g. Nishime 2014), and mixed-race studies (Washington 2017b). Challenging our field to consider hybridity in conjunction with international communications, Kraidy draws on the many intellectual streams that converge in cultural production. I am informed by the mapping of the field of hybridity by Kraniauskas (2000a, b), who identifies a cultural/anthropological strain (Canclini 1995) and a more psychoanalytical literary version (Bhaba 1994), both of which circulate as globally influential versions of hybridity. Mapped over Media Studies, from where I write, this bimodality of contemporary theories of hybridity reminds me of a constructed binary within my field that had largely, but not totally, been abandoned by the late 2010s. The US academy's tendency toward binaries, as well as its rejection of paradigms that criticize structural inequalities, resulted in the 1980s in a juxtaposition between cultural studies and political economy. This fiction was difficult to sustain, as global intellectual traditions inextricably connected these two areas of study (e.g. Cardoso and Faletto 1979; Lowe 1996), and had done so for many decades (O'Connor 1991). I find that the bimodal approaches to hybridity – in literature and anthropology – inherit traces of this divide, which partly is informed by a US academy that despite statements to the contrary, has not fully embraced global intellectual perspectives (see Shome 2016). In terms of the interdiscipline Media and Cultural Studies, there is still relatively little research on Latina/os (Valdivia 2004b), and most of that which exists is medium-specific rather than broad, sweeping across the terrain of mainstream popular culture. Additionally, much – though not all – of the research on media issues is currently carried out by scholars outside of Media Studies, and often reveals a lack of familiarity with sophisticated approaches to the study of media. This project thoroughly combines Latina/o and Media

Studies, taking both interdisciplines as foundational to the study of contemporary popular culture. Moreover, it takes both the textual and the industrial seriously.

Hybridity is not a new term or concept. Though its original use in the 17th century was in a biological sense, much of the resistance to it stems precisely from its racist social applications. Hybrid agricultural plants, for example, are not only more resistant to disease but are also infertile. However, when applied to populations in the 18th century, hybridity was often "invoked by those hostile to racial difference" (Labanyi 2000, p. 56) – usually in conjunction with the term "miscegenation," which connoted unwanted and often illegal reproduction between white women and men of color. This concern was all the more intense in a historical period marked by colonial expansion, which brought many previously separate populations in contact with one another (Young 1995). Miscegenation was legally precluded in some settings so as to preserve both purity and colonial authority, but in others it was encouraged so as to improve, Westernize, and whiten the local population in a positivist quest for racial breeding. Of course, the latter strategy always simultaneously generated fears of the tipping point where the native blood, stock, and bodies would outnumber the racial purity of the white colonizer. Fears of mixing were voiced both by the colonizers and the colonized. For instance, hybridity was reviled by Octavio Paz (1959), who identified the pachuco, a young masculine Mexican American resistant subject, as an instance of depravity. For Paz, this depravity resulted from the mixing of the purity of Mexico with the pollution of the United States. Fears of the contamination, dilution, and disappearance of the pure-white subject continue today, and are central to understanding the contemporary sociopolitical situation wherein Latina/os have become the largest US minority, with some demographic projections showing us becoming the majority sometime in this century. From a Latin American perspective, Paz's sentiments toward US Latina/os have not altogether disappeared. Given that so many producers of mainstream US Latina/o media are actually Latin Americans, this historical trace is not inconsequential. As well, these fears demonstrate the endurance of a biologically and anthropologically untenable belief in purity – though, when people implicitly refer to "purity," this has to be treated as a floating signifier.

Contemporary scholars continue to contribute to this language of cultural tension, collision, mixture, erasure, and displacement. Thus, Mary Louise Pratt uses "zones of contact," Gloria Anzaldúa speaks of "nepantla," Homi Bhabha writes of "mimicry" and a "third space," and Nestor García Canclini uses "hybrid cultures." While its application to population and cultural form is undeniable, there are still many who caution against the wholesale adoption of the concept of hybridity. Foremost among their concerns is the depoliticizing potential of accepting that there is an inevitable mixture and hybridity in everything and that if everything and everyone is hybrid then there is no theoretical validity to the term. Sommer (1991) worries that the deployment of hybridity duplicates national unity movements that seek to rewrite the violent and uneasy history of many Latin American nations. Others are concerned that concepts such as hybridity, mestizaje, syncretism, miscegenation, and assimilation are being used carelessly and interchangeably, flattening historical, geographical, and cultural specificity. Shohat warns that a "celebration of syncretism and hybridity per se, if not articulated in conjunction with questions of hegemony and neocolonial power relations, runs the risk of appearing to sanctify the *fait accompli* of colonial violence" (1991, p. 109). When coupled with a critical assessment of hegemonic relations, the concept is foremost a rejection of essentialist notions, either of gender or of ethnicity and race, as well as an acknowledgment that there is no purity to be found at the level of culture, the body, blood, or DNA.

Since Latina/os represent an instance of radical hybridity, drawing the boundaries around this ethnic group proves to be most challenging. Focusing on Latina/o television, Levine (2001), drawing on Naficy (1993), reminds us that hybridity is unstable and uncomfortable. Not only is it verifiably evident that cities are not the sites of national (let alone ethnic or class) purity – Miami is not purely Cuban American, Los Angeles is not purely Mexican American, New York is not purely Puerto Rican – but also the in-between space (the Midwest, the South, etc.) is populated by fast-growing heterogeneous Latina/o populations that are, in turn, reproducing across the ethnic and racial spectrum. Yet, a range of Latina/o Studies scholars, such as Fusco (1995) and Lugo (2000), remind us that it is far easier for cultural forms to cross borders than it is for human beings, for whom hybridity is often a wrenching lived experience. The lived experience of Latina/o bodies remains a hybrid one, full of ambivalence, tension, and pain despite celebratory and messianic messages of the joys and pressures of globalization. Whereas music, food, and style may cross borders unchecked, bodies are continuously inspected, even after legal and successful border crossings, as Latina/os remain the eternal outsiders within the US political psyche and system. Against this context, media strives to portray and reach the Latina/o audience.

Applying hybridity to US Latinidad and mainstream popular culture must rely on a combination of both versions and take up inherent tensions in locating the concept of US Latina/o within a nation while simultaneously acknowledging that Latinidad cannot be contained by national boundaries and is influenced by hybrid cultures and populations. Historically, at least as far back as the 15th century, Latin American populations were already hybrid, with a mixture of indigenous and settler colonialists, in both South and North America. Therefore, hybridity is not new to Latinidad. Indeed, hybridity may be the most authentic element of US Latina/o culture. Considerations of cultural mixing, as well as of textual hybridity, are inextricably entwined in the commodification of Latinidad. Throughout my work, I draw on the canonical writings of Levine (2001) and Naficy (1993), who usefully outline the difference between hybridity as an unsettled and difficult-to-harness cultural mixture and syncretism, which is a manageable, fixed, and domesticated identity. All through the violent history of the Spanish in the Americas, syncretic outbursts of local populations were allowed to manage indigenous resistance to Roman Catholic imposition. An indigenous deity, for example, would remain behind the painting or sculpture of a virgin or crucifixion. Similarly, the Virgin of Guadalupe and her attendant representations combine Mexican with Spanish religious symbols, and are further infused with feminist iconography (Latorre 2008). Syncretic appropriation is an ongoing process. The effort to domesticate and fix ultimately fails, but at least it slows a tendency toward hybridity. Unsurprisingly, mainstream media industries prefer to produce easy-to-manage syncretic Latina/o material culture and to visualize Latina/o audiences as settled and fixed. Neither the production, the visualization, nor the targeting of the audience engages with the complexity of contemporary Latinidad.

Media scholars, focusing across the racial spectrum, warn us that mixed race is a reality often ignored but nonetheless quite common. For example, in *Undercover Asian*, LeiLani Nishime (2014) seeks to understand how "ideological narratives of race, sexuality, gender, and nation intersect to create or erase multiracial representation..." Kraidy (2006) reminds us of hybridity's controversial history and charges that it represents the lives of elite intellectuals more than providing a useful tool to analyze contemporary global popular culture. However, hybridity is not synonymous with cosmopolitanism, and cultural mixture is not only the province of the rich and well-traveled. To begin with, millions of people engage in involuntary mobility across regions and nations, and there is nothing elite about this forced migration. Along with migration comes hybridity – and US Latina/os, our culture, and our population bear out the mixture of culture, blood, and populations. Hybridity is not an effort to erase power from the equation of mixture and migration. Rather, a major task of media scholars is to tease out the many possibilities of hybridity in the production and consumption of media at each step, given that hybridity does not erase power differentials. Neither the temporary stability achieved by syncretism nor the fluidity of hybrid processes resolves power inequalities. Rather, the syncretic settlement can be called a truce – with the vanquished retaining some form of presence, albeit a negotiated one, as they continue to prepare for the next assault. Hybridity represents a combination of low- and high-intensity cultural conflict. It can be harnessed toward democratic and social-justice goals just as it is more often harnessed to buttress the status quo. It can, as anything else, be used against social movements and segments of the population. Just as some people can voluntarily and luxuriously shop for ethnicity (Halter 2000), others are forced to make do with what is available, to consume from limited options or with limited resources, and to engage with similarly displaced but differently rooted populations.

Thus, hybridity between cultures and populations is inescapable and undeniable, though potentially unacknowledged. Ethnic studies used to be treated as drops of oil on pools of water. African Americans, Asian Americans, Latina/os, and Native Americans were treated as coexisting yet separate groups. While historical and geographical roots differed, they sometimes overlapped. Moreover, given the segregation prevalent in the United States, minoritized groups often share less desirable living locations. As a result of this long-term process, we can begin to discern the acknowledgment of inevitable mixture. For instance, the *Latino Media Gap* (Negrón-Muntaner et al. 2014) notes the presence and incorporation of AfroLatinos as a positive trend. Concordantly, recent research on mixed race and media (Washington 2017b) explores the mixtures that challenge previous assumptions about discrete ethnicities, and expands the possible mixtures beyond white and whatever else. For example, Washington examines Blasians – black Asians. The controversy over the casting of Zoe Saldana as Nina Simone demonstrates mainstream media's tension toward African Americans and the strategic casting of Afro-Latinas (Molina-Guzmán 2013b). Despite the backlash from the African American community at having one of their heroes played by a Latina, the fact remains that Saldana is and identifies herself as a black Latina. Saldana herself is subject to an industry that prefers to cast light Latinas such as Jennifer Lopez for ethnic roles. Industry practices also continue to avoid casting African Americans, especially dark-skinned ones. So, Saldana is too dark to be Latina, and African Americans are too dark to be cast as African Americans. Here is a case that clearly illustrates the uses and abuses of hybridity. The hybrid Afro-Latina body cannot be used for Latinidad, yet it displaces the black body. Consequently, these casting practices pit ethnic communities against one another. Possible interethnic alliances are undermined by the favoring of light skin even for African American roles.

Hybridity is deployed through gendered bodies. Ideally, one of the uses of hybridity could be to reach a space beyond gender binaries. Predictably, one of the abuses is to reinforce gender binaries as natural. Ethnically hybrid characters, when they exist beyond a mere suggestion of more than one ethnicity or race, fall firmly within cisgender categories. We are firmly embedded in a gendered mainstream wherein Latinas sign for Latinidad much more so than Latinos. Latina bodies are sexualized or relegated to abnegation narratives, such as spitfires and dedicated asexual mothers. Ultimately, Latinas are much more visible than Latinos in mainstream popular culture, especially in spectacular forms (Molina-Guzmán 2010). Latinos appear more often as specters of violence and criminality within the current political administration of the United States.

In the 2016 US presidential election, the Republican party, which for decades has courted a section of the electorate that retains whiteness as a premium, generated a successful candidate who combines tendencies to simultaneously racialize and criminalize with a reality television approach to decision making. A love of social media and Twitter rounds out his novel idea of national governance. This toxic mixture of media and narrative results in a rapidly evolving terrain of belonging, whose terms of engagement disfavor US Latina/os regardless of citizenship, race, location, and socioeconomic status. While discrimination is suffered most heavily by those with darker skin, no browned body is safe in this political climate (Silva 2016).

In a book drawing on hybridity, it must be mentioned that we cannot assume homogeneity of political conviction within Latinidad. While it's true that more Latina/os are either Democrats or Independents, there are Latina/o Republicans – especially, though not solely, a powerful and vocal Cuban-American community in Florida. Thus, it came to be that in the thick of the 2016 presidential election, amidst all of the ratings-driven TV coverage that the Republican candidate received, an unexpected supportive statement from Marco Gutierrez, founder of the group Latinos for Trump, appeared. Latinos come from a very dominant culture, he warned. If you don't watch it, you might have "taco trucks on every corner"! Gutierrez's interview with Joy Reid, broadcast on MSNBC on September 1, 2016, immediately went viral on social media and mainstream news. His statements trended for days on Facebook and Twitter, and became a favorite subject of gifs and memes. Classic and contemporary art were recruited for ironic commentary. For instance, a widely circulating visual added a taco truck to Hopper's classic painting, "Nighthawks"; another added one to Munch's "The Scream." Visualizing technologies were added to the debate: a gif showed taco trucks spreading from south of the border throughout the continental United States. The taco truck incident also became a major news item on legacy media – newspapers, television, and radio news. As well, it inspired taco trucks throughout the States to position themselves in front of or close to Trump campaign headquarters (e.g., in Denver). Mostly, people voiced a desire to have more taco trucks in their lives and neighborhoods. Some people posted that they would welcome a taco truck in every corner of their living room. Others outed Marco Gutierrez, the originator of this statement, as a real-estate scammer preying on poor Latinos (Kuns 2016).

This ironic reaction can be read as a repudiation of anti-immigration policies and support for Latina/os in general and Mexican Americans in particular. However, if we heed Coco Fusco's (1995) warning that culture has an easy border crossing whereas the bodies that produce it face stiff barriers, and combine this with a neoliberal preference for a global extraction of wealth transferred to the imperial private sector, then it makes sense that people voice support for tacos while not necessarily supporting amnesty, DACA, or any of the other policies opposed by the current administration's efforts to engage in wide-sweeping immigration reform/rollback of immigrant rights. In other words, one can be pro-tacos and anti-Mexican. President Trump has famously celebrated Cinco de Mayo by eating tacos even as he dedicates himself to policies to restrict the rights and possibilities of US Latina/os and immigrant bodies. Cinco de Mayo itself is a stereotypical US made-up holiday marketed as a national Mexican holiday for the purposes of cultural commodification. As well, salsa surpassed ketchup as the condiment of choice in the United States over 20 years ago. Yet, public embraces of Latina/o culture have not necessarily elicited increasingly humane approaches to Latina/o immigration in the US Congress. To be sure, there is also undeniable backlash, and Mr. Trump's successful candidacy points to the political and cultural value of rhetorical attacks on Mexican Americans in particular and Latina/os in general. Actually, "Mexican" functions as a metonym for all Latina/os in a classic deployment of the flattening of difference. Mexicans serve a unifying function for a political party whose anti-immigration platform serves as its *raison d'être* in the face of irreversible population flows and the changing domestic balance of forces they generate. Mexicans serve as a rhetorical tool to attempt to reverse decades of ambivalently inclusive racial and immigration policies. The return to the mythically pure Mexican body belies the diversity and hybridity within Latinidad but yields a simple figure to be attacked in a concerted effort to return to an imagined past of racial purity. Unfortunately, some Mexicans, such as Marco Gutierrez, contribute to this misplaced hysteria.

We could engage in a slightly more gendered analysis of the taco truck incident by asking who makes up Latinos for Trump. It's hard to tell, as the website was taken down right after the "tacos on every corner" interview. Yet, it deserves to be asked: Why are Latina/o spokespeople in the news almost inevitably male? For example, in the Joy Reid segment on MSNBC, Adriano Espaillat, New York senator and former undocumented youth, represented the counterpoint to Marco Gutierrez, author of the taco comment. No Latinas were interviewed. Soledad O'Brien, one of the few major network television Latina news broadcasters, was relieved of her CNN position in 2013, and currently anchors a political commentary show on Hearst Television Network, a part of her own Starfish Media Group. Even the taco truck rhetoric presumes a male-gendered labor force. Though some of the memes included female cooks, by and large the representational terrain of the taco truck workforce was male. The fear and the discourse about Latinos continues to focus on working-class or unemployed, mostly undocumented males. The fear of rapists, clearly articulated by Trump and displaced on to non-white bodies, is about men. The attempted moral panic over lesbian farmers orchestrated by conservative radio host Rush Limbaugh (August 16, 2016), which preceded and was displaced by the taco truck fiasco, focused only on white women. In the contemporary news environment of fear of the criminal Latino body, men figure prominently and women are nearly absent. The difference with the news coverage of the epidemic of mass shootings is worth mentioning. Whereas most of the recent mass shooting in the United States have been carried out by white males, the mainstream news media seldom calls out the race and gender characteristics of the perpetrators of this violence. On the other hand, with little evidence, both the current administration and Fox News repeatedly and continuously construct a narrative of Latino male criminality.

Latinas largely fall out of the news prism, both as news sources and as news subjects. In comparison, when it comes to celebrities, Latinas sign in as spectacular bodies, as theorized by Isabel Molina-Guzmán (2010). Spectacular Latinas in the mainstream include major figures, enduring names, and new stars. These women can carve out long-term careers that remain remarkably normative in terms of whiteness but show ruptures illustrating the presence of a hybrid and heterogeneous population whose numbers and influence continue to increase. Feminist Media Studies has long tracked the many and ingenious ways in which mainstream media genders populations, genres, and bodies as a discursive means of parsing out power, empowering some and disempowering others between and within ethnic categories. Thus, not surprisingly, we are witnessing a gendered division of Latina/o visibility in mainstream media. There is a fear of Latinos in the news and a desire for curvy Latinas in entertainment. In terms of sources of authority (news anchors and reporters), neither gender is prominent, but Latinos appear more often than Latinas.

The Gender of Latinidad addresses the contemporary situation of Latinidad, the dynamic process of signifying and performing Latina/o peoples and cultural forms, in the United States and, by implication, globally, as US popular culture is exported throughout the world. Focusing on three sites of intervention – historical and contemporary efforts by Latina actors who entered the mainstream as spitfires to construct an enduring career in entertainment; the ambiguous Latinidad constructed by Disney; and an exploration of the tensions within Latinidad about implicit and explicit utopias through the media – this book addresses Latinidad as a constant low-intensity conflict of cultural engagement, negotiation, and deferment carried out by unequally empowered forces. On the one hand are individual Latina actors, who function as representatives of labor and cultural forces, and who seek to carve out a space of presence, belonging, and, hopefully, success. Some major examples are discussed individually in Chapter 2. On the other hand is mainstream media as a whole, with its global power and resources. In particular, Chapter 3 focuses on the Walt Disney company, arguably the biggest global media conglomerate, as it engages in avowal and disavowal of Latinidad. The push and pull of forces come together in the desire for an ideal place, a utopia, whose internally contradictory contours are discussed in Chapter 4.

The book explores the concept of hybridity and applies it to the study of contemporary Latina/os. In particular, it seeks to complement documented demographic and political evidence of increased Latina/o presence with an understanding of the complex terrain of representations and narratives in the mainstream media. *The Gender of Latinidad* investigates some of the many ways that hybridity as a concept is strategically deployed in a range of contemporary media, with strong tendencies to resolve tensions by settling for syncretism. Hybrid launches land as syncretic culture. The energy that sends hybridity off settles in a domesticated manner. Efforts to contain hybridity and to harness it toward increased profitability, the commodification of Latinidad, coexist with unruly bodies and messy categories that threaten to interfere with neatly planned advertising and marketing campaigns, as well as official government efforts to account for, regulate, and service the Latina/o segment of the population. Indeed, the ongoing debates and controversies about Census categories reveal the fissures over both the definition of Latinidad and the acknowledgment of mixed race and hybridity as a challenge to that most official of population accounting. The tendency to "snap back" – that is, to retreat to old-school ethnic categories – is great. It is always easier to rely on outdated yet neat categories than to engage in the far more difficult process of trying to understand and include heterogeneous populations whose lumping together originally occurred out of historical exigency and oppressive undemocratic goals, and not necessarily due to any empirical accuracy. Borders to the north and south of the United States effectively divided pre-existing communities in the name of unifying the nation. Despite an undeniable increase in representation of Latina/os, production and representational analysis, findings are examined in terms of the gains in visibility against the costs, displacements, and erasures generated through it. Visibility is not the only goal. The questions of whose visibility and toward what purposes overlap with hybridity, as, in representing mixed cultures and populations, decisions have to be made as to what to foreground, and *ipso facto* what to displace or leave out.

Nonetheless, Latina/os compose a statistically significant percentage of the US population: 17.6% as of 2019. Projections predict Latina/o population growth, Latina/o consumer power growth, and Latina/o media consumption growth. Historical attention to the Northeast and Southwest has transitioned to acknowledgment that Latina/os are present in every region of the country. In addition to the "flyover" zone of the Midwest (not only Chicago, but other cities and the rural area), there has been Latina/o growth in the Southeast and the Northwest. In sum, Latina/os are part of the fiber of the United States. Latina/o presence has great implications for mainstream media, which prefers the male 18–34 age group as both media and general product consumers. Latina/os are a young demographic, and that fact could have positive expenditure implications for media industries, should they choose to exploit it, in terms of sheer ratings for television and box office receipts for movies. The gendered preference of mainstream advertising rhetoric about the most desired segment of the audience implicitly undervalues women. Exploiting this gender blindspot would be a great asset to media industries, which are constantly actively seeking new "niche" audiences, and would be an opportunity for Latina audiences to assert symbolic ruptures and cultural citizenship (Molina-Guzmán 2010, 2018; Báez 2018).

Because viewership is but a point of entry into the synergistic merchandising, product placement, and tie-ins accompanying any mainstream media circulation, media produced by conglomerates derives profit from integrated global marketing and advertising campaigns. The 18–34-year-old age group has been found to devote more time to media and to have the discretionary income to purchase the products and services implied by the media that it consumes. As the *Latino Media Gap* (Negrón-Muntaner et al. 2014) documents, Latinos are overrepresented (in relation to their percentage of the population) as radio listeners, moviegoers, and social media participants. Thus, including Latina/os in general, and Latinas in particular in the production of media, in their representation and narratives, and in their target audiences seems like a win–win proposition. That this strategy is not being widely deployed once again illustrates that media production is not always about the bottom line but implicitly derives from ethnic and gendered omissions.

The Gender of Latinidad investigates specific representational strategies used in mainstream popular culture that differ, sometimes drastically, from previous efforts to account for and to reach ethnically diverse populations. Drawing on a wealth of research (Molina-Guzmán and Valdivia 2004; Valdivia 2004a, b, 2005a, b, c; Harewood and Valdivia 2005; Calafell 2008; Moreman 2008; Molina-Guzmán 2010; Cepeda 2015, etc.), the book seeks to map the deployment of particular ways of representing the "radical and dynamic relationality" resulting from population and cultural mobility (forced and voluntary). As Shohat (1991) has so brilliantly noted, ethnicities only make sense in relation to other ethnicities, and this is all the more true in the contemporary global situation. Ethnicities are discursive, in that they are deployments of power. They are not natural, as a brief tour of what constitutes Latina/o or blackness in separate nations will reveal. There is no such thing as an absolute ethnic identity or position. Ethnic positions shift across time and space. There is no such thing as a particular skin color – for, the very fact of identifying and naming a skin color results from a political, historical, and cultural context.[5] In the contemporary US moment, Latinas, for example, make sense in relation to whiteness and blackness. They/we occupy an in-between location, regardless of our heterogeneity. Despite the fact that some Latinas are Afro-Latinas, others are China-Latinas,[6] and so on, we have been coded, for cultural purposes, as light-brown Latinas. Our hybridity is erased in favor of that very useful in-between location that serves many purposes at once. Light-brown Latinas provide the US mainstream with a rationale of inclusivity. They can say, "hey, look, we are diverse." This inclusion often displaces blackness, because why stop at that in-between, why not just redraw the spectrum to white and light brown? It also excludes many if not most Latinas, as it displaces blackness and foregrounds whiteness as normative (Shuggart 2007). It coexists uneasily with other ethnicities, such as Asian Americans, Native Americans, and Arab

Americans, whose skin color and ethnicization also place them between the white and black poles that rule the United States' racial spectrum.

Within US history, and really anywhere else in the world, ethnicization as a project has served not only to categorize but also to segregate. Government and marketing efforts to control and profit from this ethnic relationality coexist with ethnic populations' efforts to gain rights and access to democratic processes – including education – as well as their political and cultural representation, ranging from political elections – both as voters and as candidates – to mediated representations – both behind and in front of the camera. The slow quantitative increase in the representation of Latinas and the qualitative change of these representations of Latinidad bear witness to the resilience of ethnic narratives of purity and binary fantasies. Both of these tactics are so entrenched that they function as default. To try anything else means going against the stream. The force of this ideological marginalization and erasure ensures their survival, despite the fact that quite possibly it would be more profitable to leave them behind. The mainstream is not very open to change, even if it promises increased profit. Latinas provide a malleable signifier of difference that at once tames the unruliness of hybridity through desirable sexualized images and provides close to a *tabula rasa* of ethnic signification for government and business purposes. In the simplest of formulations, Latinas provide an in-between space of representation for a nation that until recently thought of itself as black and white. The recurring and unavoidable reminders of a far more complex and violent history, culture, and population – that is, the inescapable heterogeneity within Latinidad and within the US population – renders such simplicity unstable and untenable. Yet, hybridity bites back. Returning the look or focus to the mainstream with the complexity of that in-between space, Latinas talk and push back (Báez 2018). Ethnically diverse Latinas can use the foregrounding of ambiguity to complicate previously binary US national imaginary. Industry and audiences understand that ambiguity simultaneously displaces, and sometimes replaces, the darker, usually black, subject (see also Molina-Guzmán 2005). Throughout the research on the subject, the attention to global circulation and hybridity has been constant. Latina/os come from everywhere and fan out everywhere – in unexpected paths. What are we to make of the Latin Americans who migrate to Europe – either Spain or the United Kingdom – and later come to the States as European citizens (Retis, 2014)? My ongoing interest in hybridity and mixed race, as a rejection of purity and an indicator or Latina/os and Latinidad, takes me back to the mainstream, a hybrid space that attempts to assert purity through contradiction and erasure – a process whose failure is yet another indication of the identity crisis facing the United States as a nation and transmitted globally through transnational conglomerate media industries.

The uses and abuses of representing ethnicities as hybrid have both potential for liberation and an expanded public sphere but also the danger of subsuming all difference into a flat ambiguous otherness for the sake of commodification and transnational profit. Therein lies the rub, in terms of production and activism. Producers within the mainstream and activists trying to make demands upon mainstream media industries engage in unequally empowered bargaining and negotiations. Demands for richer and more textured narratives are met with resistance and outright avoidance. Industry executives claim that the profit motive guides development, and as such it makes little sense to alienate a large segment of the audience. Even when production of a television show including a range of Latinas somehow comes to be, the perceived tensions between mainstream (read: white) and Latina (read: brown) audiences appear to producers as a liability rather than a possibility. Exploring the production of *Devious Maids* as a more Latina version of *Desperate Housewives*, Báez (2015) concluded: "Ultimately, in trying to simultaneously appeal to a broader female audience *and* a narrow Latina/o audience segment, *Devious Maids* illustrates the difficulties cable networks like Lifetime experience in trying to diversify programming that will attract highly segmented audiences, while also maintaining their larger audience base" (p. 54). Internal contradictions abound.

The long history of representations of Latina/os in the US mainstream reveals far more continuities than ruptures. Felix Gutiérrez (2012) summarizes the range of possibilities:

> Greasy bandidos, fat mamacitas, romantic Latin lovers, lazy peons sleeping under sombreros, short-tempered Mexican spitfires, violent revolutionaries, faithful servants, gang members, and sexy señoritas with low-cut blouses and loose morals have long been staples of Latin images in fiction, films, and television. When seen on the screen or page, the stereotyped characters quickly trigger a picture in the heads of the audience of what the character is like and what role she or he will play as the plot unfolds.
>
> *(p. 100)*

This neat summary of production leading to representations leading to audience reactions maps out the continuities. Yet, we also have some presence in the mainstream, which sometimes brings along ruptures. In the entertainment realm, we have the continuation of Jennifer Lopez as the reigning Latina mogul whose ethnic presence does not preclude her othering of other ethnics, such as a recent incident on *The Voice* with an Asian American contestant (Washington 2017a). As mentioned previously in this chapter, ethnicities between the white and black ends of the spectrum are positioned in uneasy relation to one another. In this particular case, Lopez deployed her agency and status as a successful mainstream Latina to pass judgment on Asian Americans striving for presence and success in the same mainstream. We have also witnessed the rise of Sofia Vergara, the breakout star from the ensemble-cast mockumentary *Modern*

Family. As the best-paid television actress, Ms. Vergara represents the latest Latin bombshell to hit US airwaves. Former Disney and Barney girls Selena Gomez and Demi Lovato continue their music, acting, and branded-products careers, with the ups and downs that follow young media celebrities. Gina Rodriguez became a breakout star through the aptly Latina-entitled *Jane the Virgin*. While the title is cheeky, it does hook to the Roman Catholicism stereotypically attributed to Latina/o populations in the United States. Cameron Diaz, Christy Turlington, Salma Hayek, Eva Longoria, Eva Mendez, Michelle Rodriguez, Zoe Saldana, Sofia Carlson, and others all remain bankable mainstream figures. Notice that these spectacular Latinas represent the multiplicity within Latinidad. Cameron Diaz is a blonde and blue-eyed Cuban American from San Diego whose Latinidad would go nearly unperceived were it not for her last name. Former supermodel Christy Turlington has used her Latinidad, as a Salvadorean American, almost as a way to stay in the limelight after aging out of her top-model days. Salma Hayek will be more extensively discussed in Chapter 2, but suffice it to say that she is a first-generation Mexican, of Hungarian and Spanish Jewish parents, who crossed over in the United States and now lives in France. Eva Longoria, Eva Mendez, and Sofia Carlson fit the bill as petite light-brown Latinas. Michelle Rodriguez is Afro-Latina, something she has said was a cause of conflict in her family, and has been typecast in a long career performing embodied and active Latina roles (Beltrán 2004). Zoe Saldana, also Afro-Latina, has removed some of the Latinidad by taking the ñ out of her name (Molina-Guzmán 2013b) and shortening it from Zoë Yadira Saldaña Nazario. She hit the big time through the *Star Trek* franchise, and has played a range of African American and ethnically ambiguous characters, gaining controversy through her casting as Nina Simone. All of these spectacular Latinas form part of the mainstream terrain. Yet, fully half do not fit the light-brown ambiguous mold, and thus are seldom discussed as Latina. Nonetheless, when it suits the individual stars or when media companies find it useful to reach out to Latina/o or ethnic audiences, white Latinas will exhort their Latinidad. Every once in a while, Cameron Diaz will assert her Latinidad, such as when she and Jennifer Lopez shared the stage while presenting an award at the 2012 Oscars. That moment, when they posed with their backs to the cameras, simultaneously reiterated their common Latinidad and differentiated Diaz's whiteness from Lopez's more ethnic body. On the other hand, Longoria and Mendez are always already Latinas, regardless of the story or role in which they appear. Unambiguous white Latinas, such as Diaz and Turlington, have the luxury of passing as white and choosing to out their Latinidad when it suits them. Light-brown Latinas play across the racial spectrum. In addition to Jennifer Lopez, Jessica Alba has proven so malleable that she has played characters from albino in the *Fantastic Four* (2009) to an African American in *Honey* (2003). The inescapably racialized Rodriguez and Saldana enjoy embodied careers, wherein they have to continuously prove their belonging within

Latinidad and African American-ness. Border crossings for these Afro-hybrid Latinas are far more inspected than for the white and light-brown ones. Clearly, Latina actors are useful to mainstream media industries for their malleability and the fact that they can displace other ethnicities.

Recent production of predominantly Latina/o shows in the post-network era provides expanded employment opportunities and roles for Latina/os, with possible ruptures in addition to inevitable continuities. The transmediated *East Los High* (2013–17), for example, provided a welcome Latina/o presence in the digital television landscape, via Hulu (Molina-Guzmán 2016). The reboot of *One Day at a Time* (2017–2019) does the same through Netflix. At an organizational level of analysis, these shows function as sites of symbolic annihilation. Were it not for them, Hulu and Netflix would have nearly zero Latina/o presence (Negrón-Muntaner et al. 2014). Latina/os are found in predictable locations, in working-class communities, yet the narratives within which they appear present novel ways of treating family structures, fluid sexuality, and productive agency. The salience of these two shows belies the overall ongoing underrepresentation of Latina/os in general in mainstream popular culture. The many critiques applied to them speak to the burden of underrepresentation – so much is expected from these shows in the absence of many others.

A mainstream that underrepresents Latina/os and maintains damaging tropes has consequences in terms of politics, education, and resource distribution. As the *Latino Media Gap Report* (Negrón-Muntaner et al. 2014) asserts:

> The consequences of this gap are far-reaching. The current data suggests persistent and unchecked job discrimination in a major US industry. The relegation of Latinos similarly deprives media consumers of innovative perspectives at a moment of rapid industry and demographic change. Equally important, as entertainment and news reports often carry more weight than do other forms of communication, the limited and stereotypical nature of existing stories about Latinos skews the public's perception of US society, sanctioning hostility toward the country's largest minority, which has already become the majority in many cities, including the media capitals of Miami and Los Angeles.
>
> *(pp. 1–2)*

I write this book 23 years after my *Feminism, Multiculturalism, and the Media: Global Diversities* (Sage, 1995), 18 years after *A Latina in the Land of Hollywood* (University of Arizona Press, 2000), and 8 years after *Latina/os and the Media* (Polity, 2010). The first, an edited collection, was groundbreaking in that it foregrounded media and gender through an intersectional range of vectors of difference and ethnicities, including Latinas, Native Americans/First Nations, Asian Americans, African Americans, Jews, and lesbians. Up to that point, most diversity gender and media studies had focused solely on African

Americans. The second book came out as Latina/o Media Studies was beginning to explode as an area of research. In addition to posing questions about audience and interpretation, which were at that time woefully understudied, it covered a broad terrain of mediated culture and analyzed issues of class as well as gender and ethnicity. The third book cohered the intersection between Latina/o Studies and Media Studies, attempting to account for the vast amount of research that was then being conducted and pointing toward future work in an area of study that continues to be dynamic and multifaceted. Mini case studies at the end of each chapter took up two separate issues to illustrate how mediation of Latinidad could be understood through the body of Jennifer Lopez, a major celebrity, and the coverage of Latino death in the *Los Angeles Times'* "Homicide Report." These two examples illustrated a continuum of production, representation, audience, and effects borne out by mediatized Latina/os and, in turn, contributing to the circulation of information about Latina/os. The Jennifer Lopez study focused on a spectacular Latina, while the "Homicide Report" analysis explored the implications of reporting the death of unnamed and unacknowledged young Latinos in the greater Los Angeles area. Overexposure of Jennifer and her butt and underexposure of Latino death coexist in the mainstream media.

In all previous and contemporary work, my focus is on the mainstream media. Never underestimating the presence, creativity, and importance of alternative media and Spanish-language media, I also acknowledge that these are very large areas of research and activity, which are beyond the scope of this book (Albarrán 2009; Chavez 2015; Báez and Avilés-Santiago 2016). My decision to keep researching what happens in the mainstream is rooted in the firm belief that Latina/os are part of mainstream US popular culture and deserve to be part of the mainstream media – as owners, producers, subjects, and interpreters. By focusing on presence in mainstream popular culture, including survival and archives, mass-produced and -marketed children's toys and books, television, popular music, movies, and celebrity culture, this book addresses Latinidad in its everyday location. The mainstream is normative and discursive – it foregrounds power through narratives, tropes, and cultures. It proposes that which "should be" through a prism of representation that in turn represents institutions and everyday signifying practices (Giles and Middleton 2008). As well, through its wide distribution and circulation, the mainstream contributes to the functioning of institutions and our personal, group, national, and transnational everyday signifying practices. Furthermore, Media Studies research suggests that we learn more from media in the absence of personal experience – so, given the segregated reality of much of our population, the mainstream provides powerful lessons about Latina/os to those not living in contact with us. The fact that Latina/os are spread throughout the United States and come from a wide range of origins, recent and ancient, and, in turn, fan out throughout the world, means that cultural production, circulation, and consumption are globally mobile. The mobility of cultural forms is also complex, dynamic, and consistent. The mainstream has implications of access to media – and also in terms of the circulation of Latina/o narratives and tropes among non-Latina/o audiences.

In 2019, Latina Feminist Media Studies contributes to many interdisciplinary streams, such as Feminist and Gender Studies, Ethnic Studies, Transnational Studies, Sexuality Studies, and the many forms that Latina/o Studies takes within the United States, such as Chicana/o Studies, Boricua Studies, Dominican Studies, and so on. Recent articles calling out gaps and omissions in mainstream communications and media studies publications point out our gendered (Mayer et al. 2018) and racialized (Chakravartty et al. 2018) citational practices. As this book is being finished, Latinas continue becoming more visible in academic research through Gender Studies journals such as *Feminist Media Studies*. As a grassroots phenomenon that continuously reacts in concert with as well as against market pressures (Cepeda 2015), Latinidad – and, more specifically, the gendering of Latinidad – has thus emerged as a key related site of inquiry for Latina/o Feminist Media Studies scholars (Cepeda 2015, p. 7). Previous erasure of Feminist Media Studies work also needs to be addressed, as by now there are decades of excellent Latina Feminist Media Studies texts (Valdivia 2018). As well, Latina Feminist Media Studies aims to be taken seriously in interdisciplinary journals such as *Latino Studies*. In conferences, the most notable inclusion lies in the recently created Race and Media conferences (2916, 2017, 2018), in which the work of Latina feminists is aired in a ventilated conversation across racial categories. As well, *The Routledge Companion to Latina/o Media* (2016), edited by Maria Elena Cepeda and Ines Casillas, includes many of the Latina feminist scholars whose work guides this chapter and this book. Moreover, in a lead article in *Feminist Media Studies*, the major feminist journal in our field, Maria Elena Cepeda (2015) clearly articulated the need to call to task practices that, unsurprisingly, center whiteness: we need to move beyond citational practices that exclude Latina Feminist Media Studies research, acknowledge the diversity within Latinidad, and admit the inescapability of transnationalism (Cepeda 2015). I take all three of these challenges very seriously. Journals that focus on the ethnic category of Latino Studies need to take Media Studies seriously as an interdiscipline, related to but different from Journalism, History, American Studies, and so on. This has long been a pet scholarly peeve of mine. No historian, for example, would conduct research without taking history seriously as a discipline. Conversely, scholars in all the fields just mentioned regularly publish books and articles about media in which media scholarship is barely included. This omission is doubled as the myth of discovery about Latinidad applies to scholarship as well as to mainstream media. Many of our feminist colleagues do not read our work, so I followed up my "Latina Media Studies" (2018) article in *Feminist Media Histories* with an exhortation to feminist media scholars to move beyond the tokenistic mention of Gloria Anzaldúa. This book contributes to a rich body of scholarship, and encourages readers to explore the other scholars, books, and articles that enrich our understanding of the world, mediated ethnic categories, and Latina/os and media in particular. It promises to extend and revise contemporary intellectual paradigms of Latina/o Studies and ethnicity. It underscores the utter necessity of understanding the tension between the need to assert an identity and the reality of the difficulty of maintaining boundaries around that identity. It also encourages the acknowledgment of hybridity as both a tool for inclusion and something to be used in the name of profit. Recognizing the uses and abuses of hybridity gives critical knowledge and potential empowering strategies to underrepresented groups.

While the flattening of difference, both within Latinidad and between ethnics, is readily apparent, so is the tacit acknowledgment that neither all Latina/os nor all ethnics are alike. Ambiguity and hybridity have been found by both the US Census, where large portions of the ethnic population feel frustrated by the discrete ethnic categories provided in census forms, and by major research projects such as the Pew Hispanic Center and Kaiser Family Foundation's report, National Survey of Latinos (2002, updated 2004), which documents that second- and later-generation Latina/os overwhelmingly (62%) do not list any single national origin as their background but opt for an umbrella category such as Latina/o. Ambiguity within Latinidad is coupled by ambiguity between ethnicities, as the Pew Foundation finds that both Latina/os and Asian Americans marry across ethnicities in increasing proportions. This hybridity is present in media culture and is represented through internally contradictory approaches. So, for example, while Dávila (2001) notes that all ethnics – Latina/os, African Americans, Asian Americans, and Native Americans – are treated as the last bastion of purity, tradition, and family, in another essay (Dávila 2001) she points out that media industries are beginning to pursue a parallel path of selective differentiation between and within types of Latinidad, often built on stereotype and essentialist national characteristics. Thus, at the level of tradition, all ethnics may be the same, but Asian Americans are the "model minority." Similarly, until quite recently – before the Elián González spectacle – Cuban Americans were treated as the model minority within Latina/os (Molina-Guzmán 2005).

The concept of hybridity is extremely useful to communications scholars for a number of reasons, yet it remains to be fully utilized by our interdiscipline (Kraidy 1999, 2002; Murphy and Kraidy 2003). Kraidy (2002, p. 317) proposes that we foreground this concept, as it "needs to be understood as a communicative practice constitutive of, and constituted by, sociopolitical and economic arrangements" that are "complex, processual, and dynamic." Beyond its merely descriptive uses, hybridity also opens up the space for the study of cultural negotiations, conflicts, and struggles against the backdrop of contemporary globalization (Shome and Hegde 2002a, b), wherein an increasing part of the global population is simultaneously becoming geographically displaced and endlessly commodified. This is precisely the framework of analysis around which this book coheres. Contemporary mainstream Latinidad will be explored against the backdrop of globalization, with an emphasis on cultural negotiations and displacements.

Notes

1 Elsewhere, many scholars have written about the history of Latina/o Studies and the previous academic formations that contributed and continue to coexist with this interdiscipline. *The Gender of Latinidad* begins within Latina/o Studies as a pan-national and pan-ethnic formation.

2 There is a long history and debate within US Latina/o Studies, and more so within Chicana/o Studies, about the mythical "bronze" race, which celebrated the indigenous elements of the Southwest Latina/o. Most powerfully articulated in the 1960s and '70s, this bronze race discourse was politically powerful and served to unify and valorize the presence and history of US Latina/os.

3 I put "voluntary" in quotes because it hides the many layers of involuntary migration due to famine, persecution, and economic dispossession. To be sure, there are fully voluntary migrants, but waves of migration usually follow push-out forces that make it impossible for populations to remain in their homeland.

4 I realize "Latinx" is widely used instead of "Latina/o." A complex conversation about terminology is beyond the scope of this book. I am still being educated about it. Whereas I am persuaded by Vidal-Ortiz and Martínez's (2018) call to challenge androcentric gendered hierarchies, I am also respectful of R. Rodriguez's (2017) questions about what is left out or eliminated by the "x." Furthermore, as Trujillo-Pagan (2018) convincingly argues, "Latinx" amounts to "genderblind sexism," echoing Molina-Guzmán's (2018) work on colorblind casting and providing yet another call for the agency to claim a gender, like the previously referenced Rodriguez (2017). Consequently, throughout the book I will use the term "Latina/o," as I continue to explore the possibilities and challenges of "Latinx."

5 This was evident in a global children's television project in which I participated. In terms of coding race, research teams across national boundaries found it impossible to concur as to what counted as "white" and what counted as "black," let alone the many possibilities in between.

6 This might read offensive to some, but in Latin America, the term "Chino" is applied to all Asian-descendant or even Asian-looking people. This usage of the term has been imported to the United States, where many use "Chino Latino" to refer to Asian-Latinos.

2

Spitfire Transition Tales

The Production of a Career

Film history can be interpreted as a process of overlapping micro-narratives – found in individual films, industrial changes, technological innovation, cultural resonance, etc. – combining to form the macro-narrative of film as an industrialized art form ... Each micro-narrative wave is influenced by dependent conditions that are mobilized independently within it, as multitudes of micro-histories move on a course determined simultaneously by their own trajectory and the trajectories of the histories that came before it, along with it, and after it.

(Alicia Kozma 2017)

As feminist film studies moves into the 21st century, it is grappling with the ongoing growth and complexity of feminist theories, as well as with the shifting boundaries around film as a category and with its relationship to other media and to other aspects of popular culture.

(Sarah Projansky and Angharad Valdivia 2006, p. 27)

It is insufficient to consider the ethnic woman as a mere stereotype, despite the fact that she has so often been represented as excessive, hypersexual, primitive, animalistic, or exotic. In fact, the ideological/cultural work she has performed has been complex and variable.

(Diane Negra 2001, p. 3)

These quotes indicate that this chapter is not about representation. It is about the material and "ideological/cultural work": the considerable effort, strategy, perseverance, and ability to navigate a presence in mainstream US entertainment. The chapter theorizes celebrity agency within the context of hybridity and various forms of difference against the political economic backdrop of neoliberalism as it inevitably seeps into the remaking of the self by ethnicized actors. Production is understood in terms of what it takes to produce media, as well as in relation to the production of media history, through archival

The Gender of Latinidad: Uses and Abuses of Hybridity, First Edition. Angharad N. Valdivia.
© 2020 John Wiley & Sons Ltd. Published 2020 by John Wiley & Sons Ltd.

practices that preserve the efforts, presence, and history of some actors while losing and forgetting many/most others. In other words, the chapter explores the classic tension between agency and structure that pervades media production research (e.g. Mayer 2013, p. 14) through recuperation of the archive of the spitfire. Furthermore, this is not an analysis of the spitfire per se, but rather an exploration of tokenism defined as parity – a definition rejected by all actors investigated in this chapter.

Nothing happens without human labor, and the labor and agency of Latina actors who crossed over into mainstream stardom via the spitfire trope has to be examined in relation to the industrial and ideological structures that they faced and continue to face. As Negrón-Muntaner (2017) reminds us, stereotypes are "complex technologies of production and desire that propel economic expansion" (p. 289). Though the chapter has to include a brief overview of the Latina spitfire trope, it does so as a way to enter into issues of production, labor, glass ceilings, archives and historical conservation, agency, and structure. How does Latina feminist intervention "envision a broader and more diverse spectrum of women in cinematic history" (Kozma 2017)? How do we theorize and document the efforts of Latina spitfire actors to branch out into more diversified labor? Kozma (2017) encourages us to unpack the "exceptional" category, as it marginalizes actors and agency in its otherizing strategies, and to take up the "generative disruptions" made by marginalized agents in order to recover and complexify film and entertainment history.[1] She adds: "However, the exceptionalism I posit here is not one of success but tokenism disguised as parity" that hides "systemic and institutionalized prejudice and oppression." Whereas Kozma applies this approach to the study of female producers in general and Stephanie Rothman in particular, I apply it to Latina actors as they seek to produce a career from a crossover begun through one of the most prominent stereotypes for the Latina/o ethnicity, the spitfire. Through the investigation of actors who have performed the Latina/o spitfire stereotype and sought or continue to seek to have a career, this chapter looks at their efforts to carve out, preserve, and survive in the cut-throat sexist, classist, ageist, and racist enterprise of mainstream US entertainment, especially – but not exclusively – Hollywood film and television. Some of these transnational and hybrid actors have managed to expand into production, activism, and a wide range of other activities as a way of prolonging their career trajectories and helping/profiting from others who seek to enter into entertainment professions and negotiate more equitably. In their crossover into the mainstream through the trope of the spitfire, we can study a range of tactics that yield challenges and possibilities inextricably linked to ethnic narratives of participation and agency within the mainstream.

Within media studies, "spitfire tales" is located at the intersection of production, audience, and representation. Latina actors have to enter through the stereotype into the mainstream to gain a foothold, however tenuous, and then try to construct a career that extends beyond the flash-in-the-pan tendency toward stereotypical work (or, really, most work in mainstream media). In mainstream entertainment industries, production takes place within an oligopolistic set of global players that use their large transnational cross-media holdings to reap profits from synergistic and convergence opportunities afforded by vertically and horizontally integrated patterns of ownership and control. The neoliberal hallmark of transferring nearly all governmental duties to the marketplace expands the geographic scope of activities for transnational media conglomerates and transfers many of the human "caring" tasks to individuals who transact them through the marketplace. Thus, conglomerates, individual actors, and entertainers function through this new prism, which is, in turn, held as a yardstick to measure actors' worth as they are constantly called upon to perform proper citizenship. Citizenship is related not so much to the nation-state as to a willingness to assume individual responsibility through the marketplace as a consumer. This newly configured "citizenship," in turn, redounds back to the marketability of actors.

The Latina spitfire is a hybrid creation with transnational traces, whose characteristics morph in accordance with changing sociohistorical markers. National origins of famous spitfires range from Mexico to Brazil, Colombia, Spain, Portugal, Puerto Rico (as part of the United States, yet thought of as outside it), and – of course – the US mainland. For a trope to encompass all of these varied national origins, it has to incorporate a serious flattening of difference and a certain degree of flexibility. In sum, the trope reiterates the mainstream construction of Latina/os and Latinidad, whose provenance ranges from the United States to the Iberian peninsula, and throughout the Americas. As well, nearly all Latina actors who have played the spitfire role are hybrid themselves, in terms of national origin and race. At its core, the spitfire trope re-enacts the binary construction of the Global North as sophisticated and the Global South as unsophisticated. The spitfire, as a trope, represents both an ethnic and a national crossover into the US mainstream (Cepeda 2000, 2001, 2003b; Ceisel 2011), which often includes national boundaries, cultural systems, linguistic traditions, and entire languages. To cross over, one needs a metaphorical bridge: a character that functions as a vehicle allowing two or more cultures to interact, if not communicate. The resulting spitfire trope is a hybrid construction that foregrounds particular elements to make the character's bridge role stand out from the other characters, on either side of implicitly cultural and geographic boundaries, and reinforces the centrality of the normative subject within the US mainstream. That normative subject is white, heteronormative, middle class, and standard English-speaking. The juxtaposition works between the spitfire and a range of gendered and racialized characters: white men, white women, and women and men of non-white, non-Latina/o ethnicities. Furthermore, that normative subject is a serious, respectable person – one who does not generate immediate laughter or ridicule. Latina spitfires thus serve the role of gender, class, and race bridge characters (Valdivia 2011).

Historical markers that influence contemporary reconfigurations of the spitfire include the discourses of post-race and post-feminism. Both are elemental to the evolution of the spitfire trope: they redraw and reinforce the structural dimensions within which the actor is able to exert agency within a historical terrain that provides opportunities for a hybrid and indeterminate racialized celebrity persona; and they challenge actors' ability to navigate a terrain that continues to privilege whiteness, as the purity and moral pole toward which their crossover is always aiming yet never quite approaching. The goalposts of inclusion keep moving, and the latest discourses of the past prevent actors from articulating these moving targets. The task of asserting presence, belonging, and agency increases in difficulty as the very language that can articulate this process is precluded if actors are to remain in the present in the mainstream entertainment business.

Furthermore, the latest iteration of spitfire navigation includes both the neoliberal requirement of celebrity philanthropy and the possibility of alternative production, delivery, and circulation channels in the post-network era. Just as media conglomerates function within a terrain of global deregulation, individual actors must perform within new rules of social responsibility and personal contributions to social welfare causes without making explicit connections to structural and historical issues of discrimination and barriers to entry in the US mainstream entertainment industries. Perhaps the post-network era allows for the inclusion and agency so difficult to achieve in legacy media. The jury is still out on that issue. The post-network era, with alternative production nodes such as Amazon Prime, Hulu, Netflix, and HBO, has been found by scholars to provide an expanded entry into presence (Molina-Guzmán 2016), though presence remains tenuous and tokenistic (Negrón-Muntaner et al. 2014; Negrón-Muntaner and Abbas 2016). For example, among these venues, Hulu had the highest inclusion of Latina/os in terms of a production line-up through *East Los High*. However, since the series is no longer being produced, its Latina/o visibility numbers have undoubtedly gone down.

Ultimately, I want to combine the study of mobility and agency within and without the entertainment industry with work on the many representational strategies used in the mainstream to domesticate, coopt, and contain racialized populations. Actors who perform as spitfires enter the mainstream through terms not of their own making, but not entirely without agency (Althusser 1971). They step into a role with imperial and colonial historical traces, contemporary negotiations about transnational forces and identity crises, and local struggles about production and audiences. Doubtless, it would be much preferable to be able to enter mainstream stardom through textured and sophisticated narratives and tropes of one's own choosing. However, given the overlapping gender, class, race/ethnicity, and age challenges facing Latina actors, few have this luxury.[2] Most often, pre-scripted, stereotypical tropes have been the only way for Latina actors to enter into and gain a foothold in this lucrative market. Once in the spotlight, a Latina actor typecast in the spitfire trope can take steps to either maximize her presence and marketability through that trope, branch out into other roles, or craft a multidimensional career that includes acting, other entertainment industry jobs, ancillary product sponsorship, and engagement with neoliberal philanthropy (Bulut et al. 2014; Molina-Guzmán 2014). In the neoliberal age, the latter has become an essential additional element of stardom.

As workers – cultural laborers who seek to make a living in the entertainment industry – Latina actors face rather high barriers to entry.[3] To enter into the business, a Latina requires strength, fortitude, amazing talent, perseverance, and luck. The glass ceiling, as a finding that applies to media industries, applies with a vengeance to intersectionally marginalized actors, and represents an invisible set of barriers that prevent them from enduring or moving up within this sphere. However, in the film industry, the consistently high barriers to entry make the concept of a "glass ceiling" sound a bit too ambitious, as entry itself is denied. This is analogous to the content finding of "symbolic annihilation." For there to be a marginalization and trivialization of gender and race, there has to be some minimal presence. Lack of presence is absence, plain and simple. Often, in Hollywood film, absence precludes the minimal finding of a glass ceiling. An additional facet of racial and ethnic discriminatory tendencies is the assignment of working-class status and roles (Valdivia 2000). From an intersectional approach, gender discrimination becomes more intense as actors age, and Latinas face ageism. All actors inevitably age as they continue their effort and ability to construct enduring careers, but much more allowance is given to aging male actors.

I want to stress that while acting is one of type of labor in the entertainment industry, many actors who carve out an enduring career – and notice I am saying "enduring" and not necessarily "highly successful" or "in the limelight" – do so by transitioning into other types of labor within and without the industry, as producers and talent agency managers, or through one of the many commodified ways of profiting and synergizing a brand identity, if one's career yields such a possibility. Taking the global into account offers yet another layer of possibility as, in addition to representations circulating across a global terrain, one can brand oneself differently across a range of global markets. This latter commodification option is open to an elite group of actors and celebrities, a precious few of whom are Latinas, never mind spitfires.

This chapter does not explore all the Latina spitfires in Hollywood film history. Rather, it selectively focuses on a number of contemporary actors whose present or history may have included a spitfire moment: Rita Moreno, Rosie Perez, Charo, Salma Hayek, and Sofía Vergara. The chapter draws extensively on previous historical research, which needs no revision, yet extends this analysis into the present through the lens of the production-of-media paradigm. Many scholars have written on two of the major historical spitfires: Lupe Vélez (Fregoso 2007; Beltrán 2009; Lopez 2012) and Carmen Miranda (Enloe 1989; Gil-Montero 1989; Roberts 1993). Mary Beltrán's (2009) research on Rita Moreno up to 2010 is definitive, and Peña Ovalle (2010) also provides a nuanced analysis of this legendary Latina. There is also burgeoning scholarship on Sofía Vergara (Molina-Guzmán 2012a; Vidal-Ortiz 2016; Fernandez L'Hoeste 2017; Contreras Porras 2017). Salma Hayek has been frontally examined by Molina-Guzmán (2010), Shaw (2010), Negrón-Muntaner (2017), and Valdivia (2000). Rosie Perez has also been researched (Valdivia 1996, 1998, 2000). Other than a one-page encyclopedia entry on Charo (Ruíz and Sánchez Korrol 2006), there is no academic scholarship on this particular spitfire.

The Spitfire

This chapter explores the arduous task that many Latina actors engage in after reaching mainstream US popular presence through the spitfire role, a process of self-invention and valorization (Negrón-Muntaner 2017). Star efforts form a diverse and multipronged assemblage (Moorti 2017). Linguistically challenged vis-á-vis dominant standard English, hypersexualized, curvaceous, loud, comical, and preferably a dancing beauty, the role of the spitfire has increased in complexity in recent years, as its bearers, the Latina actors who play this character, have sought to imbue it with texture and intelligence. It is unclear whether these attempts are interpreted as such by general audiences; that would require an additional and separate research project. Nonetheless, the trope survives even as Latina/os become the dominant minority in the United States and as the US population continues to change in ethnic composition. Charles Ramirez-Berg (2002) calls the role "the Latina harlot" because of its sexualized dimension, and includes it as the one feminized role in a list of four Latina/o tropes, the other three being the Latin lover, the bandido, and the clown.[4] The spitfire sometimes spills into the three other roles, as none are mutually exclusive. It predates the talkies and silent film, and can be traced back as far as frontier literature (Ramirez-Berg 2002, referenced in Beltrán 2009, p. 62). Research on Latina spitfires[5] dates back at least to Lupe Vélez and continues up to Rita Moreno, Rosie Perez, Charo, Salma Hayek, and Sofía Vergara, all of whom entered the mainstream consciousness as spitfires and have attempted to cross over – or to make a border crossing, if you will – into mainstream popular culture, and from there into a long-lasting career (though not necessarily in the spotlight or the mainstream). Latina spitfire performances provide Hollywood with a female clown trope that "focuse[s] on the comedy of errors created by intercultural communications and the comedic tensions inherent in the romantic relationship between the Latina star and her white US paramour" (Molina-Guzmán 2014, p. 67). This trope relies on two recurring and continuous ethnic representation characteristics. First, the dyads are always in relation to whiteness: in this case, a Latina and a white paramour. Second, there is flattening of difference within Latinidad, wherein elements of US, many Latin American, Portuguese, and Spanish cultures are blended together to create an amalgamated comic character.

Much of the spitfire comedy stems from language and accent issues, with the stereotype gaining traction once Hollywood began to make movies with sound (Beltrán 2008b, 2009).[6] Despite the fact that spitfire actors, including Carmen Miranda and Rita Moreno, often speak English quite well or even as natives, the trope relies on language misuse/malapropism, mispronunciation, and loudness. These linguistic elements are combined with bodily performance of excessiveness: loud and accented mispronunciations accompany sexualized dancing and suggestive dress. One of the many handicaps from entering the mainstream through this role is that an actor can be typecast as an accented English speaker even when they actually speak without an accent. Of course, actors who do have an accent find moving beyond the trope even more difficult. Nonetheless, whether an actor has an accent or not, crafting an enduring career – beyond ridicule – proves challenging. The "eternal foreigner" status of Latina/os in the United States is predicated on our inability to learn and speak English or to speak it imperfectly, with a thick, perceptible accent. This linguistic handicap remains an element of stereotypical construction of Latina/os in the mainstream despite the fact that most US Latina/os are first-language English speakers – due, in part, to the fact that most of them have lived here for more than one generation (Taylor et al. 2012). Language remains a core element of the construction of the spitfire. The purposeful inclusion of malapropisms leading to comedic misunderstandings is a scripted, rehearsed, and staged component of their performance. The performativity of accented English remains foregrounded with Gloria Delgado-Pritchett/Sofía Vergara and the ever-resilient Charo, whose "cuchi cuchi" trademark comment has contributed to her visibility in and out of the US mainstream for four decades. Branding techniques, incursions into media production, and differential commodification contribute to contemporary strategies. Spitfires who are already positioned as nonthreatening/comedic in character have to assert themselves as agent workers within an industry that clearly prefers timeworn tropes over transgressive gendered and ethnic performances.

Once in the mainstream, some Latina stars attempt to move beyond the spitfire role, to craft an enduring career. Others mine the trope as long as possible. There have been many spitfires, and many have been such a flash in the pan that they have nearly disappeared from history. We know of the successful ones. Thus, one of the concerns of this chapter is the issue of the archive. Another is strategies for survival and endurance. Most of the spitfires mentioned here managed not only to enter into the mainstream but also to craft a long enough career that they form part of the archive – we generally remember them and note them as forming a history and legacy. Even becoming part of the archive takes agency, and some of the spitfires in this chapter have penned autobiographies or self-help books in order to leave their their personal history on the record.

The archive: how to remember and how to rescue the forgotten

1) What stories currently exist in the archive, in the record, in a collection? In whose interest do those materials serve?
2) Which stories are missing? What can be added to the historical record? What is significant about these stories?
3) How can I collaborate with others to make the record more complete, dynamic, multi-vocal and inclusive?

(Aguayo 2017)

As scholars of minoritized populations, our labor intersects with archival issues, as record keeping so often dovetails with power. In 2005, I wrote "Film Producers," an encyclopedia entry for the *Oxford Encyclopedia of Latinas and Latinos in the United States* (Oboler and Gonzalez, Eds.). Within a historical approach, this entry sought to assess whether early Chicana/o film production contributed to the professional development of a Latina/o film-producing workforce. Drawing on the foundational and canonical research of Fregoso (1993) and Noriega (1992a, b), the findings for this entry were not surprising. Dating back to the Chicano movement in 1969, the first wave of Latina/o film production, there were a few, iconic products. Most of these consisted of film shorts, because the resources for a feature-length film were beyond the means of all of these early producers. Nonetheless, male producers actually turned their early revolutionary production forays into enduring Hollywood careers. For example, Luiz Valdez adapted an epic poem of the early Chicana/o movement into the audiovisual short, *Yo Soy Joaquin*. "Acknowledged as the founder of modern Chicano theater and film, (Valdez) went on to direct, write, and act in a number of other movies and television shows. After his original twenty-minute film, Valdez directed some feature-length films with considerable mass appeal" within and without Latina/o audiences (Valdivia 2005a). Iconic films such as *Zoot Suit* (1982), *La Bamba* (1987), and *The Cisco Kid* (1994) spanned two decades of limited yet enduring Latina/o production, now known as the first and second wave.[7] Luis Valdez remains active as a voice actor, most recently voicing Tio Berto in the animated film *Coco* (2017).

Within the first wave, Jesús Salvador Treviño was also actively producing Chicano-themed media for PBS, including *Chicano Moratorium Aftermath*

(1970), *The Salazar Inquest* (1970), *América Tropical* (1971), and *Yo Soy Chicano* (1972). The latter film, whose title clearly resembles Valdez's *Yo Soy Joaquín*, was a 1-hour, multimedia-collage, documentary-style film attempting a counter-historical project that foregrounded aspects of Chicano and Chicana experience and history. Treviño, who was already embedded within television production circles, followed *Yo Soy Chicano* with a Mexican feature-length film, *Raíces de sangre* (1979), as well as another made-for-television movie, *Seguín* (1982). Treviño has since had an extremely successful career as a mainstream television producer and director. His credits include such widely known series as *Star Trek, Chicago Hope, ER, Sea Quest, NYPD Blue, The Practice, Dawson's Creek, Crossing Jordan*, and *The OC*. More recent efforts include *Prison Break, Reunion, Vanished, Bones, Lincoln Heights, Law and Order*, and the documentary *Vision of Aztlán* (2010). His co-producing credit for Showtime's series *Resurrection Boulevard* (2000–03) earned him an ALMA Award, and he is the recipient of several other entertainment awards.

You may note that all these early Chicano film producers were male and that the subject of their films centered the masculine experience through indigenous male heroes, among other elements. Following that first wave of production, Esperanza Vasquez and Sylvia Morales, two Chicana filmmakers, produced more women-centered films, featuring everyday themes. In *Agueda Martínez: Our People, Our Country* (1977), Vasquez directed a film (produced by Moctesuma Esparza) about the famous Mexican American multi-skilled artist and matriarch (Fregoso 1993). Morales expanded a slide show by Ana Nieto-Gomez into a film entitled *Chicana* (1979). Drawing on her expertise as a television producer with KABC-TV in Los Angeles, she was able to challenge masculinist approaches to Chicano and Chicana history, including a revision of La Malinche as a central figure. However, whereas both Valdez and Treviño went on to have successful long-term careers in the mainstream entertainment business,[8] Morales and Vasquez nearly disappear from historical archives and other mediated resources (e.g. IMDb.com) after their initial films. Fregoso (1993) documents that Sylvia Morales directed *Esperanza* in 1985 (p. 87). After that, she transitioned into a career in television production; among her credits are *Love and Long Distance* (1985), *Hearts on Fire* (1987), *SIDA Is AIDS* (1989), *Real Men and Other Miracles* (1999), *A Century of Women* (1994), and, most recently, *A Crushing Love* (2009). One can only find Esperanza Vasquez as a film editor on *Only Once in a Lifetime* (1979) and an uncredited member of the crew on three largely unknown movies produced between 1971 and 1972.

The issue of archive is central to these female producers' – or anyone else's – enduring presence. There are three easily available online archives, if you will, where one can try to learn about these women in film. If one googles them, one is usually directed to the major mainstream archive, IMDb.com (the Internet Movie Database), to Women Make Movies (wmm.com), or to Wikipedia. Vasquez disappears from IMDb.com after 1994, while Morales appears in several entries from 1979 to 2009. Moreover, Morales appears on wmm.com, where we find that she has maintained a very active career for the past 30 years – participating in well-known premium television shows such as Showtime's *Resurrection Blvd.* and *Women: Stories of Passion*. In 2009, she produced a sequel to *Chicana* entitled *A Crushing Love* (http://www.wmm.com/filmcatalog/makers/fm258.shtml). She has since held a number of academic posts throughout Southern California, has earned numerous prestigious fellowships, and has an extensive entry on Wikipedia.

Esperanza Vasquez is a bit more difficult to trace beyond IMDb. Her canonical 1977 film is listed as co-produced with Moctesuma Esparza in 2009 and 2010. Not much appears between 1979 and 2010, a span of 31 years, nor thereafter. She does not appear on Women Make Movies, nor as an entry on Wikipedia. Her only presence on Wikipedia is through the listing of Agueda Salazar Martinez – the artist/matriarch about whom she directed a documentary – which names Morales without a hyperlink. On the other hand, producer Moctesuma Esparza is hyperlinked into his own long entry, and he frequently appears in encyclopedic entries and Latina/o media research (e.g. Puente 2011).

Clearly, these early Chicana filmmakers did not have the career that their male counterparts enjoyed. Consequently, it is very difficult to trace their trajectory outside of a dedicated academic research project. They are discussed in Rosa Linda Fregoso's *The Bronze Screen* (1993), but only in terms of their initial contributions to Chicana film and not in relation to further contributions, since that was not the book's task. As producers, these women's careers were not prolific. Their initial forays into Chicana/o activist production did not translate into a major mainstream career. Their presence in the mainstream never materialized. Vasquez's *Agueda* is more linked to Moctesuma Esparza than to her. Morales' continued involvement in television production is a bit more prolific that Vasquez's, and led to opportunities in higher education. Yet, it is undeniable that the career trajectories of early Chicano and early Chicana producers were vastly different. Granted, these women chose to work behind the camera, which is an easier type of labor to subsume in the archive. Nonetheless, they were foundational cultural workers. This comparative discussion of gendered early Chicana/o film producers serves to lay some of the groundwork for the career of another type of cultural worker: the Latina actor who plays or has played the spitfire.

Our Mediated Latina Spitfires

The history of spectacular Latinas (Mendible 2007a, b; Beltrán 2009; Molina-Guzmán 2010) includes many stars who entered US mainstream entertainment as spitfires, and many scholars have written extensively on iconic and canonical Latina spitfires. In particular, research on Maria Guadalupe Villalobos Vélez, a.k.a. Lupe Vélez (Lopez 1991, 2012;

Rodriguez-Estrada 2006; Fregoso 2007; Beltrán 2009), and on Carmen Miranda (Roberts 1993; Valdivia 1998; Trujillo-Pagan 2006) greatly informs work on Latina Feminist Media Studies in general and spitfire research in particular. We know that we cannot impute the spitfire construction and performance to the lived experience of actors (Fregoso 2007), yet Vélez has been treated as a real-life spitfire, while Miranda has received more careful analysis. Certainly, both actors attempted to carve out careers beyond the stereotype, but both died soon after their stars waned, so we are left with their potential and the history of their lives interrupted. Nonetheless, Miranda had begun to engage in philanthropic activities – a harbinger of the philanthropy that would become *de rigeur* in the neoliberal age – while Vélez was still in the throes of career navigation at the time of her death.

Rita Moreno

> I have no objection to play an Hispanic. I have every objection to play a stereotype … My biggest accomplishment is being here. I am eighty and I am working!
>
> *(Rita Moreno at http://www.makers.com/rita-moreno,*
> *retrieved June 27, 2017)*

> Rita Moreno remains one of the busiest stars in show business. She's currently juggling performances of her own one-woman stage show, Life Without Make-up, with television appearances as Fran Drescher's mother in TVLand's Happily Divorced. In addition, Ms. Moreno is preparing to record a new album as a follow up to her self-titled CD and is currently at work penning her autobiography.[9]
>
> *(www.looktothestars.org, retrieved*
> *July 10, 2017)*

> I did not want to keep playing the Conchita Lolita roles
>
> *(Rita Moreno, lecture to Notre Dame students,*
> *February 20, 2019)*

At 87 years old, Rita Moreno is arguably the oldest living and one of the most enduring former spitfires in US mainstream entertainment.[10] Her legacy continues to grow, and her visibility is undeniable. In fact, a photograph of Moreno in classic 40s pinup pose graces the cover of one of the core Latina/o Media Studies books, *Latina/o Stars in Their Eyes* by Mary Beltrán (2009), as well as that of Pricilla Peña Ovalle's *Dance and the Hollywood Latina* (2010). Both Beltrán and Peña Ovalle devote an entire chapter to this Latina icon. Beltrán begins with a quote from one of her biographies (Moreno as quoted by Beltrán 2009, p. 62), in which she acknowledges that she settled for the role of the spitfire because there weren't other options for her at the time. Beltrán traces the star's professional trajectory back to 1950, when she was aged 18, whereas Peña Ovalle goes back further to the age of 5. Moreno was conscious of the stereotype she had to play to remain in the limelight and of the roles and opportunities she could not access because of her heritage. Moreover, she was trying to enter the entertainment industry during a conservative time in which Puerto Ricans were constructed as outsiders, foreigners (which they had not been since 1917, when the United States granted citizenship to the island's residents), and trouble makers. Within this environment, Moreno, a talented singer, dancer, and actor, knew she had to perform the role of the spitfire in order to find employment. Her spitfire typecasting included a heavy accent, which she later clarified was part of the act: "Hell, no. That wasn't my real accent. I learned to speak English very early. That Latin accent was a put-on" (Martin 2008). Peña Ovalle (2010) highlights Moreno's critique of Hollywood Latina typecasting, which she claims paved the way for more recent Hollywood Latinas such as Jennifer Lopez, while simultaneously tracing a strong aural, vocal, dancing, and sexual continuity in Moreno's roles. Whereas Peña Ovalle partly attributes Moreno's typecasting to her brown skin, Moreno is in fact quite light-skinned, something she brings up in conversations and interviews. In fact, Moreno repeatedly tells the tale of confronting her make-up artist during *West Side Story* for slathering brownface all over the actors playing the Sharks.

After Moreno earned an Oscar for *West Side Story* (1961) as Best Supporting Actress, she was more typecast than ever.[11] A 7-year hiatus followed, in which she acted in only one film, as she hoped to transition into roles with "dignity and integrity," which meant largely dropping out of the mainstream film and television entertainment industry. Moreno literally left the country to escape the spitfire character that she could not avoid within the United States. Living in London from 1964, Moreno transitioned into theater roles in the West End, which she experienced as liberating and beyond the spitfire stereotype: "This was a wonderful time of my life ... As a bonus, I was not cast as a stereotype" (Moreno 2013, p. 203). Eventually, Moreno returned to the States, for a 5-year stint with the Children's Television Workshop's *The Electric Company* (1970–75), which earned her many awards. By 1981, Moreno realized she was facing yet another barrier: "I had battled racism and sexism all my life. Now I had to battle the worst enemy of all: ageism" (Moreno 2013, p. 242). Moreno relates that she was at once too old for young roles, and too young-looking to play older ones. After she turned 70, her career received a boost when she was cast as Sister Peter Marie Reimondo, a nun, in *Oz* (1997–2003), a made-for-television HBO first dramatic series. Despite the grim stories on this show, set in a prison, Moreno remembers it fondly: "It was so great that I longed to be a lifer" (Moreno 2013, p. 272).

Moreno has continued to act in movies, theater, and television series, both as an actor and as a voice actor, and is one of only 15 performers to have won an EGOT: an Emmy, a Grammy, an Oscar, and a Tony. She has been recognized nationally as a performer and contributor to cultural arts by a Presidential Medal of Freedom, granted by President George W. Bush in 2004; a National Medal of the Arts, granted by President Barack Obama in 2009; and a Kennedy Center Honors Lifetime Achievement Award, given in 2015. Moreno forcefully reminds us that she has a KEGOT, which includes the Kennedy Center Honors. She published her memoir in 2013, in which she had a chance to put her own spin on her storied career, and she currently accepts invitations to give university talks, wherein she discusses her history and the role of the spitfire.

In the teens of the 21st century, Moreno has experienced a rare revival. A nearly seven-decade mainstream entertainment career seldom results in a return to the limelight. Due in part to the opportunities offered in the post-network era, Moreno has re-entered the mainstream. At the 2018 Oscars, she attended and presented an award in the same dress, slightly altered, that she wore to accept her Oscar in 1962. In addition to roles in the Netflix series *Grace and Frankie*, as neighbor Lucy Chambers (2016), ABC's *Grey's Anatomy*, playing Gayle McColl (2016), and the CW and Hulu's *Jane the Virgin*, as Liliana De La Vega (2015–16), Moreno has a leading role in the Netflix reboot of the Norman Lear series *One Day at a Time* (2017–19). Interestingly, whereas both *One Day at a Time* and *Jane the Virgin* are Latina/o-themed television shows and therefore feature Moreno playing a Latina, neither Lucy in *Grace and Frankie* nor Gayle in *Grey's Anatomy* is racialized. In fact, Moreno's publicity photographs showcase a lean woman with silver spiky hair and not a hint of any stereotypical Latina/o features, jewelry, make-up, or hair style. As of March 2019, *One Day at a Time* has been canceled. Only a large and concerted campaign from fans and "even the National Hispanic Media Coalition" (Nguyen 2018) resulted in its third-season renewal. In this final season, the show, which has received rave reviews for its intersectional treatment of issues of gender, class, and sexuality in relation to Latinidad, tackles immigration and history as Lydia, Moreno's character, resists getting US citizenship, especially since it means renouncing her original Cuban citizenship – which Moreno claims she did not know immigrants had to do (Hill 2018). As well, Moreno will have a part in Steven Spielberg's forthcoming remake of *West Side Story*.

Drawing on her long trajectory as well as her recent comeback to the mainstream, Moreno remains active in a number of ancillary activities:

> In addition to film, stage, television and concert commitments, Ms. Moreno fills her spare time by lecturing to various organizations and university audiences on such varied topics as The Value of Diversity to our Culture, The Power of Language, Getting Older without Getting Old and A History of the Arts in Film TV & Theatre. She is also involved with a number of civic and charitable organizations and events.
>
> *(www.looktothestars.org, retrieved July 10, 2017)*

As do other celebrities, Rita Moreno engages in product endorsements. Given that she has been active in entertainment longer than any of the other spitfires in this chapter, Moreno's endorsements date back to the 1980s, prior to the full-blown celebrity branding of today. Film stars have endorsed products such as cigarettes and beauty creams since the early days of Hollywood. As a waning star, Moreno endorsed Pepsodent toothpaste in 1980 and Pizza Hut in 1996 – not exactly the sexiest or most glamorous of endorsements. She appears at the top of the fourth stage of celebrity influence through medical product endorsement in an industry report (Phoenix Reports 2016). However, her endorsement stature has not always been so strong, as illustrated by a comment about the relative value of endorsements of cheaper celebrities: "Sums of 100 000 or less ... would buy perhaps three days of work by lower-level celebrity such as actor Rita Moreno" (Phoenix Reports 2016, p. 121).

Perhaps because of her unlikely return to the limelight at such an advanced age (87), Moreno is outspoken about Latina/o issues and other political matters. Since the 1960s, Moreno has engaged in political activism in broad causes such as the March for Jobs and Racial Justice. In fact, she was present during Martin Luther King Jr.'s "I Have a Dream" speech. Since then, she has remained active in more specific causes, such as actors' rights (Actors Fund of America, Screen Actors Guild Foundation), health issues (HIV/AIDS, breast cancer, heart disease, diabetes; American Heart Association, American Stroke Association), and race and age issues (Jackie Robinson Foundation, the National Association of Insurance Commissioners' Senior Education Campaign). In sum, Moreno remains an active actor, speaker, and celebrity political activist. As of June 2018, she represents the successful transition from spitfire to productive, nonstereotypical, diversified, long-lasting career. Moreno's engagement calendar is full of events, including university lectures,[12] entertainment awards, and sponsorships. She has transcended the spitfire trope to achieve one of the longest-lasting successful careers of any Hollywood star.

Rosie Perez

Most of the criticism I got early in my career was from the Latin community. They used to take me out to lunch and tell me, "Can you go and take lessons to lessen your accent?". Or, "When you're on a talk show, can you not be so funny and loud?". People gave me so much crap about my voice, and I tried. I really did try to change, but it was the way I spoke. As I got older, the octaves dropped, thank God. Now I find it flattering if a sixteen-year-old comes up and starts imitating me.

(http://www.imdb.com/name/nm0001609/bio?ref_=nm_ov_bio_sm)

Her roles and the resulting oppositional readings suggest she thickens, complicates, and deconstructs her own stereotypical representation, thereby undermining the very parts she is brought in to play, at least for some members of the audience.

(Valdivia 2000, p. 105)

Rosie Perez was part and parcel of the late 1990s Latina/o boom,[13] and is one of the few spitfires discussed in this chapter who was born in the continental United States. She was a dancer before she became a film star, and has remained a choreographer. Her major film breakthrough came in Spike Lee's *Do the Right Thing* (1989), wherein she opened the film dancing to Public Enemy's "Fight the Power" and played the role of Tina, protagonist Mookie's girlfriend. Subsequently, she was cast in a string of mainstream Hollywood movies, and was even nominated for an Oscar as Best Supporting Actress for her role in *Fearless* (1993). Following a flurry of movies in the 1990s – such as *White Men Can't Jump* (1992), *Untamed Heart* (1993), *Somebody to Love* (1994), *It Could Happen to You* (1994), and *The 24 Hour Woman* (1999), in only some of which she played a spitfire – roles became scarcer, so that by 2001 she played Shirley Perro, the absolutely shrill, trailer park-resident wife of the drug-addict in the Drew Barrymore vehicle *Riding in Cars with Boys*.

Of all the actors discussed in this chapter, Rosie is the least typical spitfire. She acted in many dramas, or even mostly in dramas. She was nearly always cast in a supporting role. However, her way of talking, which has been offi-cially attributed to a speech impediment as well as being very much a collo-quial way of speaking in Brooklyn, has marked her roles and career. Whereas the classic spitfire is a comic character, with her mispronunciation and exag-gerated and sexualized performance domesticating her ethnic or national difference, Rosie's roles have foregrounded her manner of speaking as well as her sensuality so as to compose an extended trope of a working-class tragi-comic spitfire (Valdivia 1996, 1998, 2000). In other words, even when she is acting in dramas, her character is so over the top that it is difficult to take it seriously within the narrative. Nonetheless, the accent/speech impediment, sexualization, excessive performance, and resulting comicality fall within the spitfire stereotype. Whereas Valdivia (1996, 1998, 2000) finds her working-class roles to be largely reiterating the working-class, supporting-role Latina, Fregoso's (1995) work on cholas and Chicano nation would cast them as transgressive and as asserting agency through solidarity and presence in an urban setting.

After her late 1990s and early 2000s salience, Perez remained active as a voice actor, with parts in children's television, and took stereotypical roles in serial television shows such as *Nurse Jackie*, *Law and Order*, and *Lipstick Jungle*, which made up most of her visibility in the mainstream. She continues to act, mostly in small supporting roles in movies such as *The Counselor* (2013),

Gods Behaving Badly (2013), and *Puerto Ricans in Paris* (2015). She voices the character of Aunt Rose in Disney's *Penn Zero: Part-Time Hero* (2014–15), the most flamboyant in a cast of generally over-the-top characters. Perez participated in the late-night show *Nightcap* (2016–17) for mostly B- and C-list celebrities. She plays a DEA agent in the show *Pure* (2017), distributed by the CBC (Canadian Broadcasting Network).

Though her Wikipedia page lists only her movie and television work, she has also acted on stage, both on and off Broadway. She played the role of Googie Gomez in the 2007 revival of *The Ritz* – the play and the role for which Rita Moreno received a Tony Award in 1975, as well as a Golden Globe nomination for the film version in 1976. Other plays include *The 24 Hour Plays* (Connie, Danita, and Carmen, in 2003, '04, and '05 respectively), *Reckless* (2004), and *The Play that I Wrote* (2003). Notably, Perez does not play principal roles and often acts in replacement roles.

As a noteworthy exception, Rosie was cast as one of the four presenters in the long-running, all-women morning talkshow *The View* (1997–), which illustrates the limits and possibilities of inclusion in the mainstream. With Whoopi Goldberg (African American) at the helm and Rosie Perez (Latina), Nicolle Wallace (white), and Raven-Symoné (light African American/queer) making up the cast, the 2014–15 season was a case study in the multicultural approach to representation. On July 19, 2015, the ladies were discussing Trump's remarks about immigration. Rosie had just commented that Latina/os agree that immigration reform is a problem that needs to be addressed. At which point, Kelly Osbourne, a guest that day, made remarks that caused a visible reaction in both Raven-Symoné and Perez: "If you kick every Latino out of this country, then who is going to be cleaning your toilet, Donald Trump?" After a pause, Rosie's response was: "Oh, that's not … oh, no! Latinos are not the only people to do that." Toussaint (2015) documents the sequence of events:

> The View's Raven-Symone then told Kelly: "There's more jobs than that he can use them for."
>
> Sensing things were tense, The Fashion Police host attempted to clarify: "In a sense, you know what I mean? In LA they always…" But before she could finish, Rosie had calmed enough to finally check her.
>
> "Latinos are not the only people doing that," explained Rosie, looking straight at Kelly.
>
> Kelly backtracked and tried to elaborate. "I didn't mean it like that! Come on, I would never mean it like that. I'm not part of this argument," she contested.
>
> As the tension built, moderator Whoopi Goldberg stepped back in and tried to take control of the segment, before ultimately going to commercial break.

Raven-Symoné's reaction has been wiped out of the public register, as that would complicate the binary Latina versus white woman narrative under which the episode has been archived. Raven not only chimed in right after Osbourne's comment, but the camera showed her repeatedly raising her eyebrows, which is one of her trademark expressions. As a result of the interaction, network executives forced Rosie to apologize. Kelly was not forced to apologize on air for being racist, though many sources reported she was very concerned that she was going to be perceived as such after her remarks. Later in the episode, Rosie apologized for being "overly sensitive" to such comments given that she is Latina. Then, again, as the episode was wrapping up, she put her arm around Kelly's shoulder and said the following:

> I want to apologize to this young woman, once again, for being overly sensitive.

Despite three separate articulations of the phrase "overly sensitive," many sources reported that network executives demanded she tweet an apology, which she did: "My apologies @KellyOzbourne, I took your point wrong- #Trump #Latinos. My bad. You're [sic] heart is so pure and righteous. I adore you. @TheView." The on-the-air apology and this "heartfelt" tweet could have been coerced performances, as Rosie did not return to the show, missing the next 2 days and a range of ancillary appearances. In addition to network disapproval, Rosie's Latina/o fans were incensed that she apologized at all, prompting Rosie to post the following tweet: "I tweeted at #KellyOsbourne in an effort to help keep her from spiraling after her unfortunate comment. I went overboard with my apology- #mybad. But I don't apologize for speaking up and calling her on it-mistake or not, it was offensive. And please don't ever question my support for mi gente... Ever." (Toussaint 2015).

For her part, Osbourne eventually tweeted the following apology (Corinthios 2015):

> I want to start by saying I ALWAYS take responsibility for my actions. In this particular case I will take responsibility for my poor choice of words but I will not apologize for being a racist as I am NOT. I whole-hearted f****d up today. I don't want to bullshit anyone with lame excuses. Although, I was stopped mid-sentence by Rosie and couldn't finish my point I will not let Rosie take responsibility for my words. I should have known better as I was on The View and it was live. I've learned a very valuable lesson. It is my hope that this situation will open up a conversation about immigration and the Latin community as a whole. By the way I clean my own f***ing toilets.

The end result was that Rosie did not return to *The View*, though there are conflicting reports as to whether she quit because of that incident or her contract was already not going to be renewed by ABC (Toomey and Malkin 2015). Season 18 was highly fraught, and there were rumors, denied by some and supported by others, that Rosie had several loud encounters with a range of hairdressers and stylists on the show. Rosie was added to the cast at the last minute, and ratings were declining prior to her joining. Indeed, that entire season, the network was considering whether – after Barbara Walters, who founded the show, had retired – to cancel *The View*. After a hiatus to participate in a previously agreed-to appearance in the Broadway show *Fish in the Dark*, it was announced that Rosie Perez would not return to the talkshow. This convenient transition ended Rosie's connection to *The View*. The episode was so disturbing to network executives, that they tried to wipe its presence from online archives – not making it available on Hulu, for example. It is much easier to find a clip of this incident on British than on US websites.

Some of the elements of this incident are so twisted that they simultaneously reveal the possibilities and the limits of ethnic inclusion and agency in the mainstream. First, the panel was multicultural according to liberal standards. Second, Raven-Symoné was the first to react to the Kelly Osbourne comment, yet that gets written out – perhaps because her queer black woman subjectivity is too intersectional, too hybrid, and therefore nearly impossible to include in a pared-down, binary controversy. For example, when Kelly Osbourne wrote a memoir in 2016, she dedicated an entire chapter to race and *The View* incident (Bitette 2016). By that time, the news coverage of the chapter retelling the panel's reaction was: "When Osbourne made her comment, co-host Rosie Perez quickly interjected to denounce the remarks before Osbourne was instantly berated on social media as a racist" (Bitette 2016). The event had been rewritten into a Kelly versus Rosie match. In fact, Rosie had barely reacted; her comments were few and quite muted. Yet, the coverage of the on-air interaction often makes it seem much more volatile and impassioned, a classic spitfire representation. Third, Kelly's reaction to the reaction and her subsequent explanations focused on the intent excuse, as in, "I did not mean to – I was not being racist." Fourth, network executives pressured Rosie to apologize to Kelly for making her feel bad and possibly portraying her as a racist; Rosie apologized on air and then on Twitter. Rosie had to apologize for politely noting that Kelly's remarks were problematic. Rosie is no longer on *The View*. Network executives, as far as it has been reported, exerted no pressure on Osbourne to apologize, though admittedly she was a guest whereas Rosie was part of the show. Fifth, immigration as an issue disappeared or moved to the distant background in relation to a catfight narrative between two women. Sixth – last but not least – the fact that the main host, Whoopi Goldberg, herself a woman of color, tried to intervene and diffuse the situation before cutting out to a commercial break, locates this incident firmly within the multicultural discourse so preferred by mainstream entertainment that foregrounds whiteness even as the host and most of the panelists were women of color.

Rosie has not had the prolific range of endorsement and commercial employment opportunities that some of the other spitfires in this chapter have been
able to deploy. This may be because she continues to be affected by her voice
and accent – which, despite much voice coaching, have remained what they
always were, minus the high octaves. Another possible reason might be that
Rosie is the only one who claims to be a "community activist." Much of her
activism is pre-neoliberal, in that she calls out structural injustices, especially
in regards to Latina/os in general and Puerto Ricans in particular. Rosie takes
an active activist role in Puerto Rican causes such as Latina/os in AIDS, and
was appointed by President Obama to The Presidential Advisory Council on
HIV/AIDS (PACHA) in 2010. In 2006, she co-directed and narrated *Yo soy
Boricua, pa'que tu lo sepas!*, a documentary whose topic varies depending on
who lists it. Wikipedia says it's about Puerto Rican history and culture; IMDb
says it's about New York's annual Puerto Rican Day parade; the reviewer comments on IMDb locate it more with history and culture than with the parade.
Actually, the documentary is a combination of ethnic pride and Rosie's personal history. Rosie is very involved in LGBTQ issues and has been a vocal
critic of the US presence in the island of Vieques, Puerto Rico. It is one thing to
be a good neoliberal citizen and perform the individualized, marketplace
philanthropy that is such a part of most celebrities' diversified entertainment
portfolios; it is quite another to call out injustice, structural inequalities, and
US imperial ventures. Explicitly political stances criticizing the US government
do not translate into the preferred mode of the product endorsement
spokesperson.

Nonetheless, like most of the other spitfires in this chapter, Rosie maintains
an active philanthropic presence, including the following charities and foundations: charity: water, Children's Rights, DonorsChoose.org (money for school
supplies), Earth Day Network, Equality Now, Felix Organization (children
without parents), Foundation for Angelman Syndrome Therapeutics, GLAAD,
i.am.angel foundation (assistance with attending college for needy students),
MusiCares, Robert F. Kennedy Memorial, The Nature Conservancy, The
Trevor Project (suicide prevention for gay teens), Urban Arts Partnership,
and We Are Family Foundation (post-9/11 respect for cultural diversity).
Furthermore, her broad range of causes includes "Abuse, Adoption, Fostering,
Orphans, AIDS & HIV, Animals, At-Risk/Disadvantaged Youths, Children,
Civil Rights, Creative Arts, Depression and Suicide, Education, Environment,
Health, Human Rights, LGBT Support, Peace, Poverty, Unemployment/Career
Support, Water, and Women" (looktothestars.com). This list noticeably does
not include the cause most dear and close to Rosie's heart, Puerto Rico, thus
illustrating this website's tendency to track only nonpolitical causes. As of June
2018, Rosie appeared in the ensemble cast of mini-series *Rise*, an NBC drama
about high schoolers in a musical. Rosie's career may not be A-list, but she
remains consistently employed in the entertainment industry. As a result of her

latest role, she has been making the rounds of morning shows and celebrity news programs, and reiterating her message that Latina/os are stereotyped and underrepresented. In particular, she advocates that Latina/o actors audition for all roles, not just Latina/o ones: "When you go out for a role, let them know that we're not just one thing ... we're human beings first and Latinos second" (Diaz 2018).

Charo

"My English is actually getting worse," she says. "We talk Spanish at home and switch to English only when we need it. Like when we go to the bank to get some money."

(People Staff 1995)

Charo, the single-word name given to the person born María del Rosario Pilar Martínez Molina Gutiérrez de los Perales Santa Ana Romanguera y de la Hinojosa Rasten, represents another flattening of difference within the category "Latina": the inclusion of the Spanish within the category and the repeated slippage between Latin American, US Latina, and Spanish. Charo hails from Murcia, Spain, a fact that she always foregrounds in her self-presentation. She cannot be faulted for backgrounding her Spanish-ness. She always explicitly and implicitly references flamenco through music, arm movement, and calling out the word "flamenco," as well as performing to classic flamenco guitar hits, some of which she has popularized in the United States. An unusual element to Charo's spitfire character, and perhaps a nod to the fact that she is of European origin, is the fact that she has maintained a large mane of blonde cascading curls as part of her self-presentation. Early photographs of Charo show her with light brunette hair. As she has aged, her hair color has gotten lighter. She also, however, performs a stereotypical spitfire Latinidad, overemphasizing many of the elements of this trope. As a result, she is treated by the US industry, other entertainers, and scholars as a US Latina, a Spanish performer, and an eternal foreigner.

Charo arrived in the United States in the mid-1960s and became a US citizen in 1977. Despite the fact that she entered the US entertainment universe in 1965, there is very little written about her in scholarly material. This may be due to her consistent over-the-top performances, which never deviate from unnuanced and flattening-of-difference repetition of the spitfire. Her only mention in a scholarly analysis appears as a brief entry in Vicky Ruíz and Virginia Sánchez Korrol's *Latinas in the United States: A Historical Encyclopedia* (2006). The encyclopedia, her presence in Latina/o entertainment awards, and her on-and-off appearances in show business illustrate her inclusion into the Latina spitfire family, albeit as a minor yet persistent player. For instance, Charo regularly attended the ALMA awards and has performed at the Latin Grammys (2013), thus asserting her belonging and presence within US Latinidad.

Of Spanish origin and US citizenship, Charo has managed to maintain a mainstream career since the 1970s. Ruíz and Sánchez Korrol (2006) note: "An accomplished musician, dancer, comedienne, actress, and singer, Charo is fluent in Spanish, English, French, Italian, and Japanese" (p. 144). Charo's skills include singing "Latin" music and playing flamenco-style guitar, in addition to being a comedian. Her seven albums have ranged from salsa to disco, flamenco to pop. Charo is a serious musician who has won numerous awards for her flamenco guitar playing. "Cuchi-Cuchi" (1977) was her first US hit, and that phrase remains a signifier of Charo, who never fails to voice and perform it in US media appearances.

While she had been a frequent performer on the club show circuit, she was introduced to a broader US audience through the hugely popular *Laugh-In* (1967–73) in 1968. Negra (2001) says of *Laugh-In*: "With their narratively fragmented style and emphasis on masquerade, such shows as Rowan and Martin's Laugh-In … were well suited to reflect and respond to social identities in flux and to stage social contestation in such a way as to re-orient difference as diversity" (p. 168). Charo, who never veers from masquerade, was one of the many representatives of "difference" on that show. Her appearances, wherein she engaged in brief banter with the two hosts, Dan Rowan and Dick Martin, illustrated the classic spitfire. In addition to highly sexualized attire, which often took the form of a bright sequined and midriff-baring halter top accompanied by a low-cut pair of tight thigh and elephant leg pants in the same sequined material, with lots of ruffles, and loud and disruptive behavior, her entire performance hinged on her accented, sometimes impossible-to-understand, and always comical English-speaking skills. For instance, in a special with Dean Martin and Danny Thomas, her answer to Thomas' "How do you do?" is, "How do I do what?"

Nonetheless, Charo consistently and persistently has maintained a hybrid performance of Spanish-ness and Latin-American/Latina. In addition to her excellence in flamenco guitar, whenever she dances, she includes flamenco arm and hand motions, coupled with a much more stereotypical spitfire hip-thrusting-with-raised-arms "cuchi cuchi" move. She also excessively rolls her r's. Throughout her career, she has continued to perform on land and aboard cruise ships, including Disney cruises, especially during her long sojourn in Hawai'i in the late 1980s and '90s, where she moved in order to raise her son away from the spotlight. This geographical move, unlike Rita Moreno's move to London, was inspired by family rather than professional, anti-stereotype reasons. In Hawai'I, she continued on the lounge circuit and opened a restaurant, as an owner.

Charo's musical career has purposefully straddled the Spanish, US Latina, and Latin American cultural tightrope. She has used her "Cuchi-Cuchi" hit from 1977, on an album appropriately touting "Salsoul" music, as a catchphrase to go along with her single-word name. Her music consistently flattens style differences. Moreover, her album covers and the titles of her singles appropriate a range of discursive struggles over Latindad, sometimes to the point of offensiveness. For example, in 1981, Charo released the single "La Mojada," with the subtitle "wet back," from her album, *Charo: Bailando con Charo*. The cover foregrounds Charo's wet head and implicitly naked body (she is covering her breast with her hand), while she stares straight at us. Appropriating the concept of wetback, a slur that refers to the bodies of immigrants who cross the border via the Rio Grande and is generally extended to brown Latino bodies, to commodify herself – and, indeed, profit from her association with Latinidad – is highly problematic. The lyrics and musical composition of the song draw heavily on Mexican cultural tradition and narrative. The music foregrounds mariachi trumpets, and the lyrics detail reasons for making the dangerous border crossing, avoiding border patrols, and seeking a way to make money to send back home, to the other side. Throughout the song, as on all others, Charo pronounces Spanish words with a Castilian accent, even as she, in "La Mojada," sings the tale of a Mexican or Latin American border crosser:

> El Rio Grande crucé
> y por el cerro subí
> y a todas partes que fui
> la Migra supo de mi …
> porque los que yo mas quiero
> necesitan el dinero
> soy La Mojada …
> como se dice I am a wetback …
> pero nunca he olvidado
> los que estan al otro lado …

[I crossed the Rio Grande, and climbed the hill, and everywhere that I went, the Migra knew my whereabouts. I'm doing this for the ones I love the most, for they need the money. I've never forgotten those who stayed on the other side.]

"La Mojada" – its cover, music, and lyrics – differs markedly from other of Charo's recordings. For instance, the much more classically Spanish "Malagueña" (2005) is a guitar solo, whose album cover shows a close-up of Charo holding a guitar against a red backdrop. The hypersexualized elements of "La Mojada" are replaced by the title *Charo and Guitar*. To be fair, Charo has been performing this popular Spanish guitar song since the 1970s. It is a difficult song that showcases her virtuosity as a guitar player. Charo's *Guitar Passion* album cover, released in 1994, is a black-and-white photo of her upper body holding a red guitar. As with "Malagueña," singles from this album are instrumental guitar music. Charo has also released holiday music albums and pop dance compilations. Her recording career embodies her Spanish, Latin American, US Latina, and hybrid approach to building a long-lasting, profitable career.

In the early years of the new millennium, Charo began to re-enter mainstream entertainment through a few appearances in commercials and on television shows such as *Hollywood Squares*. In 2010, her new single, "Sexy, Sexy," written by her son, generated a new round of appearances on talkshows, such as *Ellen*. In 2016, she appeared in three episodes of *Jane the Virgin* as herself, complete with "cuchi-cuchi" hip thrust. This, in turn, generated a new round of talkshow interviews, in which she demonstrated that she had not veered from her spitfire performance. Commenting on her appearance in *Jane the Virgin* (2014–) to Larry King, Charo recounted that she was afforded the opportunity to play on the guitar her "beautiful concerto, *Recuerdo de la Alhambra* ... it was difficult to play and it was an answer to destroy the image of cuchi cuchi." However, simultaneously with vocalizing a critique of her stereotype and desire to move beyond it, she raised her arms and shook her upper body, saying, "cuchi cuchi" – a decidedly ambivalent approach to moving beyond typecasting. In that same interview, she illustrated the following Charo-wisdom in response to King's questions about Latina/os: "Larry [accent on the rolled r's], Latino is hot tamale and spice and came to this country with one dream – work, work, work – and improve the life." She also referred to her son as a "hot tamale" and revealed that, on and off, she had bulls on her property. Her anti-bullfighting cause gives her a platform to assert her Spanish-ness through her delight in enunciating in Spanish many of the elements of bull fighting: "matador," "rejoneador," "parenderillero," and so on. A member of PETA, Charo adopted a bull named Manolo, who then gave birth to a calf, Manolito. A YouTube video featuring this bull (Reyes 2015) gave her a chance to have a close up in which she "runs" in place, offering an opportunity for breast bouncing and hair movement. To sum up: an appearance on *Jane the Virgin* generates an opportunity to appear on *Larry King*, which, in turn, allows her to talk about her support for PETA and speak in Spanish, and this opens up an opportunity to post a video of her bull, which includes a close up of her running, reminding us of her sexualized body. Other than her crusade against bullfighting and her support of PETA, Charo's only other current philanthropic activity is with the Muscular Dystrophy Foundation, and she participated in the 2010 *Jerry Lewis Telethon*.

A 2010 guest appearance on *Dancing with the Stars* (DWTS) led to her becoming one of the competitors in Season 24, in 2017. Coupled with professional dancer Keo Motsepe, Charo was the second to be eliminated from the competition, but this nevertheless allowed her to continue to appear on the show through the grand finale. Covered in the press (Davies 2017) as "salsa and sass" from the first episode, Charo contributed to the stereotype by her frequent use of particular Spanish words, such as "cucaracha." Notice that the representation of Charo as "salsa" elides the difference between flamenco, an Andalusian Spanish dance/music, and salsa, a Caribbean/New York dance/ music. The difference between these two cultural forms is huge – unless it is flattened and categorized as "Latin sass." Charo did not correct this flattening. Doing the round of morning talkshows, the morning after her elimination from DWTS, Charo entered ABC's *Good Morning America* with an "Hola!", and performed her English-accented and silly warm-up routine, while Keo Motsepe looked uncomfortably on. To the question of how he would describe working with Charo, he replied, "Cuchi cuchi!." Charo shared her pre-performance ritual with the audience:

> Standing up, she begins to shake her hips and says:
> *If you want to have a good body, you run, o.k.?* [she pretends to run in place]
> *Then wear a basier* [sic] *or underwear in to where your maracas will be hanging down to the floor.*
> *Then you do that after running* [turns to the side and places hands together in between her chest and squeezes]
> *Mirrrrro mirrrrro on the wall, make my maracas 44* [not sure if she says 44 or forty fall?].
> She proceeds to hop and face forward now, while she slowly squats up and down and holds her rear end.
> *Por favor, por favor, lift my butt up off the floor*[14]
> As her former DWTS dance partner Motsepe covers his face in the background, Charo is shameless.

Another layer to her five-decade career, drawing on her excessive and spectacular performances in Las Vegas and Hawai'i, is her status as a gay icon, as well as a supporter of LGBTQ causes (Ferber 2011). Charo has appeared on *RuPaul's Drag Race* (2016) – playing herself, of course.

By the 2000-teens, Charo was exhibiting indications that she had had extensive cosmetic surgery, especially on her nose – something that is a troubling yet expected aspect of an aging female celebrity (Negra 2001). Charo represents the spitfire who banks on typecasting throughout her US career. She herself remarks quite explicitly that her global persona as a serious musician does not cross over into the United States, where she realizes she's known as "the cuchi-cuchi girl." Nonetheless, she seems unperturbed by this typecasting, as it has taken her "all the way to the bank" (Ruíz and Sánchez Korrol 2006, p. 244). Her official website lists her attributes as "witty humor, lovable accent, and her mastery of the flamenco guitar" (www.charo.com). The website has a background of fire-engine red, the classic color in flattened stereotypes of "red hot" Latinas and flamenco dancers. There is very little in her own presentation that does not foreground the trope that has economically sustained her all these years: the spitfire.

Charo remains a reference for over-the-top, ridiculous Latinidad and accent. For example, she appeared in three episodes of the *Donnie and Marie Show* (1976–79) during the 1976–77 season. In one of these episodes, Donny Osmond introduces her as follows: "You probably wouldn't go to our next guest for English lessons. And when it comes to comedy and music, you still won't understand it" (laugh track) (*The Donny and Marie Show* 2017). In *The Carol Burnett Show* (1967–78) comedy hour, Charo appeared as the character "Chiquita," with every component of her over-the-top spitfire characterization. Carol Burnett not only cast Charo in her show but also mocked her through "Chiquita," "Nadine," and any number of characters that explicitly spoof her. Charo is remembered by many as a frequent guest on the popular ABC television show *The Love Boat* (1977–87), where she played the character April Lopez, whose first scene had her carrying a piñata and guitar as a stowaway, with the final line, "America, here I come!" Charo guest-starred eight times on this show, with her character becoming a performer on the titular cruise ship. She even performed her own hip-thrusting rendition of the theme song, now available on Spotify and YouTube. She has also appeared, as herself or a fictional form of herself, in many other television shows, including *That '70s Show* (2000) and *The Suite Life on Deck* (2010).

If Latina actors or actors playing Latinas receive negative feedback for their accent, they are likely to be compared to Charo. For instance, Marissa Tomei's performance in *The Perez Family* (1995) is criticized by comparing her Spanish accent to Charo's (Negra 2001). Similarly, in the first-season episode of *Modern Family*, "The Incident" (2009), Jay's first wife, DeDe, played by Shelley Long, actually refers to Gloria as "Charo," further underscoring DeDe's disapproval of Gloria, as well as situating Sofía Vergara's character within a historical tradition of spitfire. Nonetheless, and despite language othering and sexualization, both of these spitfires – Charo and Sofía – are laughing all the way to the bank. Whereas one might argue that they are forced to play this role, and, indeed, are the butt of many jokes, they exploit self-tropicalization for fame and profit.

Salma Hayek

> Do celebrity philanthropists and social activists harness their status and cachet to benefit others, or do they use the philanthropic-activist image to benefit and brand themselves? ... Can it be both?
>
> *(Trope 2012, p. 156)*

Salma Hayek's trajectory differs a bit from that of Rita Moreno, Rosie Perez, and Charo. First, Hayek was born and grew up in Coatzacoalcos, in southern

Mexico. The difficult name for non-Spanish speakers adds authenticity to Hayek's self-fashioning as an exotic and authentic "Latin" star. Second, Hayek came from a wealthy family and crossed over into the US mainstream as an already successful Mexican actor, in the early 1990s. She first appeared in a very small role as a jilted girlfriend in Allison Anders' *Mi Vida Loca/My Crazy Life* (1993), and then in mainstream Hollywood film by the mid-90s – about the time that Perez's stardom was beginning to wane. Third, while her native accent/ manner of speech reduced her viability in the mainstream in a similar way to Perez, Hayek's is a result of her being a second-language speaker. Nonetheless, her thick accent, in combination with her perfect Coca Cola-bottle body (Báez 2015), resulted in a number of movies wherein she played "the bikini girl," as she herself has said. Trying to move beyond typecasting, in the late 1990s Hayek created a production company, Ventanarosa. Lucrative modeling and product endorsements, in addition to participating in her own productions, have kept her in the limelight. Furthermore, Hayek, already born into wealth, married the billionaire François-Henry Pinault, a scion of the Pinault family, in 2009, which has both added to her resources as a commodity activist and kept her on the red carpet at many occasions that other spitfires do not have access to, such as fashion weeks and even royal events throughout Europe.

Hayek founded Ventanarosa in 1999, to expand the production and representation of "Latin" material and actors. Her strategic use of the word "Latin" muddles the line between US Latina/o and Latin American, something Hayek continues to do throughout her career. Through Ventanarosa, Hayek produced films and television shows in which she cast herself in roles other than the spitfire. For example, Ventanarosa produced Julia Alvarez's novel *In the Time of the Butterflies* (1994) into a feature length drama in 2001, including major Latina/o and Latin American ("Latin") talent such as Edward James Olmos, Demian Bichir, and Marc Anthony, in addition to Salma Hayek in the lead role of Minerva. Hayek produced and played the protagonist in the *Frida* biopic (2002), for which she was nominated for an Oscar as Leading Actress. She executive produced the hugely successful US *Ugly Betty* (2006–10), whose global circulation displaced many other countries' productions of that originally Colombian show, acting the role of Sofía Reyes in the 2006–07 season. This show pretty much took up Ventanarosa's entire production schedule for the years it ran. Negrón-Muntaner (2017) argues that these productions "allowed Hayek to simultaneously modify her star text, increase her worth in the industry, extend her influence beyond it, and re-invest her star capital to political forces" (p. 296).

In 2007, MGM announced a partnership with Salma Hayek to create a new company called Ventanazul. MGM COO Rick Sands asserted, "Hayek will be running the company … To the extent that it makes sense for her to act, she'll do that; to the extent that it makes sense for her to produce, she'll do that" (Gilstrap and Gilstrap 2007). The announcement, placed in *Variety*, used the word "Latin," as in "Latin talent" and "The Lion is going Latin" – the latter in reference to MGM's iconic symbol. Ventanazul aimed to cross over into both English-language and global markets in relation to Ventanarosa's target audience of US Latina/os with bilingual or monolingual Spanish skills (Molina-Guzmán 2012a). However, while Ventanarosa continues to exist, there is no indication that Ventanazul ever existed. Most of the news coverage about that venture was published in 2007, and no more follows it. *Variety* has two articles on Ventanazul, both in April 2007, and *The New York Times* has but one, also in April: "Hollywood has had little success so far in appealing to the large and growing Latino audience in the United States, with flops like Fox's 2003 effort, 'Chasing Papi.'" Apparently, Hollywood has also had little success in creating successful production ventures by and for Latina/os, as Ventanazul never got off the ground.

Hayek's acting roles have diminished since the 2000s, other than in Ventanarosa productions, with her largely unable to break the mold of the spitfire Latina. For example, she played Elisia Padriera on the hit television show *30 Rock*. Cast as a voluptuous and beautiful working-class Puerto Rican, with her cleavage often foregrounded, bright red lipstick, luscious long brunette hair, big hoop earrings, strong Catholic devotion, heavy-duty accent, and a propensity to speak in fast Spanish depending on the situation, she captured the heart of main character Jack, played by Alec Baldwin. She appeared only in six episodes in 2009, and one episode in 2013, but was undisputedly a spitfire. Granted, the role, and the entire show, was tongue-in-cheek, but we do not know if audiences read this double-entendre ironically or not (Báez 2018). Salma Hayek continues to be cast as Latina, with supporting roles in nearly unheard-of films and some television shows – for example, as Olivia, the Mexican sister in *Some Kind of Beautiful* (2014), which went straight to video release, and the voice of Teresa[15] del Taco in *Sausage Party* (2016). Recently, she was Sara in *How to Be a Latin Lover*[16] (2017), the main character's sister, a working-class single mother. She is also cast in a range of non-US roles, such as in *September in Shiraz* (2015), a film about the Iranian revolution, in which she is billed as Salma Hayek-Pinault, perhaps because the film was mostly released in culturally conservative countries. Given that Hayek is part Lebanese, she is quite credible as an Iranian, with a bit of an accent. She also played the Queen of Longtrellis in *Tale of Tales* (2015), produced in England and mostly distributed in Italy. She starred in the title role in *Everly* (2015), a violent thriller, which was not released in the United States but received limited release in a number of countries, such as Bulgaria, Estonia, the United Arab Emirates, Singapore, Lebanon, Nigeria, Turkey, and Jordan. This film returns Hayek to a bikini-girl character, albeit a highly violent one, who can handle many types of weapons and is proficient in hand-to-hand combat.

In July 2017, Hayek starred in the drama *Beatriz at Dinner*,[17] in which she played the title character, a holistic practitioner. *Beatriz* trenchantly skewers the superficiality and lack of ethics of contemporary wealthy Los Angeles real-estate developers. Hayek portrays a Latina whose difference from all the other characters is palpable, yet whose character is far from stereotype. In fact, the movie contains a maid whose presence "represents the invisibility of the visible" (Hurtado 2017, p. 329), a classic Latina stereotype, played by Soledad St. Hilaire, who seems to have inherited the trope since Lupe Ontiveros[18] passed away. In *Beatriz*, St. Hilaire's character does not merit a name, and her interactions with Beatriz/Salma are minimal, though suggesting solidarity while maintaining distance – after all, Beatriz considers herself a health-care professional. Hayek's Beatriz is fully unspectacular, dressed in grays, made up to look like she is not wearing make-up, and slightly overweight – the camera often shoots her from the back and focuses on her ill-fitting tight pants, almost as a counter move to the lingering camera shots that so often focus on Jennifer Lopez's butt (Negrón-Muntaner 1997; Barrera 2002; Molina-Guzmán and Valdivia 2004). Unexpectedly, Beatriz ends up part of a real-estate celebratory dinner at one of her clients' mansions. The sharp dialog, especially between Beatriz and John Lithgow/Dough Strutt, proves to be highly timely, as their respective roles remind audiences and critics of current US political debates. Goldstein (2017) titles her film analysis piece, "'Beatriz at Dinner' Puts a Trumpian Mogul and an Immigrant at the Same Table":

> Hayek is riveting and so far from the trope she often gets trapped in (and, as she did on 30 Rock, occasionally subverts): Instead of playing an alluring sexpot – a male fantasy – she's almost childlike in her mannerisms and unyielding moral purity. She's totally disinterested in appealing to others, which makes her a man's nightmare, and she has no love interest to speak of but adores her goats so *much she lets them sleep in her bedroom.*

The review's fixation on the character's heteronormative subversion, juxtaposing her celibacy with her focus on her pets and coding her asexuality as "childlike," reads more as unmet expectations on the part of the reviewer than a careful analysis of the movie itself. Other reviewers note that Beatriz purposefully avoids the usual typecasting. The following interview with Mike White, the movie's writer, in a Parade.com article, explicitly addresses the effort to go against typecasting:

Salma Hayek's performance in this film is phenomenal. Did you have her in mind for the part from the beginning?
Yes. Early on, I had a great meeting with Salma. She was a fan of *Enlightened*. She has a lot of great cultural and political opinions, and it seemed like we were very like-minded. It was a lot of fun. I left the meeting thinking it would be really cool to write something for her. Then I started trying to figure out what that

would be, and what that character would be. Salma is such a force of life. *She plays a lot of spitfire characters. I thought it would be really interesting to have her dress down into something more simple and reserved, and to do something different.* Obviously she is capable, and a great actress (Murrian 2017, emphasis mine)

Through this role, in conjunction with the *Frida* role in 2002, Hayek has managed to demonstrate that she is "a great actress," as Mike White states. It has been difficult, however, for her to stay active in leading roles in mainstream US entertainment.

Since her crossover into the US mainstream, Hayek has had lucrative contracts with a number of major globally recognized brands, such as Lincoln cars (marketed through tropes of wealth and Spanish hacienda iconography; Valdivia 2005c), Revlon, Avon, Le Chopard luxury watches and jewelry, Campari, and Cartier jewelers, all of which foreground her beautiful body. She has transcended class in the commercial sphere, managing to endorse upper-middle-class and luxury goods. This self-branding in relation to products cannot be underestimated, as many Latina actors have generally been linked to more down-market products.

Hayek further extended her commercial ventures from 2011 to 2018 through her make-up and hair products line, Nuance, marketed exclusively through CVS drugstores. Apparently, she took 3 years off from acting to work on this line (Trionfo 2015). Promoted as natural and authentic, the products touted that they used the power of "exotic"[19] botanicals such as acai, buriti oil, aloe vera, acacia senegal gum, monoi flower butter, blue agave, mamey fruit (sapote), jojoba oil, cotton blossom, annatto seed oil (achiote), avocado oil, amaranth protein, and algae extract. Many of these ingredients had to be explained on the Nuance website as they were not generally known to mainstream US consumers. In particular, Hayek mentioned and identified tepezcohuite (mimosa bark extract) as central to the products: "used by the Mayans for hundreds of years to rejuvenate skin" (Nuancesalmahayek.com). In a pseudo-interview on the website, staged to foreground Hayek sitting on a white couch, with a white-haired white man taking notes, Hayek asserted that "every woman should be entitled to preserve their youth and beauty ... tepezcohuite is used in Mexico because it's the strongest regenerator of skin cells ... they call it the miracle plant in Mexico; it's something I used for years to keep my skin young." Blue agave, she claimed, grows in Jalisco, Mexico; "the women in my family have been using these exotic ingredients for generations, and with Nuance I'm passing them onto you."

Coverage of this partnership was highly positive. CVS's transaction size growth has been partially attributed to the Salma Hayek line (CSA 2011). In fact, sales of Nuance products were the "highest of a proprietary brand in CVS's history" (Vora 2013). Nuance was successful enough that, in 2015, the brand launched updated packaging and an extended facial products line. As well, CVS expanded its aisle space for the collaboration (Born and Brookman 2015). WWD notes that "on the day of the product presentation, [Hayek stood] before a roomful of young beauty editors … dressed in a Gucci outfit with an Yves Saint Laurent hat (both part of the Kering luxury group overseen by her husband, François-Henri Pinault)," thus acknowledging that she used her personal wealth to promote the beauty line. She also drew on her Mexican heritage and personal beauty to promote her profitable collaboration.

While news coverage of her Nuance products foregrounded Hayek sounding like a chemist as well as the actor and model that we all know her to be, both it and Salma's presentation of the product line referenced her grandmother, the use of traditional, natural, and organic ingredients, and a discourse that set the modern chemistry of make-up development against a more holistic, organic, and green approach to beauty and health. In the Nuance venture, Hayek's commodity activism linked her products back to Mexico, to natural ingredients, to her female ancestors, and to health. This is an interesting marketing tactic that brings up some questions vis-à-vis Hayek's personal history. First, Hayek is a first-generation Mexican. Her mother is Spanish-Mexican and her father Lebanese-Mexican. Her grandparents are from Spain and Lebanon. In fact, press releases mention that her grandmother was a cosmetologist who studied in Paris (Trionfo 2015). Second, as with most beauty products, the first few ingredients remained water, alcohol, and a range of words ending in "glycerides." Third, no mention was made at all in this entire venture about Latinidad – rather, Hayek firmly located her identity, provenance, and holistic knowledge, as well as her ingredients, in Mexico, in a product targeting all women, not just Latinas. This self-branding through strategic essentialism proved quite profitable, both for Hayek and for CVS. However, in 2018, without an announcement, Nuance products went on deep discount and the line was discontinued. As of April 2018, some of the products were still on the CVS website, but none could be ordered. As of June 2018, one can only purchase Nuance products at a steep mark up on eBay and other such online vendors.

As is the case with most major contemporary stars on the global stage, Hayek also includes philanthropic work in her self-branding portfolio. She is active in a wide range of foundations, charities, and causes, foremost in relation to violence against women and immigrant issues. Since the birth of her child, she has added children's issues to the list. Her own Salma Hayek Foundation has branched out from originally raising aid and awareness for battered women to working with disadvantaged children in Mexico. In addition to collaborations with major conglomerates such as Procter and Gamble (to fund, through the sales of disposable diapers, a vaccine against maternal and neonatal tetanus), she has worked to eradicate violence against women, advocate breastfeeding, spread female empowerment, and promote women's rights in Afghanistan (Wikipedia). Look to the Stars, a website dedicated to publicizing celebrity philanthropy, lists the following as Hayek's charities and foundations: 10 × 10 (girls' education), American Foundation for AIDS Research, Children's Defense Fund, CHIME FOR CHANGE (education, health, and justice for girls and women), Chrysalis (economically disadvantaged and homeless individuals), Clara Lionel Foundation (health, education, arts, and culture), Conservation International, Entertainment Industry Foundation, First Star (child victims of abuse and neglect), Fulfillment Fund (helping disadvantaged students finish high school, graduate from college, and find a job), Global Green, Legacy of Hope Foundation (health care for children), Natural Resources Defense Council, Oceana, ONE Campaign (global AIDS and extreme poverty), Peace Over Violence, Raising Malawi, Room to Grow (babies born to poverty, from newborn to age 3), Salma Hayek Foundation, Solar Neighbors Program, Speak Out Against Domestic Violence, Stand Up To Cancer, The Art of Elysium, UNICEF, and V-Day (violence against girls and women). It lists her "causes" as: Abuse, Addiction, Adoption, Fostering, Orphans, AIDS & HIV, Animals, At-Risk/Disadvantaged Youths, Cancer, Children, Conservation, Creative Arts, Education, Environment, Family/Parent Support, Health, Homelessness, Human Rights, Hunger, Mental Challenges, Oceans, Peace, Physical Challenges, Poverty, Rape/Sexual Abuse, Senior Citizen Support, Slavery & Human Trafficking, Substance Abuse, Water, and Women. While there is very little research on the recipients of this philanthropy, or on the NGOs and other organizations with which Hayek works, Castañeda (2012) has interviewed Avon ladies who have worked with Avon's "Speak Out Against Domestic Violence" campaign and experienced a conflict of interest in this endeavor. On the one hand, they support the cause and try to promote it; on the other, if customers purchase products branded by it, the Avon ladies lose commission. Alongside Academy Award-winning actor Reese Witherspoon, Hayek has worked to fund this campaign (Castañeda 2012, p. 281).

Like our next Latina actor, Sofía Vergara, Salma Hayek has astutely shifted to production of media, product endorsements, licensing deals, beauty products, and an extensive philanthropic footprint. Control over production has enabled her to play less stereotypical roles. She has somehow managed to promote upscale products. Her marriage into the Pinault family, purveyors of luxury brands such as Gucci, Yves Saint Laurent, Bottega Veneta, Balenciaga, Boucheron, Alexander McQueen, and Stella McCartney, has ramifications in terms of her visibility at major events in fashion and elite circles. Her most recent role as Beatriz, while casting her in the character of a working-class immigrant – a Latina/o stereotype in news narratives – nonetheless veers far away from the bikini-girl-with-an-accent role taht marked her crossover to the US mainstream. While she is not one of the top A-list Hollywood stars, Salma Hayek has certainly managed to remain in the global mainstream entertainment circuit.

Molina-Guzmán (2012b) further analyzes Hayek's labor in the production of authenticity, in which the star seeks to define the representational landscape of Latinidad, nationally and transnationally. Staking a claim to represent Latinidad on a global level (p. 142), Hayek, through her commodity activism, produces a commodification of Latinidad: "She must circulate a media discourse about herself that reinforces her privileged authority as an authentic Latina/Mexicana to produce media texts that both colonize and rupture media representations of Latinidad" (p. 139). In sum, Hayek harnesses US and Latin American talent, targets US Latina/os, commodifies Latinidad in general, and markets this construct globally, while simultaneously marketing herself as an authentic Mexican to mainstream popular culture, not necessarily Latina/o consumers.

As a coda to her self-fashioning as an authentic purveyor of global Latinidad, and in connection to the issues of language so central to the spitfire trope, Hayek conspicuously chooses very difficult Nahuatl words to mark her provenance and authenticity. For example, she reiterates that she hails from Coatzacoalcos in Mexico. She identifies tepezcohuite as the featured ingredient in her now-defunct Nuance product line. In *Beatriz at Dinner*, a movie in whose script and development she participated, her character comes from Tlaltecuhtli, which Beatriz tells Don Strutt "is on the Pacific." Actually, Tlaltecuhtli is the name of an Aztec mythical figure, usually represented in birthing position, but not of an actual place. Whether in self-representation, in naming ingredients for her product line, or in collaborating on movie dialog, Hayek continuously deploys her authenticity partly through usage of difficult Spanish words.

Sofía Vergara

> While Gloria Pritchett is well known for her curves and sex appeal, Vergara uses the role as an opportunity to question the relativity of cultural constructs associated with language and gender, setting most of the weight of her acting on her accent.
>
> *(Fernandez L'Hoeste 2017, p. 223)*

> At a moment of deep global economic anxiety, Modern Family recuperates middle-class whiteness through a subtle narrative of resentment
>
> *(Molina-Guzmán 2012)*

> Sofía Vergara's embrace of the loud, curvaceous, and accented Latina therefore can't be understood solely as a passive response to Hollywood pressure – it is also a self-conscious performance in service of increasing star power
>
> *(Contreras Porras 2017, p. 311)*

Sofía Vergara was the highest-paid television actress the United States in 2011, 2012, 2013, and 2016, and is the latest and last spitfire included in this chapter. Born in Barranquilla, Colombia in 1972, Vergara was "discovered"[20] on the beach by a talent agent at the age of 17, and cast in a Pepsi ad distributed throughout Latin America. According to multiple sources, none of which mention a specific university, Sofía Vergara moved to the United States even though she had already completed three years of dentistry studies at a university in Colombia to pursue an entertainment career and escape political unrest in her home country.

Latina/o Feminist Media Studies scholars have begun to build a body of scholarship on Vergara (Molina-Guzmán 2012a; Vidal-Ortiz 2016; Fernandez L'Hoeste 2017; Contreras Porras 2017; Casillas et al. 2018). Scholars historically situate her in relation to Carmen Miranda in the forties: "Whereas the Good Neighbor-era spitfire [was] meant to ease foreign relations in a time of war, Vergara's spitfire needs to effectively manage her difference during a moment of growing US public anger towards Latino immigration and increasing white economic resentment in the post-race era, when race and racism are frequently presented as irrelevant" (Molina-Guzmán 2012). Furthermore, Contreras Porras (2017) argues that despite the historical lineage between Miranda and Vergara, the former remained a comedic figure whereas the latter is reduced to a sexualized trope. Nonetheless, Vergara's self-presentation as a US Latina in the English-language part of her website and as a Colombiana in the Spanish-language version suggests an effort to represent herself to a transnational audience through multivocal strategies. Through her role as Gloria Delgado-Pritchett in the hit ABC network docudrama *Modern Family*, a show that as of February 2019 has been announced to be in its last season, Vergara remains in the throes of her fame as the most recent Latina spitfire while simultaneously building a diversified entertainment portfolio extending far beyond the role that has made her rich and famous.

Since the beginning of her entry into any type of public performance, Vergara has capitalized on her body. The Pepsi commercial that introduced her to the world via Colombia and Latin America had her stripping down to a tiny bikini as she attempted to navigate very hot sand on a hot day at the beach. The camera followed the then-unknown actor as she used her clothes and other items, such as her book and bag, to avoid the hot sand on her way to a Pepsi stand. The commercial shifted between Sofía's body and the approving gaze of male sunbathers. Thus, from the outset, Sofía was cast as a hot Latin American woman. After crossing over into the United States, Vergara, naturally blonde, had to dye her hair dark brown to fit into the structure of stereotypical mainstream Latina, simultaneously reiterating the trope and avoiding the misunderstanding experienced by the Brazilian actor Xuxa when she attempted a crossover without dyeing her own blonde hair (Valdivia and Curry, 1996). Vergara's lush mane of (blonde or brown) hair, curvaceous body (especially her breasts), and comedic aptitude have generated ample opportunities for her. Fernandez L'Hoeste (2017) notes, "A blonde, coquettish teenager with substantial comedic aptitude, who clearly rejoiced in the playful potential of her femininity to achieve her ambitions, stood a tad beyond the imagination of Colombia's cultural establishment, anchored in the mountains" (p. 229). As a result, Vergara has had to cross over multiple entertainment barriers in her career. Within the terrain of difference, Sofía Margarita Vergara hails from Barranquilla, on the Caribbean coast of Colombia. As such, she is known within Colombia as a Costeña, rather than the more normative Colombians who hail from Bogota, the Andeans, who by virtue of privilege get to pass as generic Colombians – what L'Hoeste refers to as "anchored in the mountains." The class and racial differences assigned to Costeños by Andeanos rely partly on the Afro, indigenous, and Middle-Eastern hybrid populations residing on that coast in relation and difference to the mestizo/light-brown/Colombian white population of the capital city. In concurrence with Fernandez L'Hoeste's (2017) accent research, women in the city of Barranquilla (interviewed by the author) do not recognize Vergara simply as from their city. In addition, these women, some of whom attended school with Vergara, grew up in her neighborhood, and know some members of her family, are very insistent about two things. First, she performs a Costeña identity in terms of her expressions, dynamism, and embodied femininity. This insistence relocates the spitfire performance into a regional Latin American local Colombian and specific coastal identity. Second, Vergara had to cross over into mainstream Colombian/Bogota entertainment before she could attempt the crossover into US entertainment. Once in the United States, Vergara first crossed over to Univision, the Spanish media production hub in Miami, where she had to assert a new subjectivity of Colombiana in relation to the Cuban, Puerto Rican, and Mexican ethnicities more prominent in US popular culture (see Cepeda 2010). In this second crossover, Vergara's performance lost the specificity within Colombian Costeña identity to sign as generic Colombian in the US Latina/o firmament. After crossing over to US English-language media, first through the movie *Chasing Papi* (2003) and eventually via ABC/*Modern Family* (2009–), Vergara came to represent the trope of the Latina spitfire in mainstream US entertainment. By the time she gained fame with *Modern Family*, she had successfully navigated three crossovers, with different regional, language, ethnic, national, and historical elements. This navigation alone represents much labor and agency.

Modern Family's ensemble cast was neither created nor written to foreground Vergara. Rather, it was a vehicle for Ed O'Neill, formerly of the hit television show *Married ... with Children* (1987–97), to extend his career. Vergara is the breakout star of this ensemble, surpassing O'Neill's popularity. Her role represents not only the classic tropicalized character (Aparicio and Chávez-Silverman 1997) but also a vocal body through which authenticity, difference, and racialized hierarchy are constructed in the show (Casillas et al. 2018).

Vergara, perhaps because she is living through the early and most lucrative point of her typecast spitfire career, or maybe because she is already set to profit from a diversified portfolio resulting from her ongoing investments in a strategy that guarantees her employment and professional opportunities beyond her spitfire stereotype, has yet to denounce the trope. She appears in curve-hugging dresses, with foregrounded cleavage, very high heels, cascading locks, large hoop earrings, and heavy make-up. Her long mane of hair has returned to blonde as she has gained popularity and agency within the mainstream entertainment industry. Recently, she has reiterated her reaction to reporters' questions about the spitfire in "What's Wrong with Being a Stereotype?" (Nelson 2017). Furthermore, without explicitly articulating her performance to Costeña identity, she affirms of her Gloria character that, "I play her the way I see my mother and my aunt behave as Latin women" (Dockterman 2014), thus concurring with the Barranquilla women who recognize her as a local representation of gendered identity. In many interviews, she excuses enduring "Latin" stereotypes in general and the spitfire in particular due to a lack of better writers. This move reduces structural issues of ethnic stereotypes to the organizational and individual levels of analysis. Vergara's use of the word "Latin" accords with Hayek's use of the same, in that both actors at once sidestep the political implication of the term Latina/o and the difference between Latin American and US Latina/o culture.

As well as with most of her acting roles, Vergara's personal appearances beyond the hit television show replay the spitfire trope. Vergara does not shy away from a focus on her body, often bringing it up herself or responding to talkshow hosts' remarks about her physique. One of the creepier interviews of her career, and the first on a major US television talkshow, was conducted on March 25, 2003. The creepiness is partly due to hindsight, because of Bill Cosby's ongoing legal issues. The interview occurred on *The Late Show with David Letterman*, when Cosby was filling in for the sick host. Vergara wore a tight, but not overly revealing, flower sleeveless dress and walked in dancing to salsa music. Cosby did not hide his delight: "What you have on is wonderful. And when you walked out many people became attentive ... Make me feel young again ... you me feel ... ahem ... very excited." All the while, he was leaning uncomfortably close into Vergara, who was 30 at the time and virtually unknown to US audiences. Without looking back at Cosby, Vergara looked straight at the audience and pushed him away while saying, "But don't die on me!", implying that his excitement was so great that he might have a heart attack – after all, he previously had told her he was 65 and that when he got excited, he went to sleep faster. Vergara deftly and subtly diffused what had become an uncomfortably creepy interview. On more recent talkshow appearances, such as ABC's *Live! With Kelly and Michael*, in an interview that pretty much focused on her attractiveness, she engages in sexualized banter about clothing, her body, and perfume: "Men love it. I let you do it. [Meaning Michael could walk over to her and smell her wrists.] I put it everywhere" – to which Michael literally dropped to the ground in a pseudo-split move (Collon 2016). In a visit to David Letterman, she revealed that everything she wore came from her licensed Kmart line – dress and earrings – "everything you see here you can get at Kmart" (she said this while raising her eyebrows suggestively) (Letterman interview, ourmarvelousworld 2011). To Ellen DeGeneres' question of "Who has more fun, blondes or brunettes?," she responded, "I would say the girls with the bigger boobs!" She often mentions that she thanks her boobs nightly for all they have done for her and her career. At least at this point, Vergara does not shy away from a focus on her body and attractiveness.

As a classic spitfire, talkshow hosts treat Vergara as if she were the same as Gloria Delgado-Pritchett, eliding the difference between acting and the self, and therefore as if her accent and malapropisms define her beyond her television role. Vergara, whose Gloria character sometimes implicitly turns the issue of language against her ensemble cast, often explicitly inverts conversations about her accent in talkshows. On David Letterman, for instance, she performed not understanding David's question about her son. She said to David: "What? Why are you talking with that accent today?" Instead of agreeing with David that she did not understand his question/the English language, she suggested he was the one speaking with a heavy accent. Similarly, when Ellen interviewed Vergara and Reese Witherspoon about *Hot Pursuit* and commented to Sofía, "Your English has gotten better, I have to say, I'm understanding you," Sofía turned to Reese and said, "Her English?", and, "Now I understand why I am so funny to the Americans, your Spanish [Reese's] sounds so ridiculous!", as if the comment had been made about Reese because she had a Southern accent, and foregrounding the fact that Reese – and, implicitly, Ellen – could not speak Spanish, thus astutely turning the tables on the English-language and accent comments.

In addition to her continuing starring role in *Modern Family*, Vergara has appeared and continues to appear in a variety of vehicles in the US entertainment mainstream. Most notably, she co-starred in and co-produced *Hot Pursuit* (2015) with Witherspoon. Vergara plays the role of Daniela Riva, the wife of a narco-trafficker from Colombia, opposite Witherspoon's uptight and unworldly Officer Cooper.[21] This role falls within US trope of Colombians as narco-traffickers (Cepeda 2018). Officer Cooper is supposed to take Daniela into the witness protection program, traveling from San Antonio to Dallas, but this turns into a road trip from hell. The movie is chock full of classic elements of a range of stereotypes. For example, Witherspoon/Officer Cooper embodies the mid-level professional[22] woman who is sexless and clueless. In fact, until the time she is assigned to protect Vergara/Rivas, Whitherspoon/Officer Cooper has a reputation in the Texas police force as an incompetent cop who is failing not only at her profession but also at femininity. At one point in the movie, she disguises herself as Justin Bieber (or José Beaver, as pronounced by Vergara). On the other hand, Vergara/Daniela Rivas embodies the Latin spitfire through dress, behavior, and dialogue. She wears tight dresses or tight pants and tops and very high heels throughout the movie, for much of which they are on the lam. She initially carries two suitcases. One of them is full of cocaine, which comically explodes in the face of a truck driver who drives into their getaway convertible. The second suitcase is full of what, at first glance, appear to be yet more high heels, but turn out to be Daniela's effort to take something of value out of her criminal husband's situation, as the shoes are encrusted with gold and gems. Dialogue includes the following intersectional gem:

Witherspoon/Officer Cooper: You have to stop treating me like I am a rookie cop who doesn't know what she's doing.
Vergara/Daniela Rivas: You have to stop treating me like a criminal.

The movie juxtaposes Witherspoon's whiteness as legally and morally straight and Vergara's excessive sexuality in connection to Latin American drug-trade criminality. At movie's end, both women come out as friends, and Vergara brings Witherspoon into the realm of heterosexual normative romance. Of course, the Colombian criminals and their corrupt US cop friends encounter their comeuppance. With a production budget of $35 million, the female-centric buddy comedy *Hot Pursuit* has earned $51.7 million at the box office thus far (June 1, 2018). It is not a major blockbuster, but it has delivered a decent profit margin despite its disappointing opening weekend. One industry analyst, attempting to explain its small audiences and lukewarm critics' reviews, offered the following wisdom:

> **Sofía Vergara Is Not a Movie Star.** Not yet, anyway. The "Modern Family" ensemble member may be the highest-paid actress on TV, but she hasn't been able to translate that level of small-screen notoriety into box office appeal. You can be gorgeous, funny, and talented and still be best-known to film audiences for playing third banana to a bunch of Smurfs. But then…
>
> *(Susman 2015)*

Susman follows this comment with an assessment of Reese Witherspoon's stardom: "Star Power Doesn't Last." Given that Witherspoon is a Best Actress winner (for *Walk the Line*, 2005), with a series of highly successful romantic comedies and dramas and an increasing production portfolio following the critical and commercial success of her HBO series *Big Little Lies* (2017), and is firmly located within whiteness, the relevance of her so-called decline to this chapter on spitfires attempting to construct a long-term career beyond their time in the limelight is strong. If this type of normative star – Reese Witherspoon – is already being declared a has-been, this serves as testament to the arduous currents that Latina actors in the spitfire trope swim against.

Vergara's most recent presence in the mainstream comes through playing the voice of Flamenca, the flamenco dancer in *The Emoji Movie* (2017), "who is the life of the party in the movie" (Miller 2017), thus making the spitfire role a full-circle endeavor, eliding together Latin American, US Latina/o, and Spanish signifiers, as well as venturing into one of the most usual types of spitfire employment, as the voice of a highly stereotypical cartoon in a children's full-length animated movie.

Vergara is often covered in the entertainment and news press – as she has been in the scholarly literature (e.g. Molina-Guzmán 2012a) – in relation to previous spitfires. For example, McDonald's (2015) article, "How Sofía Picked Up Carmen Miranda's Legacy – and Ran With It" implies a high degree of agency for Vergara and historical knowledge of the trope. Even Charo has reacted to her in relation to the spitfire trope, and her own (Charo's) connection to it. To an ALMA Awards comparison with Vergara, Charo responded, "Sofía Vergara is Charo with diarrhea" (Moreno 2013). Later, while being interviewed by Larry King, Charo referred to that comment by saying, "I talk without I think," and mused over whether she should apologize, to which Larry King replied that she should (Fernandez L'Hoeste 2017). This comment received a ton of coverage on Fox, by Larry King, and in *Latina, Cosmopolitan, The Huffington Post*, and the *National Enquirer*, to name a few media outlets. The gaffe served to circulate both spitfires in the celebrity news, to relink their careers, and to reiterate their currency as spitfires.

Endorsement and licensing deals have proven much more lucrative to Vergara than her income as television's highest-paid actress, according to *Forbes* magazine and her manager and partner Luis Balaguer. Balaguer says Sofía knew she would not make huge amounts of dollars as an actor, and the pair realized early in her career that "endorsement deals provided much more steady income than acting." Early diversification began prior to her becoming a household name. Balaguer and Vergara first experimented with a highly profitable bikini calendar in 2000, and they have not stopped exploring the wide world of endorsements and (even more lucrative) licensing agreements. This has meant endorsing a wide range of products an audience might want through companies wishing to link themselves to Vergara's star persona. One of the most frequent elements of a celebrity diversified portfolio is perfume. For example, Elizabeth Taylor's perfumes still bring millions of dollars to her heirs long after her death (Robehmed 2015), and Jennifer Lopez has developed highly lucrative perfume lines. Not surprisingly, then, Sofía Vergara has developed a fragrance collection with Perfumania, whose "Tempting" fragrance comes in an hourglass-shaped bottle – in distinction to Jennifer Lopez's "Glow," which is more guitar shaped, in accordance with the way she has commodified and branded her booty.[23] Other fragrances are called "Love" and "Sofía." As well, female stars secure beauty and cosmetic product endorsements, which in Vergara's case includes the dandruff shampoo Head and Shoulders, which was seeking to glamorize its image. Similarly, in 2011, Vergara picked up an endorsement contract as one of the faces of Cover Girl make-up. In addition to a licensing agreement with Ninja coffee bar,[24] a clothing line for Kmart, and ongoing commercials with Diet Pepsi, Vergara has worked with fast-food giant McDonald's, gym chain Bally Total Fitness, and beer brand Cerveza Aguila, and "promotes a line of scrubs for Careisma, including, of course, one of a Cheetah-print variety" (Berg 2016). *Forbes* magazine credits these endorsement and licensing agreements with the star's standing as one of the top-grossing earners in US entertainment. On August 2012, Vergara graced the cover of *Forbes* Magazine as television's best-paid actress. She does not endorse mostly upscale products. In fact, the Head and Shoulders deal arguably could only be attempted by someone atop their celebrity game, yet with a sense of humor.

Much of this endorsement and licensing labor has been carried out behind the scenes in collaboration with her partner and manager, Luis Balaguer. With little fanfare outside the "insular Latino media community," they have shrewdly built their company, Latin World Entertainment (latinwe.com), from a Miami talent-management firm into a licensing, marketing, production, and new-media powerhouse. The history of this collaboration is a bit fuzzy as to its initial date. For instance, McDonald (2015) reports that Sofía Vergara had already begun to branch out into other aspects of the entertainment industry by 1994, when, at the age of 22, she co-founded LatinWE with Balaguer, initially as a casting agency to help Latina/o talent negotiate better deals than Univision was providing. Representing itself as "the premier Hispanic talent management and entertainment marketing firm in the United States":

> The multi-service company offers a 360 degree approach that includes publicity, licensing, endorsements, brand integration, production and content development. 100% Hispanic owned, LatinWE has the reputation of being the number one Hispanic talent agency in the country and the strongest multi-service and synergy provider in its kind in entertainment.
>
> *(latinwe.com, retrieved July 7, 2017)*

However, Luis Balaguer's biography[25] on IMDb.com lists him as CEO and founder of LatinWE (http://www.imdb.com/name/nm2230500/bio), with no mention of Vergara until 2010, when the talent agency worked on her product line with Kmart.

Casserly (2012) reports that Vergara and Balaguer have been building their company "for 16 years." Subtracting 16 from 2012 takes us back to 1996. As matter of fact, Casserly reports that the pair met in 1996. Nevertheless, and regardless of when Balaguer and Vergara actually became partners, a source inside the firm pegs 2011 revenues at $27 million, with a healthy profit margin of nearly 20%. Clients include Disney and Paramount. The company's YouTube channel, NuevOn, premiered in April and immediately sold out ad inventory to Procter & Gamble through 2013. Having crossed over to the United States via co-hosting two Univision shows in the late 1990s, Vergara has continued collaborations with that powerful player in US Latina/o media production and distribution. The announcement of NuevoMall, for instance, foregrounded the new venture's collaboration with the network.[26] NuevoMall was scheduled to launch in 2012 as a digital location connecting Latin stars with brands. Though it was an elaborate partnership with Univision, it seems to have disappeared from public view.

In January 2017, still working with long-time partner Sofía Vergara and incorporating Emiliano Calemzuk, former president of Fox television studios, Balaguer announced the formation of Raze, a Latino Media Digital Startup (Spangler 2017). According to Balaguer, Raze is "a great tool for advertisers and products to connect with transforming Latino audiences, and will benefit from the shifting of audiences from traditional platforms to mobile video." Promotional video coverage of its launch party in July 2017 (produ.com) foregrounds Balaguer and Calemzuk as the driving forces, conceptually and financially, and shows Vergara schmoozing as a celebrity. She is not mentioned by anyone interviewed in the tightly produced promotional video, though she is prominently featured backgrounding interviews with several people involved in producing Raze material. As of July 2017, Raze.com was up and running, producing and circulating a tightly edited segment on Daddy Yankee's global megahit "Suavecito" (https://www.facebook.com/Raze/videos/1754869937861555).

Like any contemporary celebrity who understands neoliberalism, implicitly or explicitly, Vergara has also ventured into the world of spokesperson or supporter for a range of causes. As a survivor of thyroid cancer, she not only promotes the drug Synthroid but is also a spokesperson for the Follow the Script campaign, which aims to raise awareness about hypothyroidism. She participated in June 2016, when the Human Rights Campaign released a video in tribute to the victims of the 2016 Orlando gay nightclub shooting; in the video, Vergara and others tell the stories of the people killed there (Wikipedia). Look to the Stars (looktothestars.com) lists the following as her charities and foundations: Alzheimer's Association, American Foundation for Equal Rights, Children's Defense Fund, Cure Duchenne, Entertainment Industry Foundation, Gabrielle's Angel Foundation, NALIP, Sandy Hook Promise, Stand Up To Cancer, St. Jude Children's Research Hospital, and THORN; and the following as her "causes": Alzheimer's Disease, Cancer, Children, Civil Rights, Creative Arts, Education, Family/Parent Support, Health, Human Rights, Hunger, LGBT Support, Mental Challenges, Peace, Physical Challenges, Poverty, Rape/ Sexual Abuse, Slavery & Human Trafficking, and Weapons Reduction. This is a partial list, as on the same website one finds a September 27, 2016 item, "Sofía Vergara and Buca Di Beppo Launch Meatballs 4 Niños," a collaboration with St. Jude's Children's Research Hospital, and mention of her participation in a December 2015 "End Gun Violence" video (https://www.looktothestars. org/news/14657-celebrities-take-part-in-we-can-end-gun-violence-video). Vergara's exemplary global citizenship, as demonstrated by her many collaborations with corporate causes, firmly places her within neoliberalism.

It is difficult to assert agency unambiguously. For example, we do not know for sure that Vergara was "discovered" on a Colombian beach by a talent agent. We also do not know whether she is trying to break away from the spitfire role at a time when it is yielding such success and profit for her. We do know that she is busy attending to the many tasks in which she is involved, several of them destined to provide her with life-long income – something that the spitfire role seldom provides for any actor.[27]

Conclusion

Sylvia Morales and Esperanza Vasquez inspired me to explore the arduous task faced by spitfire Latinas in maintaining a career. Alicia Kozma's research on Stephanie Rothman informs my analysis about these two vanishing Chicana film producers. As such, this is partly a chapter about method: what gets archived, what scholars have access to, what we have to dig for to get the answers, and the unexpected places where we have to look for material. Representation research is often critiqued for being an easy archive, and this chapter illustrates the difficulty of conducting work on undervalued producers. As a way of framing data throughout this book, what looks easy is actually hard because we have to do extra work to find out what it is that needs to be analyzed, as even basic figures are not recorded in accessible ways or locations. I have triangulated Wikipedia material, not as a stand alone archive but in relation to books, articles, and encyclopedia entries, especially in the case of the underexplored Charo. The archives of film history have not been sensitive to the production by women of color. For every book about representation of women of color in film (e.g. Negra 2001; Beltrán 2009), there are very few articles, let alone books, on women of color or ethnic women as producers. Molina-Guzmán's work on Salma Hayek as a producer of authentic Latinidad (2012a) stands out nearly alone in terms of recognizing the labor that women of color perform within mainstream entertainment.

Beginning with the canonical work of Chicana film producers and their relative disappearance, especially in relation to their male counterparts, I expanded this mini-project into an investigation of the staying efforts by actors playing one of the most enduring and stereotypical tropes of Latinidad, the spitfire. Neither Morales nor Vazquez – nor, for that reason, Rothman – was in front of the camera, and they sought to produce counter-stereotypic representations of women, which generated both canonical productions and vanishing careers. Spitfires, on the other hand, perform, by definition, in front of the camera. Yet, often their efforts at longevity of career involve being able to function behind the camera, as well as in other domains. Rothman was not able to cross over into mainstream production, and eventually dropped out of the film industry altogether. Morales and Vazquez had less success in production than Rothman, and also largely dropped out of the entertainment business. We need to fill out the archive on these three women, for further scholars and generations to learn from their labor, agency, and resulting industry indifference.

My efforts to begin to construct a cartography of agency and labor for Latina actors usually dismissed as passive recipients of one of the most offensive stereotypes reserved for this ethnic category seek to make an imprint on the history of an industry that remains stubbornly sexist and racist. Moving beyond exceptional women to chart their laborious effort to maintain a career, this chapter resituates the spitfire from the realm of representation to the area of production, agency, effort, and intervention. The Latina actors in this chapter represent a group of performers still present in mainstream entertainment, with different histories, ages, ranges of origin, and overlaps, as well as particular strategies for staying afloat in the turbulent waters of mainstream entertainment. They all face, or will face, gender and ethnic prejudice, as well as age discrimination, which is insidiously gendered in Hollywood film. They also all share amazing talent and hard and arduous labor, as they managed to cross over into the mainstream and have since attempted to continue to have a lucrative career.

Sofía Vergara recognized early on in her career that a diversified portfolio would lead to greater earnings and, perhaps, more control over her career. Vergara and Charo welcomed the opportunity to play the spitfire role, as it provided employment and stardom. Moreno, Hayek, and Perez voiced a preference to leave the role behind, with differential intensity and different strategies to do so. The latter three experienced the trope as a complicated opportunity, but also as a barrier to be overcome and left behind.

Contemporary stardom bears its own cross-platform synergies and a huge industrial branding process, in addition to a required presence on social media. For instance, in decreasing order of followers on Twitter, we have: Jennifer Lopez, 41.6 million; Sofía Vergara, 9.3 million; Salma Hayek, 198 000; Rosie Perez, 99 300; Rita Moreno, 15 500; and Charo, 4019. Jennifer Lopez is the contemporary Latina star against whom all others measure their popularity. The descending numbers are a mixture of popularity, contemporaneity, and age (of the performer, and therefore of their target audience). The fact is, all of these actors have a Twitter account and other social media presence, as one must in contemporary celebrity culture.

I explored Rosie and Salma because, in my previous work, I have argued that their career paths would differ from that of someone like Jennifer Lopez primarily because their accents make their crossover always deferred and difficult. In fact, Rosie continues to talk about her voice as an element of tension even within Latina/o audiences. We do not know if it is due to her accent – I doubt it, since many of the ad campaigns in which Salma is present are only visual – or to personal choice – as Rosie classifies herself as a "community activist" rather than a philanthropist – but Rosie does not appear to have as highly diversified a portfolio as Vergara and Hayek. Salma Hayek's film career has arguably not been that much different than that of Rosie. However, she has been able to parlay a global presence through her product endorsements, charity work, and elite wealth-enabled visibility on a range of red carpets. Salma is much more globally ubiquitous than the other actors in this chapter. One could say that by taking a feminist activist role, Rosie has not chosen to or gotten to participate in the spoils offered by a postfeminist, postracial, neoliberal presence. Either way, these two actors have had to transition into roles that arguably allow the former to keep acting, albeit onstage and in supporting roles, and the latter to maintain a presence behind the camera, on the global philitainment stage, and in the occasional juicy starring part in front of the camera.

Hayek and Vergara partly have banked on production in general and on organizing and representing "Latin" talent in particular as a way to explore a broader range of roles and opportunities for themselves and to pave the way for their possible eventual displacement from the limelight. Ideally, one could envision for them a career like Moreno's; the latter is enjoying full employment well into her 80s, and arguably paved the way for this to be a possibility for all the other spitfires discussed in this chapter.

In terms of endorsements and licensing agreements, there is such a wide range of products and services that generally endorsing within a price range would appear to be a strategy or a check on agency. Salma Hayek's upscale endorsements in relation to Sofía Vergara's mid to low-market products, while equally lucrative, represent differential branding for the Latina stars. Rosie Perez and Rita Moreno's nearly nonexistent presence in this realm represent either a choice made by the actors or a choice made by companies not to affiliate with their celebrity. It is difficult to parse this out as we are faced with evidence at the level of effect. Philanthropic ventures also bear some of these same characteristics of agency or structure. Wealthy philanthropists such as Salma Hayek are able to fund their own charity as they contribute to many others. Four out of the five actors in this chapter have an extensive philanthropic footprint, as this is nearly required in the present neoliberal moment. Charo remains alone in her trajectory of mining the stereotype with little discernible effort to branch beyond it. One cannot dismiss Charo, as it must not have been easy to keep the "cuchi-cuchi" act going for so long. In terms of consistency and nondeviation from the trope, Charo stands alone.

The transnational circulation of popular culture adds another layer of opportunity to the careers of these Latina actors. Given that many of these hybrid Latinas have roots or family beyond the United States, they can develop their connections into another element of their ongoing strategy. Salma Hayek markets her

Mexicanidad and can return to Mexico for lucrative endorsements even as she draws on her membership in the Pinault family to extend her networks and appearances on a European and a global stage. Some of her films have been released or produced through a transnational set of players outside of the United States. Sofía Vergara, though now a US citizen, remains a Colombian to Colombians and thus has that country, and indeed all of Latin America, as her terrain of possibility. Charo, though underconnected to neoliberal philanthropy, has maintained a reputation as a serious flamenco guitar player on the Spanish, European, and global stages – something of which she is explicitly aware and separates from her spitfire persona within the United States. Rosie Perez is currently acting in a Canadian series. The world at large seems much less interested in perpetuating the spitfire stereotype of these actors than does the US entertainment industry.

Post-network opportunities have played a large role in Rita Moreno's career revival at the age of 87. One of her favorite roles was in the HBO series *Oz*. While it is true that she never stopped working, surely not even she could have predicted a leading role in a Netflix Norman Lear sitcom at this age. Similarly, her role in *Jane the Virgin* is available to audiences through Hulu and Amazon Prime Video. While it's too early to tell, scholars and activists hope that the expanded production terrain will mean more inclusive and expanded narrative in the post-network landscape, so as to introduce talent that has heretofore remained untapped and to provide already known talent with more and less stereotypical roles.

In *Be Creative: Making a Living in the New Cultural Industries*, Angela McRobbie (2016) writes of "the euphoria of imagined success, relative untainted by a reality of impediments and obstacles in the creative labor market" (p. 4) in relation to her master's students at a university in England. Latina actors enter US mainstream success euphorically, to be sure, as they have all endured all sorts of trials and tribulations before even getting to that stage. For many, the crossover is transnational. Their hybrid impure roots, in relation to the fantasized purity of the white subject, make them both exotic and suspect. They are tainted before their crossover, and the reality of impediments and obstacles rise above them – huge, yet somehow scalable. This chapter contributes to an archive for understanding some of the strategies these actors have pursued in order to build a long-lasting career; their efforts to transition beyond token and exceptional into a parity that would include them in the mundane – the ever-employed successful actor.

As a way to end this chapter, I return to Rita Moreno and her recent (February 18–19, 2019) visit to Notre Dame campus. Many people, faculty and students, continually praised her on her creativity and perseverance in carving out a long career. She eventually answered that she wished she had not had to be so creative and to have had to exert so much perseverance. She just wanted a career like Meryl Streep's, where she would have been offered juicy roles throughout her life because she is a great actor. This is the utopia of a former spitfire.

Notes

1 Kozma (2017) asserts that, "For Derrida the archive is another way of maintaining hegemonic power through exclusion and erasure."
2 Indeed, few Latina actors ever achieve meaningful employment in the mainstream entertainment industry.
3 I have to reiterate that barriers to entry in the mainstream entertainment industry are high as it is – and much recent research, media reports and – even – a department of labor investigation – continue to document the fact that mainstream US entertainment industry has a glass ceiling for women and minorities in nearly every type of job category – a glass ceiling that is much lower in the film industry.
4 It is interesting to note that the gendered trope is a minority among more options for male stereotypes. A similar categorization occurs within African American "new minstrelsy" tropes which include the coon, the buck, the Uncle Tom, and the Mammy.
5 As with many of the ethnic tropes applied to Latina/os, the spitfire was also used to represent African American femininity.
6 Prior to the talkies, many Latin American actors enjoyed lucrative careers due to their ability to make expressive performances in popular exotic narratives. As Beltrán documents, some non-Latina/o actors actually changed their names to sound Latina/o in order to cash in on the popularity enjoyed by the likes of Dolores del Rio and Lupe Vélez. However, even then, actors' ability to cross over into the mainstream depended on "whether they had fair skin and European facial features" (Beltrán 2008b, p. 31). With the introduction of sound, Latina and Mexican stars either lost their careers or were reframed through highly intensified stereotypes.
7 Categorization of first and second waves can only be made post-facto, when we have the hindsight of historical production patterns.
8 Fregoso (1993) adds that these Chicano producers represented Chicanas as metaphors or in gendered stereotypes.
9 This actually would be her second autobiography, as she published her first in 2013.
10 The best analysis of Rita Moreno's career is a chapter in Mary Beltrán's *Latina/o Stars in their Eyes* (2009).
11 Much has been written about this role and this Oscar. While it was an undeniable achievement for Moreno, the fact is that the lead role given to Natalie Wood, a white US actor, illustrating that in Hollywood's eyes, a Latina could not be trusted to play the lead in a major Hollywood film about Latina/os. Thus, Moreno's Best Supporting Actress Oscar was a bittersweet win, in that it was the first Oscar for a Latina, playing second fiddle and a spitfire to the protagonist role.
12 In the spirit of full disclosure, I and my colleague Isabel Molina Guzman were invited to a panel and participated in a 2-day visit with Rita Moreno at Notre Dame University on February 18–19, 2019.

13 A Latino boom is part of the "myth of discovery." Basically, Latina/os and our "hot" culture are rediscovered every so often as mainstream popular culture commodifies our ethnicity. There have been previous booms, for example in the 1940s, and there will surely be others in the future.

14 Research assistant Diana Leon-Boys had the unenviable task of transcribing this segment. She adds the following to the transcript: *I think she meant to say "so that your maracas are not hanging down to the floor."

15 The fact that the name is Teresa, without an H, signifies Latinidad. Were the character an ambiguous ethnic, the name would be Theresa (please see longer discussion of this in the Disney chapter).

16 Produced by Pantelion Films, which also distributed *Instructions Not Included* (2012) in the United States. Both are Eugenio Derbez vehicles and are designed to appeal to US Latina/o audiences through highly stereotypical representations of Latin Americans and Latina/os. It doesn't get much more stereotypical than a film called *How to be a Latin Lover*.

17 In terms of genre, many reviewers classify it as a dark comedy or drama. Within those two genres, the most often mentioned subgenre is the "guess who's coming to dinner." In fact, Mike White, the screenwriter, admits to being inspired by *Who's Afraid of Virginia Woolf*, the mother of all "guess who's coming to dinner" books and movies (Murrian 2017).

18 Lupe Ontiveros died in 2012. She estimated that she had played the role of the maid in Hollywood film and television nearly 200 times. St. Hilaire plays other roles, such as "Hispanic woman on plane" in *Graceland*, but mostly gets cast as the maid or nanny.

19 This word is used often by Salma Hayek in interviews about the product line, YouTube clips on the Nuance website, and descriptions of the ingredients both on the actual products and on the Nuance website, as well as any other websites that sell the products.

20 This narrative of "discovery" appears often in stars' histories. I repeat it here as it is often reiterated in relation to how Sofía Vergara entered into media employment. I am not convinced by it, since it appears too easy of a vehicle to efface the labor that it takes to land one's first lucrative contract.

21 Reese Witherspoon's character, Officer Cooper, is mistaken for a meter maid due to her size and gender. This is strangely similar to Disney's *Zootopia* (2016), in which protagonist Judy Hopps, also a police officer, is treated by nearly everyone as a meter maid, partly because her duties include issuing parking tickets. While beyond the scope of this chapter, this coincidence speaks to the deep ambivalence of gender gains in traditionally male professions such as police work.

22 A police office would be a mid-level professional in relation to a lawyer, doctor, or professor.

23 An internet search leads us directly to perfumania.com. Searching for "Sofía Vergara" on google.com yields a first option of Sofíavergara.com. However, when one clicks on that, the perfumania website opens up, with the three Sofía Vergara perfumes.

24 This combines the star's sexy persona with her provenance from Colombia, a country partly known in the US imagination as a coffee producer.

25 There is also discrepancy in terms of Luis Balaguer's origin, with his IMDb bio listing it as Cuba and Casserly (2012) claiming it's Madrid, Spain.

26 NuevoMall appears not to have materialized. There is no trace of it online as of July 2018. Raze, on the other hand, is actively producing and disseminating on Latina/o popular culture topics.

27 Based on a conversation with a fellow scholar who has had the opportunity to visit Sofía Vergara and her husband, Joe Manganiello, at their home, I trust her observation that this couple works nearly round the clock. That even at home, in what most people consider after-work hours, they have a team of handlers who constantly make demands on their time. Furthermore, they are not at liberty to make scheduled visits and appearances, as these are all managed for them, with less of their input that we might have in our own lives. I am not saying this to suggest that Vergara and Manganiello are unusual in their degree of agency vis-à-vis their careers, but rather to bring out the fact that cultural workers at this level of celebrity work very hard and have a very complicated relation with issues of "agency," as they have to rely on handlers and managers, who, in turn, respond to studios, advertising agencies, the parent companies of endorsed products, and media conglomerates – not to mention the elusive audience – in managing their celebrity clients.

3

An Unambivalent Structure of Ambivalence

Disney's Production of Latina Princesses

Preface: Disney Does *Moana* – Cultural Politics in 2016

In September 2016, Walt Disney Animation Studios was preparing for the release of its newest princess movie, *Moana*. With an opening date scheduled for the US Thanksgiving weekend, known to bring huge audiences to theaters, Disney was following its release playbook by, among other things, beginning to market a huge range of products through its Disney stores, website, and the many licensed agreements customary to this level of global publicity campaign,[1] as well as pursuing a complex set of pre-release cross-promotional activities worthy of a conglomerate that basically invented the concept of synergy (Meehan 2005). One of the items available through the Disney stores was a $34 costume sold as a "Maui costume for kids – Disney Moana," which consisted of a full body suit with tattoos, an "island style skirt," and a rope necklace. In essence, the costume was a brownskin body suit. Activists charged that the characterization of Maui, a Pacific Island demigod, and the sale of the costume were instances of cultural appropriation and "brownface," referencing the concept of blackface wherein white actors, such as Al Jolson in *The Jazz Singer* (1927), portray African Americans by literally painting their white skin black. Such impersonations of African Americans are now deemed racist, as the debate following *Saturday Night Live*'s "honeyface" impersonation of Obama demonstrates (Beltrán 2013). After Pacific Islanders asserted that the sale of the body suit amounted to a modern version of blackface only in brown, Disney pulled the costume from sale (BBC News, September 22, 2016), making the following statement:

> The team behind *Moana* has taken great care to respect the cultures of the Pacific Islands that inspired the film, and we regret that the Maui costume has offended some … We sincerely apologize and are pulling the costume from our website and stores.
>
> *(BBC News September 22, 2016)*

The Gender of Latinidad: Uses and Abuses of Hybridity, First Edition. Angharad N. Valdivia.
© 2020 John Wiley & Sons Ltd. Published 2020 by John Wiley & Sons Ltd.

This chapter investigates the intersection between princesses, tween fictional characters, and tween starlets as they contribute to Disney's contemporary ambiguous and hybrid representations, as well as their avowal and disavowal of Latinidad. Disney conducts seemingly contradictory processes of stereotypical ethnic and lack of ethnic specificity through mixed-race characters and actors relying on ambivalence and ambiguity. Disney scholars have identified ambivalence and ambiguity as an audience response to the pleasure of Disney narratives in relation to distrust of Disney as a global for-profit behemoth (Wasko and Meehan, 2001). I propose that Disney produces an *unambivalent structure of ambivalence* within its narratives and global marketing through representation some characters and situations as ethnically ambiguous and simultaneously unambiguously ethnic (Valdivia 2016). Given that Latina/os are an in-between ethnic category and tweens an in-between age category, this chapter highlights ambiguity as in-betweenness 3.0. The in-between or bridge role that Latinas play in popular culture (Valdivia 2011) translates into Disney Latinas being both can-do and at-risk as they represent as characters, navigate as actors, and are interpreted by girls (Projansky 2014). Furthermore, building on Shields Dobson and Kanai (2018), the lives of the starlets appear to express affective dissonance that bubbles over into mental and physical health issues, a decidedly dystopian outcome. The can-do Disney princess utopia embodied by the animated princesses and tween fictional characters cannot be sustained by the live actors in the flesh.

In keeping with the conceptual themes of this book, and as illustrated by the *Moana* vignette, this chapter extends the application of hybridity and transnationality to the analysis of this threesome of Disney princesses. Mainstream visibility of Latinidad seldom goes beyond the impulse to flatten difference, which takes up hybridity and transnationality implicitly. In pursuing a strategy of minimizing risk while maximizing profit, Disney avows ethnicity and global heterogeneity while simultaneously disavowing cultural demands for respectful inclusivity. Nationally and globally, Disney takes deliberate steps to expand its ethnic register through distribution and engagement with global audiences, characters, and narratives. Latinidad and Latina/os present both an opportunity and a challenge to Disney, as illustrated by its confusing attempts to target the US Latina/o audience and the global brown audience.

I began this chapter with the recent controversy about *Moana* because it illustrates so much about contemporary mainstream media, in particular Disney, and its approach to issues of ethnicity, Latinidad, and gender. One would think that with all of its huge personnel and resources, Disney would have been able to anticipate such a guffaw and avoid the bad publicity and controversy. From an economic standpoint – the most important one to Disney as a major media conglomerate run according to the principles of capitalism – it is not efficient to develop a product, such as the body suit, that will generate a backlash and have to be pulled off the shelves. I dare not estimate the cost of this mistake, though in relation to the billions that the company is worth, the hundreds of millions that the movie is expected to generate, and the $150 million the movie cost to make, it is probably not a significant amount to the company. As of March 2019, *Moana* has generated $643.3 million worldwide[2] (Box Office Mojo 2016), well surpassing its production costs and rendering huge profits through its national and global release. Moreover, this figure does not include all of its ancillary products and licensing agreements. As contradictory as it may sound, the extra press coverage that the incident generated may have been worth the price of trashing the brownskin costume.

Moana, in terms of cultural politics and ethnic visibility, represents yet another Disney effort at utopian inclusion/cooptation of the global within its hugely profitable princess franchise. Hybridity in Disney iconography, curated out of a large intellectual property archive, incorporates the labor of a wide range of hugely talented hybrid cultural workers. Creating a narrative based on the already existing Pacific Islander tale of Maui the demigod, voiced by Dwayne Johnson,[3] foregrounds an actor whose own hybrid identity has been the subject of academic research (Washington 2017b). In addition to Johnson, *Moana* introduces Auli'i Cravalho, a soprano music student from Hawai'i, as Moana. The casting call auditioned hundreds of girls throughout the Polynesian Islands and Hawai'i. In typical Disney fashion, some of the auditions and the reveal to Auli'i that she had been selected were taped and used as promotional material for the movie.[4] Additionally, "Polynesian singer and composer Opetaia Foa'i (performing with his band Te Vaka) anchor the film's cheery globalism in a specific South Pacific milieu" (Scott 2016). Perhaps even more notably, *Moana* features Lin-Manuel Miranda, of *Hamilton* fame, who is experiencing a Midas-touch moment in his career. Miranda wrote the musical score, which many reviewers single out as "infectious." Given that nearly nobody can obtain a ticket to *Hamilton*,[5] the fact that Disney managed to hire Miranda for this movie illustrates the power and deep pockets of the global media conglomerate. Hypothetically, had Lin-Manuel known about the body suit, he probably would have made an intervention, but the large size of the Disney empire yields many instances of the hands not talking to the brain.

The market-driven inclusion of the "other" (Valdivia 2017) through tokenistic visibility represents a capitalist impulse toward utopian inclusivity in representation, casting, and production that usually generates a dystopian response from those being represented. This dynamic, in turn, contributes to an ambivalent strategy of diversity that comes off as avowal and disavowal of the ethnic group and narrative that Disney gingerly dares to represent in an effort to interpellate expanded audiences and therefore generate increased profit. Resistance to this latest addition to the profitable Disney princess franchise began with activist response to the sheer size of the Maui character. While Dwayne Johnson is a large, lean, and muscular actor, Maui in *Moana* is extra-large – much larger than circulating representations and figures of this demigod. On the heels of the size controversy came the brownface body-suit fiasco. *The Moana Syllabus* (https://moanasyllabus.wordpress.com) summarizes many of the responses, contextualizes the movie in relation to a Disney history of representing the global South, signals the broad range of issues that Polynesian activists had with the movie, and presents an alternative archive of history and culture.

In *Moana*, we have a Disney princess franchise movie, which seeks to represent the global in a hybrid production and representational mode, stepping on ethnic landmines while generating profits for its parent company. *Moana* also foregrounds the gendered deployment and commodification of globalized hybridity. In addition to the landmines of ethnic representation, *Moana*, as all Disney princess movies do, foregrounds a girl as the bearer of the action, as the main protagonist. As such, Moana is a can-do girl, an authentic postfeminist heroine (Kennedy 2018). Indeed, *Moana* reviewers contextualize the movie in relation to the tween princess. Peter Bradshaw of the *Guardian* brings it all together: "Disney has contrived an amiable new animated musical that speaks to the tween-princess-sleepover demographic while tapping into Polynesian myths and making a modest, decently intentioned gesture at diversity" (2016). Rolling out the occasional brown girl has become part of the Disney playbook.

Not surprisingly, mainstream reviews of the movie were generally rather positive. Reviews of the movie range from the "this is what we expect from Disney" variety – both amiable and pleasurably predictable (e.g. Bradshaw 2016; Scott 2016) – to the more celebratory, "*Moana* is a Big, Beautiful Disney Smash," written by Christopher Orr for *The Atlantic* (2016), which concludes that "The movie is an absolute delight, a lush, exuberant quest fable full of big musical numbers and featuring perhaps the most stunning visuals of any Disney film to date." Assessing the post-Thanksgiving box-office returns, one reviewer sums it up as follows: "For some Americans, it looks like only Disney movies will get them to theaters" (Levine 2015).

From a circuit-of-culture approach, Disney commodifies ethnicity (Halter 2000), deploys it through tween bodies in princess movies, develops hybrid narratives with hybrid talent, and cultivates (hopefully) growing and lifelong audiences. The domestic and global articulation of content and related products contributes to contemporary popular culture in general, and girl culture in particular. Arguably, inclusion of previously ignored groups, such as brown girls, has the potential to create spaces for historically underrecognized groups to be represented and to recognize themselves (Seiter 1995, referenced in Roman and McAllister 2012). Despite the overwhelming profit motive and tendencies toward white heteronormative content, Disney's efforts to domesticate and include diversity yield contradictory results. Navigating the turbulent hybrid streams that push and talk back to the mainstream befuddles even Disney.

The *Moana* mini-case study illustrates that Disney, along with other major media/toys marketers of children and family products, such as Mattel and its

American Girl line, attempts to attract new audiences by trying to commodify and sell gender and ethnicity, in a controlled and domesticated manner. However, ethnicity is a tricky construct, and commodifying it comes with many issues. Disney walks a tightrope of inclusion and exclusion – seeking out ethnic audiences through complex industrial and representational strategies, while reassuring its traditional, implicitly white audience that all is well and the same as ever in the white normative Disney universe (Real 1977; Wasko 2001; Wasko et al. 2001; Blue 2017). This tension becomes difficult to manage, even for Disney industries, with their massive PR and research budgets and untold numbers of highly talented creative artists. Despite the carefully orchestrated production and release of content franchises and the construction and circulation of stars, in the process of gingerly articulating ethnicity, Disney, like other media/toy makers, unwittingly enters into controversy – but its size is an asset in weathering representational and activist storms, allowing it to bravely soldier on. Relying on hybrid specificity, such as in *Moana*, and in ambiguity and barely perceptible hybridity in Latinidad, Disney exploits a gendered and racialized formula, designed to include and appropriate a global range of tales and characters, ideally avoid any controversy through this Disneyfication process, and sidestep controversies if and when they arise through its size, influence, and managed amnesia. In this process, the uses and abuses of ambiguous hybridity toward the marketing of gendered Latinidad prove to be quite profitable, while simultaneously engaging the imaginations of girls, increasing the visibility of Latina/os, and potentially generating a complex and internally contradictory cycle of self-esteem, agency, and marginalization.

Media ↔ Toys

The convergence and synergy industrially exploited by a media conglomerate such as Disney begins with the media–toy symbiosis. In the contemporary entertainment mainstream, there are no children's toys without children's media or children's media without children's toys. Griffin (2000) reminds us that Walt Disney learned the licensing lesson early in his career, but that it took Kay Kamen, a toy licenser, to teach him that increased sales worked both ways: licensing toys increased movie audiences and movie releases increased toy and other product sales. In fact, licensing revenue helped Disney sail the turbulent economic waters of animated film production. We can thank Walt Disney for exploding the potential of cross-promotion/synergy and of product placements.

The case studies in this chapter explore the construction of ambiguous and hybrid Latinidad by Disney from girlhood into tweendom and the promised land of long-lasting adult stardom. It is essential to begin at the media–toy nexus in order to understand the commodification of audiences and stars.

Implicitly referencing the classic Dallas Smythe (1977) "audience as blindspot" argument that what media produces and commodifies is the audiences sold to advertisers, Blue (2017) correctly asserts that both audiences and stars are laborers. Chavez and Kiley (2016) further break down the labor that children perform in the Disney universe, as audiences, actors, and corporate social responsibility (CSR) recipients. In today's integrated merchandising environment, major global media companies and other conglomerates are able to work together to synergistically promote a children's, tween's, or young adult's product, link it to a branded character or narrative, and further link it to the big brand of Disney itself. Of course, the Disney company, with its many converged holdings, ranging from television, film, sound, digital, and print media to theme parks, toy stores, and vacation cruises, can synergize a mediated product in a way that no other toy or media company can. The result is that a children's or tween's television show or movie is made with ancillary marketing in mind, where toys are the mere beginning of a wide range of products, including – for the more successful franchises, such as *Dora the Explorer* and the many Disney princesses and other media vehicles – clothing, digital gaming, food (gummy bears, cookies, crackers, specially shaped noodles for macaroni and cheese, soups, granola bars, ice cream, chocolates, etc.), sheets, furniture, wallpaper, lunchboxes, telephones, backpacks, watches, toothbrushes, toothpaste, adhesive bandages, shampoos, soaps, thermoses, coloring books, crayons, coloring pencils, stickers, and so on. Moreover, many ancillary products profitably combine a brand-name product with a toy/media character, such as Minion Band-Aids. Another primary way in the United States to provide a tie-in for a children's media product is through the toy in a McDonald's Happy Meal – what is known in marketing as a "premium." Thus, a transnational fast-food company and a global media conglomerate co-market their food and media products via a specially produced toy with a limited time availability. In fact, in February 2018, after more than a decade, Disney re-established its ties with McDonald's, which had been severed when childhood obesity statistics made the media conglomerate wary of a connection with purveyors of fattening foods. Now that McDonald's had more "healthy" items on its menu, and with *The Incredibles* sequel about to be released, the two conglomerates were once more collaborating in cross-promotion (Whitten 2018). Additionally, Happy Meal toys often become collector items, so that sales include not only the children who might watch the movie, but many an adult looking for a trophy or an investment.

McDonald's may be the most prominent brand that seeks to profit from the children's mediated product market, but it is far from the only one. For example, Campbell's Soup sold a "Healthy Kids" chicken noodle soup with noodles in the shape of Dora the Explorer, thus simultaneously hailing busy parents concerned about their children's health and child fans of Dora. In the same Campbell's Healthy Kids line, packaging and noodles featured Woody and Andy from *Toy Story* and Princesses Belle, Tiana, and Cinderella[6] from classic and modern Disney princess movies. Similarly, Band-Aid strips feature Dora the Explorer, Princess Tiana, a group of Disney princesses (foregrounding Ariel, with Cinderella and Belle in the background), *Toy Story*, SpongeBob, Mickey Mouse, Hello Kitty, Spider-Man, Barbie, Diego Márquez,[7] Scooby-Doo, and Minions – to name a few.[8] A third and final example[9] of the marketing of children's media, toys, and a wide range of other products is the ubiquitous US children's food, macaroni and cheese, wherein the leading brand, Kraft, has partnered to distribute versions with noodles shaped like SpongeBob, Spider-Man, the Cat in the Hat, Super Mario, and characters from *Stars Wars*, *Cars*, *The Flintstones*, *Rugrats*, and *Looney Tunes*, among many other examples. In sum, the "tie-ins" between children's media, fast and "healthy" food, products such as Band-Aids, and specially produced toys illustrate some of the many possibilities for co-marketing between transnational conglomerates, among which Disney is the top media player.

In addition to the many products mentioned in the previous paragraph, a toy line also looks for media presence (in addition to media exposure through advertising), such as in a television show, digital gaming, a website, a movie, recorded music, or magazines. Looking back to the wildly successful Bratz dolls, by the time they spun off the Bratz Babyz and Bratz Kidz lines, they had generated a television show, a feature-length Hollywood film, recorded music, digital games, many books, an app, and a web series (Valdivia 2011; McAllister 2007). Evidently, children's toy and media companies seek to expand their markets by forging an ever-increasing set of economic relationships across the rapidly expanding media technology terrain, to try to reach new segments of the audience nationally and globally. In this process, the lily-white vision of the 1950s, when media companies could pretend that the world was white or that it was not economically imperative to reach multicultural audiences, is no longer sustainable.

Disney Tales

This chapter combines Latina/o Studies, Media Studies, and Girls Studies to explore the multimodal release of Latina princesses by Disney. Exploiting its successful track record with children, expanding it to the recently constructed marketing category of *tweens*, and continuing its reach to the young-adult market, Disney wholeheartedly reaches out to as much of its audience's lifespan as possible, while simultaneously expanding the ethnic register. Including tweens, a hybrid age category full of ambiguity for the girls who are supposed to inhabit it (MacDonald 2016), functions as a bridge between the children and adults that constitute Disney's diversified target audiences. Blue (2013, 2017) reminds us that through representations of girlhood, Disney promotes and reproduces hegemonic ideologies of heteronormativity and conventional gender roles and expectations (2013, p. 660), which Robinson (2005) traces back to early childhood viewing and play. Similarly, Projansky (2014) asserts that all girls are spectacular, yet some are represented as such and many others – especially ethnicized girls – are represented as lacking luster. Nearly all Girls Studies scholars build on Harris' (2004) foundational categorization of the can-do girl and the at-risk girl to parse out contemporary depictions of this age group. Combining Girls Studies with Postfeminism reveals that can-do authenticity in the tween universe can only be achieved through postfeminist practices of individualism, working on the self, and self-surveillance. Taking into account the strategic ambiguity that black and racialized women must perform in the public sphere (Joseph 2013) and turning it upside down – as in something with which Disney infuses their Latinas princesses – furthers the analysis of tween Latinas in the Disney universe.

Beginning with a brief overview of Latina/os and Latin Americans in Disney,[10] this chapter takes us through the turn of this century and up to the new millennium in terms of Disney and Latinidad. While, admittedly, there are many more instances of Latin American and Latina/o Disney than the ones mentioned here – as well there should be for such a prolific producer of media across the mainstream spectrum – I focus on the moments of tween and girl culture interventions, as these signal efforts to manage the multicultural, multiracial, and hybrid presence of populations while simultaneously luring ethnic audiences and assuaging mainstream (read: white) ones with narratives that reaffirm the normative whiteness that has been a part of the Disney universe since its inception.

Even before the field of Media Studies existed as such, sociologists and art critics (among others) paid attention to Disney's narratives, representations, and industrial moves. Much of the Disney research has either textually analyzed content or explored the national and global expansion of Disney as a business. Given the company's global reach, some of the research has focused on imperial and transnational implications. For instance, Ariel Dorfman and Armand Mattelart authored *Para Leer al Pato Donald/How to Read Donald Duck* (1971) in the midst of the Allende presidency in Chile (1970–73). The Chilean experiment included efforts to decolonize its mass media in terms of ownership, production, and content within an historical context. In the early 1970s, US mainstream media circulated freely and plentifully in Latin America, with very few nodes of contra flow. Dorfman and Mattelart offered a content analysis of 100 Disney comic books widely available in Chile (Wasko 2001), and concluded that Disney represented a universe of consumerism, colonialism, classism, and imperialism (Phillips 2001). This critical investigation, arising out of a socialist political process attempting to regain national control of the mainstream media while incorporating a global ideological critique, remains a classic in the field. Its scathing critique generated swift reaction from Disney, successfully delaying its English-language translation by 10 years.

Perhaps inspired by the global reach of Dorfman and Mattelart's work, Michael Real, in his *Mass Mediated Culture: Case Studies in Contemporary Communications and Culture* (1977), includes a chapter based on a questionnaire concerning Disney's vices and virtues. Participants, mostly students, were frequent visitors to Disneyland, given that they lived within proximity to the theme park in Southern California.[11] Real combines a thorough literature review of Disney scholarly critique, a semiotic analysis of the park itself, and a questionnaire with 200 respondents, utilizing the paradigm of Disneyland as a moral play. Among his many findings, which reveal gendered preferences about parts of the park, this study shows remarkable consistency between the respondents in regards to the virtues and vices in the Disney universe. Regardless of positive or negative affect, respondents agreed on the vices and virtues, underscoring the pedagogical thrust of the Disney universe.

Twenty-five years later, Real's chapter inspired another group of scholars, led by Janet Wasko and Mark Phillips, to an expansive global analysis of Disney audiences entitled *Dazzled by Disney? The Global Disney Audiences Project* (Wasko et al. 2001). Moreover, Wasko published an entire book about Disney entitled *Understanding Disney: The Manufacture of Fantasy* that same year (2001), extending research about the global conglomerate from a wide-ranging Media Studies perspective and documenting the growing influence of the Eisner "Renaissance" period (1984–2005), in which Disney expanded globally and diversified greatly (Lustyik 2013). Ambitious in scope, both books explore global aspects. *Dazzled by Disney?* includes major communication scholars in 12 countries, exploring a wide range of issues, all of them focusing on audience research – representing a time when scholarship on the audience was booming in response to previous reliance on content and political economy. The elegant results draw on a range of theoretical paradigms to illuminate the global reach of Disney products and experiences, expanding Real's Southern California sample and reiterating the strong presence of global Disney. Both books provide a continuous research program of Disney media from a diverse media studies perspective, extending the previous books by Dorfman and Mattelart (1971) and Real (1977). The recently published *Global Media Giants* (Birkinbine et al. 2017) features a chapter on Disney, which brings us up to date on Walt Disney Company's latest CEO, Bob Iger, whose three identifiable strategies have been: "investing in creative content, international expansion, and technological innovation" (Wasko 2017, p. 17). This latest update underscores the continuities of the global behemoth, as well as its ability to morph along with new technological realities. Finally, Iger was one of the many CEOs who resigned from the President's Business Council during the mid-August 2017 series of events in which the 45th President of the United States backtracked on his denouncement of white supremacist groups. I bring this up not necessarily to suggest a progressive political stance, but to show that the Disney CEO is important enough to be included in the President's Business Council.

Ambiguity as a complex concept comes up in the results from a wide range of country case studies in *Dazzled by Disney?* (Wasko et al. 2001). The researchers mention issues of global representation and problematic aspects of racialized Disney, and report on the tension felt by audiences between the pleasure of the narrative and the business aspects of the global conglomerate. They also report ambivalence in the empirical discrepancy between owning up to how much Disney participants in the study had consumed and what they originally reported. The discrepancy arose after participants were prompted to answer questions about engagement with a long list of Disney experiences and products. Phillips (2001) proposes the concepts of ambiguity and ambivalence on the part of those interviewed to explicate the tension voiced by global audiences between the narrative pleasure of Disney and the company's less innocent business practices, as well as between participants' acknowledgment of engagement and their actual and far more extensive Disney experiences. Some members of the audience reported an ability for pleasurable engagement with the content while simultaneously critiquing the industrial, profit-motive, and global expansion of Disney industries. Other participants placed Disney in a state of exception from transnational capital influence, as reported by the authors of the Mexico case study (Molina y Vedia 2001). Korean audiences developed ambivalent feelings toward Disney "following the globalization process of the early 1990s" (Kim and Lee 2001, p. 198). Wasko and Meehan (2001) subtitle their conclusion chapter "Ambiguity in Ubiquity," tracing the "ambiguities and contradictions that exist among Disney audiences" (p. 329) in relation to the "symbolic ubiquity" of Disney products. This attraction and repulsion generated by the global Disney universe also applies to the symbiotic relation between gender and ethnic representations and the audiences that Disney attempts to cultivate in its consistent strategy of audience expansion.

Latina/os and/in Disney

By the late 1990s Latina/o boom, coinciding with the 2000 Census documentation of Latina/os as the most numerous US minority, the presence of Latina/os within the United States (in addition to within its sphere of influence) was undeniable.[12] As well, global audiences, especially those with economic means, had access to a broad range of programming and characters within ABC (owned by Disney since 1995) and the global expansion and rise of the Disney television channel, as part of premium cable packages. However, Disney was thinking in terms of a global, synergistic, and convergence strategic plan long before these became buzzwords in the 1980s version of globalization. In the 1940s, Disney was part of the Good Neighbor policy in Latin America,[13] circulating *Saludos Amigos* (1942), followed by the *The Three Caballeros* (1944), in addition to other movie plots, magazines, stamp books, and a range of other media (Miller and Kraidy 2016). Thus, dating back to the middle of the last century, Disney represented Latin American cultures and characters through the recurring, continuous, and still familiar tropes of the bandido, the señorita/ spitfire, the Latin lover, and the dark lady (Ramirez-Berg 2002), with heavy doses of dancing, colorful tropical settings, happy natives, and talking animals. Disney did not claim to produce Latina/o shows and movies until recently, given that Latinidad, as defined within contemporary politics and Latina/o studies, is a nation-specific category, yet Disney historically and purposefully courted the Latin American audience, and by implication, the US Latina/o audience. The success of the Latin American marketing strategy is partly illustrated by the fact that coming to Disney World or Disneyland has become a rite of passage for the Latin American middle class.

The narrative device of these movies consisted of following Donald Duck[14] around Latin America as he opened birthday presents, allowing Disney to represent a narrow pan-Latin American range of locations (Brazil, Argentina, Uruguay,[15] and Mexico) that included stereotyped places and characters. For example, in Mexico, Panchito welcomes Donald and José Carioca,[16] the Brazilian bird, using nearly every element of the Mexican bag of stereotypes, most of which have morphed into the US Latina/o traditional discourse: huge sombreros, classic Mexican accent, mariachi music, guns in the bandido tradition, serapes, a piñata, and the silhouette of a red curvy señorita with hoop earrings. The films drew on and reiterated the classic tropes about Latin Americans that have been largely transferred to the representation of Latina/os in the United States, replete with frequent inclusion of song and dance. Notably, whereas in the 1940s Brazil figured prominently in the United States' imaginary of the Latin American region, Brazilians contemporarily occupy a far less central location in discourses of US Latinidad.

Like other media producers of mainstream popular culture, Disney flattened differences in the many countries and regions of Latin America by treating them as similar and exchangeable, without paying much attention to geographical, climate, historical, population, and language specificities actually existing in the Latin American region. The flattening of difference results from a range of nationalities and ethnicities being compared to one nation, rather than examined in relation to one another in more or less polyvalent terms. Both sides of the flattening process suffer from simplification: the implicit superior part of the dyad (in this case, the United States), and the inferior part (Latin America and US Latina/os). The flattened others provide a *tabula rasa* on to which the self-designated superior culture can project its fears and desires, based not on fact but on partial and sometimes purely fantastical perception. The superior culture suffers from a reduction of sophistication, as its presentation of the implicit better opposite to the flattened other results in reduced engagement and knowledge. Disney, and most contemporary mainstream US popular culture, continues to flatten difference by combining symbols, places, characters, and actors from a range of US Latina/o and Latin American origins in relation to the United States, rather than in relation to one another. In the case of Latin Americans and Disney, one of the outcomes is that Latina/os are represented as generic Latin Americans, not only without national or regional specificity, but also with the commonality of being eternally foreign within the United States.

Continuity, rather than rupture, characterizes the high-flying times of the Disney Eisner/Renaissance era of the 1990s, the historical moment when Disney propelled itself into global media conglomerate status, and the contemporary Iger era, when Disney is purchasing other content franchises and figuring its way through the new digital, post-legacy mediascape. The contemporary ambiguous representational moment ushered by the tween princess is the latest iteration, bearing continuous residues of that history but also embodying the discursive weight of postfeminism, postracism, and neoliberalism. Through the 1980s, a new epoch of globalization asserted itself, changing the mass mediascape and communications through the transfer of ownership from government stewardship to market-driven and privately-owned media enterprises; in sum, the neoliberal move. These global media enterprises in turn had to compete in a global terrain, make global alliances, market their products through a global strategy, and – especially for image-rich cultural producers – begin to understand that their possessive investment in whiteness (Lipsitz 1998) might not work in this new global situation. The recent purchases of Marvel and Lucas/*Star Wars* content contribute to an expanded Disney content library. The huge hit that *Black Panther* has been – with a global box office of $1.344 billion as of March 16, 2019 – is but the beginning of increased profit potential for this media conglomerate.

Yet, in the United States and abroad, Disney faces a population that bears out complicated flows and hybridities due to historical voluntary and forced mobility, as well as the forces of the latest neoliberal wave of globalization. Furthermore, technological platforms upset the brief (in historical terms) but highly profitable moment when what we now know as legacy media – television, radio, and film – garnered most of the attention of mainstream audiences. In turn, the prominence of US media conglomerates in the global circulation of their media products is somewhat lessened. I use the word "lessened" because cries of the demise of US prominence are quite premature (e.g. Schiller 1992; Morley 2006; Thussu 2006; Birkinbine et al. 2017). Nonetheless, the nature of capitalism requires increasing profit with minimum risk, dictated by economies of scale and expanding markets. Logically, when national and normative audiences have been exhausted, conglomerates look elsewhere and fabricate new categories of people they construct as "audiences" in hopes that interpellation will generate more attention and therefore purchase of media and ancillary products – either the ones advertised or the licensed products bearing the media characters and franchises being rolled out (or re-rolled out, as conglomerates do with their invaluable archives). In this necessary expansion, Disney begins to recognize previously ignored elements of the audience while gingerly varying its usual stock of representations.

Simultaneously, Disney does not stop producing highly stereotypical representations of other cultures, including the engagement with the flattening of difference in, for example, spin offs of its highly profitable *Cars* (2006) franchise. Released originally as a television mini-series, currently playing on Disney Channel as well as on Netflix, *Mater's Tall Tales* (2008–12) includes episodes stereotyping the Japanese in "Tokyo Mater" (2010) and the Spanish "El Materdor" (2008), the latter replete with flamenco-and-castanets soundtrack; bull-fighting pick-up truck matador (Materdor) with red cape and montera cap; Spanish señoritas with comb, veils, and fans yelling "ay-ay-ay"; crowd yelling "olé"; priest with sacristan, including rosary and Latin benediction; and bull ring. When Disney wants to do full-throttle stereotyping, it can draw on nearly all the elements for any given region, even when its protagonists are cars.

Disney Princesses

From *Snow White and the Seven Dwarfs* in 1937 – its first feature-length animated film – to *Moana* in 2016, Disney has developed a very successful princess franchise with an 80-year history. The relevant bits of this larger history are the continued investment in the Disney princess franchise, as well as in female-protagonist animated movies by the Walt Disney Company and its subsidiaries, such as the recent megahits *Frozen* (2013), *Zootopia* (2016), *Moana* (2016), and the hybrid live-action/CGI remake of *Beauty and the Beast* (2017). The acknowledgment of diversity within the national and global population by Disney, its global expansion of children's television through over-the-air, cable, and live-streaming options, and the postfeminist postracial/colorblind culture circulated by mainstream media all contribute to the current representational moment. Disney princesses date back to *Snow White*, though the franchise was not officially launched until 2000 by Disney Consumer Products Chairman, Andy Mooney (http://disneyprincess.wikia.com/wiki/List_of_Disney_Princesses).[17] Disney has to classify a character as a "princess" for it to join the official pantheon of Disney princesses, which can be divided into three distinct but continuous categories. The Classic era began with S*now White* and includes *Cinderella* (1950) and *Sleeping Beauty* (1959). The Renaissance/Eisner era includes Ariel from *The Little Mermaid* (1989), Belle from *Beauty and the Beast* (1991), *Pocahontas* (1992), *Mulan* (1998), and Jasmine from *Aladdin* (1995). The Modern era[18] includes Tiana from *The Princess and the Frog* (2009), Rapunzel from *Tangled* (2010), Merida from *Brave* (2012), and *Moana* (2016). Thus far, Mulan is the only modern character that has joined the princess pantheon despite a lack of royal blood or connection. Conversely, Elsa and Anna from *Frozen* (2013) have yet to be added to the official princess list, even though they were real princesses within their narrative. The most recent Disney princess is Moana, a Polynesian. Judy Hopps, the protagonist of 2017 Academy Award winner *Zootopia* is neither royal nor marriage-minded, and thus veers too far from the princess character for inclusion. Disney adds new princesses to the pantheon as the marketing power of an individual princess begins to wear off so that adding her to the larger "princess" line reinvigorates purchasing and profits.

Within the pantheon, the first ethnic princess outside of fantasy unspecific whiteness was Pocahontas, a Native American. She was followed by three more ethnic or foreign/historical princesses: Mulan is Chinese, Jasmine is Middle Eastern, and Tiana is African American. Most princess narratives are borrowed from Brothers Grimm fairy tales, though others, such as *Pocahontas* and *Mulan*, come from other sources (US history and Chinese ballad, respectively). Regardless of provenance, after the Classic princesses, most of those who followed, other than Rapunzel and Ariel, are rooted in actual countries or identifiable global regions. Princesses have transitioned from being passive victims waiting to be saved by a prince to spunky heroines who sometimes end up with their "prince" (e.g. Mulan), sometimes watch him sail off (e.g. Pocahontas) (England et al. 2011), and sometimes don't have a prince at all (e.g. Moana). The transition from passive princess to spunky princess to nonromantic spunky princess responds to feminism and postfeminism. Currently, postfeminism describes contemporary Disney princesses through individualism, beauty, and performance as part of the narrative iconography. "Spunky" or "can-do" heroines abound in postfeminist popular culture, so their appearance in Disney is part of this cultural moment, when beautiful (in relation to whiteness) young women use their feminine guiles to forge ahead (Tasker 2011; Kennedy 2018). Some of the princesses may be spunky and some of them many end up single, but all of them are "beautiful,"[19] have huge almond eyes, have tiny waists, and possess a mane of hair almost as big as they are. Moana's body has been touted as less stereotypical, but she still has the eyes, the mane, and the tiny waist of previous princesses – only, her legs are less skinny than those of other princesses. Of the many continuities that Disney princesses share, the ideal of (white) beauty remains similar despite their national or ethnic origin.

The spunky heroine also perfectly suits the tween audience category. Most of the princesses are mid-teen years, which makes them too old for adolescent audiences but just perfect for late-childhood and tween ones. In this global marketing approach, Disney draws on its franchise in combination with local stars, settings, dance moves, and so on to produce *glocal* material. The movie and its sequels, television shows, musicals, ice shows, televised reality shows, digital games, and licensed clothing and other products target girls and tweens across the globe, in addition to the family audience, which includes viewers from all generations steeped in Disney fare (Lustyik 2013).

Latina Disney Princesses?

Whereas huge budgets, special effects, major movie star voice overs, and animated characters form a central part of the Disney princess universe, the Latina princess or identifiably Latina girl or tween has proven to be an elusive member of the Disney family, signing through absence or very subtle presence. Her location within the Disney universe has been encoded through subtle ambiguity, avowal and disavowal, and highly profitable franchises. Disney princesses come in many forms. For the purposes of this chapter, I will consider three. First, while there is yet to be a Latina Disney princess of the official feature-length animated film variety, there are two Latina television animated princesses, Sofia the First and Elena of Avalor, who have been presented and represented differentially by Disney. Second, Disney has rolled out two ambiguous Latinas within their juggernaut tween vehicles *Lizzie McGuire* and *High School Musical*, both of them beginning in Disney television and graduating to motion-picture film-release status in addition to a huge range of ancillary products. Third, real-life actors/celebrities Selena Gomez and Demi Lovato round out the presence of subtle and ambiguous Latinidad on contemporary Disney. None are classified within the official Disney princess pantheon, yet they sign in as Disney's efforts to represent Latinidad and court the brown tween audience, including Latin Americans and US Latina/os, through princessly strategies.

Disney's gingerly inclusion of contemporary Latinidad must be understood within its approach to representations of multicultural populations. Multicultural and multiracial characters and their inclusion in media representation are a fairly recent phenomenon, as is the US government's acknowledgement of the presence of multicultural and multiracial individuals within the population (DaCosta 2007). Media Studies scholars have noticed the many ways that multiracial actors can be used by mainstream media (Beltrán 2005; Nishime 2005; Valdivia 2013, 2015, 2016; Washington 2017b). Unsurprisingly, Disney has produced highly successful franchises exploiting this multicultural aesthetic. For example, Disney Channel's *The Cheetah Girls* (2003, 2006, 2008) illustrates the company's multiracial/multicultural approach to girl-power representation through the use of a multiracial cast comprising multiracial actors playing ambiguously multiracial characters. In the franchise, Galleria (Italian and African American upper-middle-class nuclear family), Chanel (unspecific mixed Latina single upper-middle-class mom), Dorinda (ambiguous white foster child to working-class African American family), and Aqua (light African American from Texas) travel the world singing and dancing to the tunes of ethnic hybridity and girl power. Disney seldom explains the ethnic specificity of its characters, and often recruits ethnically mixed actors to represent Latina/os and other racialized characters. In the first *The Cheetah Girls* movie, Chanel actually tells Dorinda that she's "a little of everything," though within Latinidad. Dorinda does not even know her ethnic background as she is adopted. Ironically, Disney includes Latina/os in this early multiracial casting by excluding highly recognizable Latina/os.[20]

Raven-Symoné, an African American actor, illustrates Disney's approach to specificity and ambiguity. Introduced to global audiences through her role as the charming little Olivia in *The Cosby Show* (1989–92), Symoné was the immediately recognizable actor playing the ethnically mixed, half-Italian and half-African American Galleria in the *Cheetah Girls* franchise's first and second movies. Symoné appeared in a number of shows until she got her own in Disney Channel's *That's So Raven* (2003–07), which ran contiguously with the *The Cheetah Girls* releases. In *That's So Raven*, Symoné was unambiguously African American, with a Disney twist of clairvoyance and stereotypical elements of embodied comedy (Blue 2017), while in *The Cheetah Girls* she was the mixed-race upper-middle-class leader of an all-girl performing group. *The Cheetah Girls* illustrates Disney's unambivalent structure of ambivalence – as does the character of Fez, from outside of the Disney universe, played by Latino actor Wilmer Valderrama, in the Fox Network's *That '70s Show* (1998–2006). Throughout the series, Fez's ethnic background is often discussed but never clarified. In other words, we know – unmistakably – that Fez is ethnic. His language/accent, skin color, hairstyle, clothing, and behavior differ notably from those of the other five normatively white characters. However, we do not know his ethnicity. *That '70s Show* was encoded with ironic intent, yet one wonders whether audiences interpret the character of Fez ironically or whether they just laugh at him, as the situations in the 8-year series seem to invite us to do. Such was the case with *All in the Family* (1971–79), once the top-ranked television show in the United States, many of whose fans identified with the misogynist, racist, and homophobic Archie Bunker rather than interpreting him ironically as the buffoon he was written to be. Similarly, audiences of the globally popular *The Cosby Show* (1984–92), created to promote positive African American images, drew on the show to blame blacks for not making it like the Cosbys – what Jhally and Lewis (1992) term "enlightened racism." Intent in media production does not guarantee the intended audience response, especially when representations of people of color are invoked to alter white audience perceptions (Hall 1972).

When Disney produces ambiguity, it is far more subtle, and perhaps more powerful, insidious, and influential. The intent to produce ambiguity – the encoding of it – aims for a multiplicitous decoding. It cannot be said that Disney encodes ambiguity without intent or purpose. Media industries have the profit motive as their main purpose and function in myriad ways to maximize profit. At the microlevel of everyday production of mediated material, the tiniest of elements are researched, rehearsed, staged, and edited to achieve a seamless and slick media product that hopefully resonates with ever-changing and -increasing audiences, with the intent to grow audience reach. So, to say that the ambiguity is accidental is highly unlikely, as every little element of media production is planned and edited. As well, media industries in general, and Disney in particular, have a long history of creating unambiguous ethnic characters and statements. From blackface on some cartoon characters, such as in *Mickey's Mellerdrammer* (1933), wherein Mickey Mouse wears blackface in a production of *Uncle Tom's Cabin*, to the scatting crows in *Dumbo* (1941), the leader of whom is named Jim Crow, to *Song of the South* (1946), wherein the main character plays the classic Uncle Tom stereotype in an unspecified time period that possibly predates the Civil War, Disney has been able to represent unambiguous characters of color. Even in its supposedly colorblind animated feature-length films populated only by animals or within the princess pantheon and its sidekicks, Disney includes characters such as Mushu the implicitly African American baby dragon sidekick voiced by Eddie Murphy in *Mulan*. Similarly, Pocahontas was unambiguously Native American, Mulan unambiguously Chinese, and Tiana unambiguously African American. The more recent ambiguous approach to representation differs from traditional depictions, yet it is nonetheless a racialized approach, even if it is only perceived as such by certain segments of the audience. Furthermore, this representational strategy can be related to Latinidad in the sense that the Latina body provides an in-betweenness – in between white and black, something not quite so different, yet different enough from whiteness; something not too close to blackness; and something lending itself to the possibility of taming, effacing, or obscuring, all the while quite legitimately claiming presence. This "something" is subtly constructed so as to include the possibility of whiteness while also entertaining the presence of light-brownness. Such seems to be the contemporary presence of Latinidad in the Disney universe.

Ethnicizing Tween Dreams

Chronologically, Disney introduced ambiguous Latinidad through subtle side-kick Latinas in television franchises, real-life Latina talent from the Disney farm system, and animated princesses, who are not yet in the official Disney princess pantheon. Thus, taking a sheet from the playbook of liberal feminism and its popular-culture backlash, postfeminism, Disney's first ambiguous Latina, Miranda Sanchez, shows up in 2001 as a sidekick in the global tween juggernaut, *Lizzie McGuire* (2001–04). The second major Disney Latina, Gabriella Montez, comes slightly later, in 2006, in *High School Musical*. Her role borders between main character and sidekick, and is much more subtly Latina than Miranda in *Lizzie*. "Anticipatory acculturation to teenagerdom" (McGladrey 2014, p. 360) attempts to lure this in-between gendered age category through the provision of spunky heroines who will ideally generate identification and stimulate consumption. As such, Miranda Sanchez and Gabriella Montez represent the new face of diversity on the Disney Channel – the ambiguously ethnic, postfeminist Latina.

Lizzie McGuire and *High School Musical* greatly contributed to Disney's coffers in the first decade of the 2000s, and both relied on tween representations to target tween audiences and ambiguous Latinas to round out a universe of light-skinned inclusivity. Miranda Sanchez and Gabriella Montez are subtle and ambiguous enough as to be literally unperceived by many members of the audience as Latinas. Miranda, a trendy and loyal best friend, hangs out with Lizzie and Gordo in the eponymous tween series, though she is written out of the last six episodes and of *The Lizzie McGuire Movie* (2003). Gabriella, a nerdy-but-cute high schooler, is paired up with popular kid, heartthrob, and basketball star Troy to form the lead couple in the titular high school musical. Though within slightly different vehicles – a regular television series for Miranda and a television movie franchise with a Hollywood film for Gabriella, both characters were part of highly successful Disney properties whose target audience – the female tween – drove their success and profits.

Before focusing on these two ambiguous Latina characters, attention must be paid to Hilary Duff, who played the main character in *Lizzie McGuire*, became the original poster girl for Disney tweenhood, and provided the vehicle through which Disney gained a foothold in national and global children's television. Lizzie's tween success was carefully orchestrated by Disney children's television executive Ann Sweeney, who was hired away from Nick Jr. in the mid-90s (Valdivia 2009b). Sweeney's tween programming mandate resulted in the production of *Lizzie McGuire* and coincided with the Disney princess franchise, which was articulated in 2000. Though tween princesses from Ariel in *The Little Mermaid* to Mulan came before Lizzie, the tween marketing impulse dates back to Zoog programming on the Disney Channel, of which *Lizzie McGuire* was the most successful show.

Lizzie McGuire focused on the trials and tribulations of main-character Lizzie, a hyper-cute, insecure, and slightly awkward middle schooler – a tween. Her appeal to middle schoolers was supposed to be universal, as Disney banked on tweens being generally insecure at that awkward age.[21] In addition to Lizzie, the cast of *Lizzie McGuire* is rounded out by her sidekicks, best friend Miranda Isabella Sanchez and guy friend Gordo. Parents, sibling, classmates, teachers, and so on form part of the Lizzie universe, which as in most Disney settings is normatively racialized as white, lush, luxurious, and very colorful. Lizzie is your classic Disney character: cute, white, and lovable. She hangs out with Miranda, her best friend and ambiguous Latina, and Gordo, who is Jewish, and both of whose parents are stereotypical psychotherapists. Lizzie's religion does not come up, but Gordo is Jewish and Miranda is implicitly Roman Catholic, simultaneously affirming Lizzie's normative every-girlness and Miranda and Gordo's ethnic difference. In its nod to diversity, Disney centers universal whiteness (Shuggart 2007) through the ethnic/religious difference of the protagonist's sidekicks.

From the beginning of the series, Miranda is relationally more colorful and assertive than Lizzie. In the first episode of the show, the first scene that shows us the three buddies has them getting their food from the cafeteria lunch line. Whereas both girls have straight hair, as a baseline difference Miranda has dark brown hair compared to Lizzie's blonde. Both Lizzie and Miranda wear tank tops, but Lizzie's hair is in a crown braid whereas Miranda's is in two spider-like pigtails, each held together by fuzzy orange pom-poms: a tarantula aesthetic. Throughout the series, Gordo dresses in what can best be called "slouch" style: baggy pants, T-shirt, oversized shirts, and stereotypically curly dark hair.

The opening credits similarly "other" Miranda, though always subtly and in relation to Lizzie. Lizzie's quirky style – tie-dyed purple shirt, orange flower-print leggings, and wavy loose hair – contrasts with Miranda's bohemian aesthetic, with midriff-showing long-sleeved T-shirt, palazzo jeans with hippie-style embroidered hem, and an elaborate hard-curl hairdo with blue ribbons. Consistently, throughout the series, Miranda's outfits and hairdos are slightly quirkier than Lizzie's. Miranda's differences – her name, dark hair, barely olive skin, and religion – subtly and ambiguously signify her Latinidad. Another element that could signal audiences to Miranda's Latinidad would be her family and home. However, the girls exist in an environment located within the private space of their bedrooms and their school (usually populated with youth and the occasional teacher or parent), spaces often devoid of any symbols of Latinidad. Of course, since Miranda is a sidekick, representations of her home and family are less visible than Lizzie's, as protagonist. Miranda is often shown in close-up on the phone when in her bedroom, so even if there were symbols of Latinidad in her home, they would be outside of the frame. Another element of difference is that Miranda is more assertive than Lizzie, adhering to the *macha* Latina (Beltrán 2004), who is more embodied and stronger than her white feminine counterpart (see also Lacroix 2004 in relation to Disney princesses of color).

In the first episode, Lizzie and Miranda are gossiping online when Miranda accidentally sends Lizzie's comment about Kate, her arch-nemesis, stuffing her bra to the entire class. Miranda assumes the blame when confronted by Kate, prompting Lizzie to remark "how lucky [she is] to have a friend like Miranda, who handles conflict so well." Miranda is not afraid of Kate, while Lizzie is terrified (for example, in another scene in that first episode, in one of the few mentions in the entire show of Miranda's Latina/o last name, in response to Miranda adding green color to her hairspray, Kate calls out "Sanchez!" in the playground/lunch room; Miranda answers Kate's threat with, "You know me," and points to the orange hairpiece she's wearing that day: "I am a big fan of color. Welcome to the club!"). This first episode marks Miranda as an ambiguous Latina through her last name, her slightly more flamboyant dress and hairdo compared to Lizzie, and her more assertive personality – markers of difference in general and of Latinidad in particular.

The first year of the show has few small elements other than the Day of the Dead ("Night of the Day of the Dead") episode. Within mainstream Latina/o representation, Dia de los Muertos, Quinceañera, and Christmas function as signifiers of Latina/o culture (Leon-Boys forthcoming). Family is nearly absent from Miranda's plot line. Miranda's mom appears in a total of four episodes – as does her dad, though her mom has more lines. Miranda's parents debut in this most Latina/o episode of the entire series. The Day of the Dead, on which some religious Roman Catholics in Latin America remember the dead with religious celebrations, and which others use as an opportunity to have parties,[22] becomes a theme for Lizzie's middle school Halloween party. Miranda offers to bring skeletons for the Halloween/Day of the Dead celebration – and warns Kate that they represent ancestors. Mr. and Mrs. Sanchez, Miranda's parents, cooperate with an elaborate ruse to pay Kate back for displacing Lizzie, who wanted to dress up as Elvira. Mr. Sanchez declares this to be one of his favorite holidays, and Mrs. Sanchez actually says in Spanish, "el día de los muertos." After this episode, Miranda's parents appear sporadically and briefly in the show. For instance, in "Mom's Best Friend," Miranda deals with her mother's wish to be closer to her; in "Gordo's Bar Mitzvah," Miranda's mother attends the ceremony and Miranda talks about her quinceañera, which she assures Lizzie will include lots of music and great food; and in "Gordo and the Dwarves," her mother appears again, but as background to the story. Other than that, Miranda's family is not present in the series. Miranda is missing from the last five episodes and from the feature-length movie, where it is explained that she is in Mexico City, visiting her aunt. Thus, just as her Latin American/Latina identity is specified and solidified, she disappears from the show. Nonetheless, Miranda remains one-third of the trio that ushered in tweendom for Disney and propelled it into a global children's television presence.

Like Miranda, Gabriella Montez debuts in the opening scene of the wildly successful *High School Musical* (HSM) trilogy in 2006. While Miranda is a sidekick, Gabriella is one-half of the main couple, though the less prominent half, and one of six main characters in the multiracial ensemble cast of the HSM franchise.[23] Gabriella's Latinidad is subtler and more ambiguous than Miranda's. Importantly, we get to know Troy's father, mother, and household far more than Gabriella's. The opening scene finds Troy and Gabriella at a New Year's Eve party in an upscale ski lodge. Troy's character as the popular jock is established, as is Gabriella's role as a studious but pretty nerd. Forced to attend a tween party and perform a karaoke number together, Gabriella and Troy realize they like each other. Much like in *Grease* (1978),[24] this vacation encounter becomes the precursor of a relationship when both unexpectedly find themselves as students in the same high school in Albuquerque, New Mexico.

Gabriella represents a very unusual Latina for mainstream US popular culture. She is an upper-middle-class science nerd. Nothing much other than her name – Gabriella Montez – signals to her Latinidad. In fact, the fact that Gabriella has two ls in her first name further muddles her Latinidad and implies an Italian-ness. Gabriella's hair is long, dark, and wavy. Her skin is ever so slightly olive color. It is slightly darker than Sharpay's, a classic white, rich, and blonde beauty who plays the scheming drama kid in relation to Gabriella's innocent and accidental high school musical lead. It is lighter than Taylor's, the light African American girl who rounds out the three females in the main group of characters. Gabriella occupies an in-between ethnic location in relation to ultra-white Sharpay and light African American Taylor. Everything from Gabriella's skin tone to her everyday clothing style is "in-between," and slightly conservative. For instance, in relation to Sharpay's over-the-top glitzy wardrobe of sequin-decorated pieces of clothing,[25] gold and silver fabrics, Chanel-like suits, and high heels, and to Taylor's utilitarian wardrobe of sometimes sporty and other times preppie outfits, Gabriella sports a wardrobe that can best be described as that of a "good Catholic girl," with knee-length skirts, loose jeans or corduroy pants, conservative and usually lace-trimmed girly tops, pastel or white-colored sweaters, and low-heeled black Mary Jane shoes. In the first movie, Gabriella's hair is always slightly wavy and styled, held back by feminine barrettes – in butterfly shape, for instance. She signs in as the in-between girl next door.

Gabriella's Latinidad is very subtly complemented by her mother's occasional appearance. Played by Socorro Herrera, Mrs. Montez is vaguely Latina. We meet her in the first scene, when she forces Gabriella, who is reading a book, to attend the party at the ski lodge. She has long, dark, wavy hair and wears a floor-length black velvet skirt and red velvet jacket. As with the conservative clothing worn by her daughter, the party outfit pretty much covers Mrs. Montez's entire body. Mrs. Montez is alone at the lodge, and there is no indication that a Mr. Montez exists. We next encounter her at the high school, when Gabriella is registering for classes as a transfer student. We hear her apologize that the job transfer means a new high school, but she promises no more moves before graduation. When Troy visits Gabriella at home, her mother answers the door. Finally, when Gabriella and Troy contrive to compete in the drama play call back, her mother shows up at the back of the auditorium. In all of these scenes, Mrs. Montez is alone and dressed in professional attire – jacket and pants or skirt – with dark long hair. The fact that she is called Mrs. Montez suggests widowhood, but this is never confirmed.

Gabriella's family situation differs from that of Troy, whose mother and father also appear in the first scene. Noticeably, his mother wears a sequined halter top for the occasion, relationally underscoring the conservative outfit worn by Mrs. Montez. After that, she appears less that his father, and her appearances suggest she is a stay-at-home mom. Troy's father, Mr. Bolton, has a bigger role in the narrative than any of the other parents, as he is the head coach of the basketball team, in which Troy is the star player.

It is entirely possible for Gabriella's Latinidad to pass wholly unperceived in HSM. The relational skin color, wardrobe, and hairstyle elements are very subtle. Mrs. Montez, though a bit more Latina-looking than Gabriella, still performs a very subtle Latinidad and appears so briefly and seldom within HSM1, not at all in HSM2, and in one scene in HSM3, that one could miss her presence entirely. Missing are the stereotypical components of mainstream Latinidad, such as accented English at the parent's generation, markers of Catholicism through either jewelry or religious icons, stereotypical Latina/o celebrations such as quinceañeras or Día de los Muertos, the presence of "Latin" music in any form, hoop earrings, red lipstick, and so on. In sum, the franchise contains the signifiers of neither the abnegated Catholic nor the spit-fire Latina. The Latinidad is so subtle that many members of the audience miss it altogether, or realize its presence only years afterwards.[26]

Miranda and Gabriella bear the classic elements of ambiguous Latina tween construction. First of all, they are girls. The tween market is driven by girls as a target audience. Second, they are light-skinned, barely-olive girls. Third, their names are ambiguously Latina. Miranda is not intrinsically a Latina name, but within the context of her family it is connected to her inferred Latinidad. Gabriella is sort-of Latina, with an extra l (kind of like Christina with an extra h). The Latina difference – to signify non-whiteness – is through the ambiguous name, the barely-olive skin, and, for Miranda, a dark hairdo, very vibrant clothing, and outlandish hairstyles. Their Latinidad thus is present through relational subtlety and absence, unless you are looking for signs. Miranda's Mexican American character specifies her Latinidad as she disappears from the series, whereas Gabriella is left as an unspecific Latina. Through tween programming, Disney introduces us to these barely-there Latinas, a construction that is repeated with live actors and animated princesses.

Real-Life Latinas: Selena Gomez and Demi Lovato

Like their ambiguous Latina fictional-character sisters, Miranda and Gabriella, Selena Gomez and Demi Lovato continue to bear out Disney's gingerly approach to Latinidad. Selena Gomez was born in Texas in 1992, to a Mexican American father and Caucasian mother with "some Italian ancestry" (Wikipedia), and was named after Selena Quintanilla, the Tejana star who was killed in 1995. Similarly, Demetria Devonne Lovato was born in New Mexico in 1992, to a Mexican American father and a Caucasian mother, whose ethnic mix includes Irish and Italian roots. Lovato grew up in Texas. Both girls bear light phenotypic characteristics, including light skin and long brown hair, which they have invariably dyed and styled in different lengths throughout their career. Their stage names of Selena and Demi could signal Latinidad to those alerted to it, or could be read as more generic Anglo names.

In 2002, both Selena and Demi were selected to be part of the multicultural cast of the children's television megahit *Barney and Friends*, and began their ascent as performers and celebrities. By 2006, the same year as the debut of *High School Musical*, Selena Gomez had begun to appear on Disney children's television, while Demi Lovato transitioned into Disney television in 2007. Their initial roles as ambiguous ethnics and/or white girls served as launching pads for their starring roles as ambiguous Latinas in their respective Disney media vehicles: the television show *Wizards of Waverly Place* (2007–12) for Selena, and the made-for-television movie franchise *Camp Rock* (2008, 2010) and short-lived television series *Sonny with a Chance* (2009–11)[27] for Demi.

Their title roles further underscore Disney's gingerly approach to Latinidad. Selena Gomez's character in *Wizards of Waverly Place* is hybrid with a Disney twist. Alexandra Margarita "Alex" Russo is a combination of Latina, through her mother, and Italian American and wizard through her father. As with the previously analyzed Gabriella and Miranda, Alex's name is not identifiably Latina/o. Indeed, it is a gender-neutral name, which befits the slightly tomboyish character. "Alexandra" is not spelled in Spanish – otherwise, it would be Alejandra. Margarita is more Latina/o of a name, but it almost never comes up in the series, so that as the main character of the show, Selena is most often referred to as Alex. Neither of Alex's brothers – Justin and Max – have particularly Latina/o names. Their mother, like Alexandra and Gabriella, is named Theresa – a potentially Latina/o name with an extra h to dilute its Latinidad. Played by Maria Canals Barrera, Theresa and her own mother (Alex's grandmother), Magdalena, played by Belita Morenos of *George Lopez* fame, are just about the only other Latina/o characters and actors within the entire series.

As has become a staple of Latina/o representation in the mainstream, *Wizards'* most Latina/o episode is "Quinceañera" (season 1, episode 20), but other than some uses of the word "quinceañera" pronounced in Spanish, there are few other elements of Latinidad in this episode. Though the maternal grandmother shows up for the occasion, her unorthodox personality is more tomboyish, like Alex, than traditional grandmotherly. A multicultural cast of silent partygoers, who serve as background props, do not have speaking roles. Other than Theresa insisting on the party and eventually – through a *Freaky Friday*-like body switch – becoming its protagonist, there are no discernible elements of Latinidad in the episode. Alex's little brother Max bears the burden of articulating stereotypes of Latinidad with two consecutive lines he utters when forced to take ballroom dancing lessons in preparation for the big party: "Salsa, were we supposed to bring chips?" and "It's not just a zesty dip." Wizardry takes far more of a leading role as a constitutive element of the plot and identity of this series.

Following a role in *As the Bell Rings* (2007–08), Demi Lovato's breakthrough role came in the made-for-television Disney Channel movie *Camp Rock* (2008). Lovato was cast in the lead role of Mitchie Torres. Drawing on the huge success of Disney's *High School Musical*, as well as on *School of Rock* (2003), *Camp Rock* presents us with tweens in a summer camp for performers. Demi Lovato plays the lead character, while Maria Canals-Barrera (the mother in *Wizards of Waverly Place*) plays her mother, Connie Torres. Whereas in *Wizards* Canals-Barrera had no accent, she has a slight accent in *Camp Rock*. Mitchie cannot afford the camp tuition, so her mom caters food, and Mitchie works at the dining hall to pay her fees. Dad owns a hardware store. The working-class element of Latinidad, a common element of the contemporary mainstream discursive construction of Latina/os, is unusual in a Disney universe populated by implicitly upper-middle-class or magical characters. Mitchie's nemesis Tess is a predictably white, rich, and blonde girl. The rest of the popular girl group comprises Peggy, a light African American, and Ella, an Asian American girl played by a Filipina actor – a classic multicultural group within the Disney universe. Through the Torres name, her family's uniformly brown hair, her ethnic relationality with the other girls, and her working-class family, Mitchie exhibits a light Latinidad. While popular, this made-for-television movie was not nearly as successful as HSM. After *Camp Rock*, Lovato signed a recording contract with Hollywood Records (a subsidiary of Disney) and was cast in the lead role in *Sonny with a Chance* (2009–11), which lasted two seasons.

Ambiguous Latinas in an Ambiguous "Latin" Movie

At the peak of their popularity, in 2009, Disney released *Princess Protection Program* (PPP), a made-for-television movie, co-starring Selena Gomez and Demi Lovato. As part of the publicity process, Selena and Demi appeared on the cover of *People* on July 22, 2009 as best friends – BFFs – whose friendship dated back to their time in the *Barney and Friends* show. Projansky (2014) notes:

> Nowhere does the issue address how Gomez self-identifies racially, or how she feels about portraying a Latina in Wizards of Waverly Place, or what it means for her to be mixed. Instead, the emotional and physical link, between Gomez and Lovato … contributes to an ambiguous racial hybridity for both of them, a hybridity that is part of their appeal, their uniqueness, and in fact, their spectacularization, but that does not seem to make any real difference in their lives or work.
>
> *(p. 75)*

Created so as to draw on the synergies available through Disney Channel, audiences were incentivized to watch PPP through access to never-before-seen episodes of *Wizards* and *Sonny*, thus synergistically linking them back to individual Selena and Demi vehicles. The PPP soundtrack included the single, "One and the Same," performed by both Selena and Demi, the music video of which was included on the DVD of the movie. The song itself was included in that year's Disney Channel Playlist. Marketed globally, PPP movie posters abounded throughout cities such as Santiago, Chile; Buenos Aires, Argentina; and Madrid, Spain, where it was billed as part of Disney television's "este verano con Disney Channel" ("this summer with Disney Channel," which rhymes in Spanish). The posters were generously distributed in places like metro stations and bus stops, in addition to billboards. In Latin America, the Disney Channel bundled the tween programming – *Wizards*, *Hannah Montana*, and, later, *Sonny with a Chance* – with the promotional message, "chicas con actitud" ("girls with an attitude").

Relationally, the marketing and framing for PPP can be compared to Disney's *Cow Belles* (2006), a made-for-tv movie starring Aly and AJ, two unambiguously white tween actors, firmly set on a dairy farm, maybe in Wisconsin. The location and the ethnicity of the cowgirls places them unambiguously within whiteness. Filmed in Uxbridge, Ontario in Canada, *Cow Belles* is a local story, despite the runaway production, about the economics of farming and teaching spoilt children the value of work and the evanescence of wealth. On the other hand, PPP is located in Louisiana and in two fictional small nations named Costa Luna and Costa Estrella. The implicit imperial narrative of banana republics is further strengthened by its filming on location in San Juan and Ponce, Puerto Rico, anchoring the film's transnational Latinidad. Rosalinda/Demi's subtle Latinidad works through her royal role, in difference to tomboy Carter/Selena, whose location in Louisiana, a region whose hybrid history includes European/French, Latin American, and African flows of populations and cultures, is nonetheless represented as nearly purely white.

The movie begins[28] with a collage of bayou scenes set to country music that introduces the Carter/Selena character, before transitioning into a bird's eye view of a castle, which in close-up has Hispanic architectural elements, wherein Rosalinda/Demi rehearses for her coronation ceremony. "Herrrrr rrroyal highness Rrrosalinda Maria Montoya Flores, Princesa de Costa Luna," announces a general (with excessive and theatrical rolling r's). The people around the princess speak either with thick Spanish accents or with none at all. Rosalinda/Demi has very few lines in Spanish (e.g. "Vamos Momma" and, when in Louisiana, "Por favor donde esta el baño? Gracias"). To be fair, the general's Spanish accent is as accented as Princess Rosalinda's English.

Once in Louisiana, the princess becomes "Rosie Gonzalez, an average American girl." Whereas she is unable to leave behind her princess ways, there is nothing that speaks any form of Latinidad, other than her very occasional English-accented Spanish. The girls are somatically similar so as to serve the narrative device of them being temporarily mistaken for each other. The bulk of the movie takes place in Louisiana, much of it within the high school setting, as is customary with Disney tween movies. At the film's end, the girls become good friends, the princess becomes a queen, and the island nation returns to its royal family. The film functions as a vehicle to bring together these two ambiguous Latinas in a tale about ambiguous Latinidad, which uses names – Costa Luna, Costa Brava, Rosalinda, Gonzalez – and very occasional accented language – both English and Spanish – as suggestive markers. The nods to Latina/o inclusivity are minor in relation to the overall tone, location, and narrative flow of the movie. PPP represents continuity of representation of banana republics, whose constant military coups necessitate US intervention to save and return their sovereignty, whose military is corrupt and incapable of holding on to power, whose male royal staff are also corrupt and implicitly gay, and whose female waitstaff are silent. The stereotypical representation of Latin America serves as a backdrop for the foregrounding and bringing together in one movie of two ambiguous Latinas who can be marketed both within the United States and globally, especially in Spain and Latin America, simultaneously providing publicity for *Wizards of Waverly Place* and *Camp Rock*, and setting these real-life princesses up for a process of ambiguous representation beyond their first individual hit shows.

Selena and Demi Grow Up

In the decade since their breakout roles as Disney television characters, Gomez and Lovato have sought to nurture long-lasting careers, or what Blue (2017) calls "the girl mogul: entrepreneurism and the new girl subject" (p. 145). Indeed, as Blue documents, the Walt Disney Company more or less requires its stars to participate in "a certain level of civic engagement ... presumably encouraging them to appear in public service announcements (PSAs) and to become spokespeople for charities and advocacy groups" (p. 115). Furthermore, Blue asserts that the Walt Disney Company "determines the causes worthy of support, who will be celebrity spokespeople, and what labor those individuals will perform on the corporation's behalf" (p. 123). Drawing on the work in *Commodity Activism* (edited by Banet-Weiser and Mukherjee 2012), in which Ouelette outlines the "do-good" impulse imposed by corporations on their stars/laborers and Hearn singles out Disney as "cynical and opportunistic" in its deployment of apolitical support of environmental activism by its stars, including Selena and Demi, Blue (2017, p. 121) provides a compelling overview of the staged production of corporate responsibility as it transitions into a discourse of corporate citizenship.

According to this templated Disney career trajectory, from their Disney children's television show perch, Selena and Demi methodically fanned out into contemporary celebrity branding efforts in old-school Disney star style, and eventually moved through and beyond Disney to enter into more grown-up and sexualized endeavors, which are usually offered to teens as they transition into adulthood. The synergistic groundwork laid by Michael Eisner in Disney's expansionary years (1984–2005), including the global deployment of Disney's children's television channel and the creation of Hollywood Records in 1998 to allow expanded recorded music possibilities, began to bear fruit through tween queen Hilary Duff with her *Lizzie McGuire* show and her recorded music hit *Metamorphosis* in 2003. The path from tween television star to tween musical performer enabled by the creation of these two synergistic Walt Disney Company properties became the road taken by Demi Lovato and Selena Gomez. In other words, Selena and Demi first appeared in small but growing roles in Disney television shows, and after securing their star turns, began to branch out into recorded music via Disney-owned Hollywood Records, as well as into fashion and philanthropy, or agential citizenship (Blue 2017).

As they have navigated the twists and turns expected of child actors transitioning into adult careers, Gomez and Lovato have pursued a path that backgrounds their mixed and ambiguous Latinidad while foregrounding their girl-next-door appeal and highlighting their neoliberal, postfeminist, and colorblind exemplary citizenship. Both have explored solo musical careers (initially with Hollywood Records) and developed their own fragrances, fashion lines, and sports clothing ventures, as well as cultivating the ancillary components of contemporary celebrity status, including philanthropy. Gomez became a UNICEF Ambassador, endorsed beauty products (OPI nail polish and Pantene hair products), promoted both luxury and global brands (Louis Vuitton, Coach, and Coca-Cola), and collaborated with Sears and Kmart on clothing lines. Lovato simultaneously launched her own skincare line, Devonne By Demi, in 2014, was named the first-ever global ambassador for NYC New York Color Cosmetics, and promoted Skechers and Fabletics athletic wear. Lovato's persona up to early 2018 centralized the pursuit of fitness, hence being a spokesperson for athletic wear rounded out a logical circle of consumption.

In addition to a brief, less-than-stellar movie trajectory, which included *Monte Carlo* (2011) and *Spring Breakers* (2012), in 2017 Gomez sought to become a media producer. July Moon Productions, which she formed in 2008, led to her being one of the executive producers of the highly acclaimed and popular *13 Reasons Why*, a Netflix series about teen suicide. July Moon Productions is one of four production agencies involved with *13 Reasons Why*, and despite the original plan to have Selena star as the protagonist in a movie version of the novel, the Netflix series features other actors but retains her as producer and consultant. Through this venture, Selena has entered the post-network era as a media producer. Additionally, she frequently appears on fashion magazine covers, red carpets, and celebrity news.

Both Selena and Demi have dated celebrities and battled physical and mental health issues. Both of these somewhat incongruous elements have served to keep them in the popular press. Selena dated Justin Bieber at the peak of his popularity and continued a highly publicized on-and-off romance with him, generating a ton of coverage for them both, until Bieber married Hailey Baldwin in September 2018. Shortly thereafter, it was revealed that Selena had returned to treatment for "ongoing emotional issues" (Chiu and Marx 2018). Among potential causes listed for her mental health issues, Bieber's wedding is identified as a "stressor" (p. 16). Blue (2017) suggests that some of Selena's productions and interventions have been subsumed under the brighter spotlight accorded Bieber by a sexist mainstream media. Healthwise, in 2015 Selena revealed she was battling lupus, and in September 2017 she had a highly publicized kidney transplant as a result of complications from this. Thanks to a kidney donation from her best friend Francia Raisa, Selena overcame this latest health hurdle, which she used to help raise funding for the Lupus Foundation, while simultaneously commodifying her own health issues. Following a few months of laying low due to recovery, Selena Instagrammed a photo of her and Francia in the recovery room of the hospital, which received more than 10.5 million likes. Francia Raisa's Instagram, called "Hermanas" ("Sisters"), garnered nearly 241 000 likes – a high number, but nothing like the more than 10 million reached by Selena's. Coverage of the transplant, post facto, included sensational titles such as "Selena Gomez's Kidney Transplant Almost Killed Her, Says Donor Friend" (Scott 2018) and "Selena Gomez 'Could Have Died' Following Kidney Transplant, Says BFF Francia Raisa" (O'Malley 2018). Selena appeared on news shows such as *Today* to discuss the ordeal. Francia Raisa continues to post photos with her "sister" – "feliz cumpleaños mi hermana" is the title of a photo featuring both of them toasting champagne. Francia is an actor in "Grown-ish," a television show on the Disney-owned network Freeform – so the two are keeping it in the Disney family. As much as Selena has commodified her transplant, Francia is commodifying her friendship with Selena through it. Moreover, Francia has done more to locate Selena within Latinidad, through invoking the Spanish language through her use of the word "hermanas," than anything Selena has done herself. Finally, early in 2018, Selena was reported to have served a brief stint in rehab. Her road to recovery is a frequent topic in celebrity news, though the reasons she was in rehab have not been revealed. Her March 2018 *Harper's Bazaar* cover story mentions battles with depression. A relapse in October 2018 contributes yet another chapter to her ongoing mental health issues. Nonetheless, coverage of this real-life Disney princess is very supportive – much more so than that of her other best friend, Demi.

Demi Lovato shares Selena's trajectory of mental and physical health issues, as well as having a well-known paramour. Demi dated the less well-known but nonetheless popular actor Wilmer Valderrama, of ambiguous *That '70s Show*/Fez fame – a relationship also regularly covered in women's magazines and celebrity news. Lovato, more so than Gomez, mines her personal issues through confessional media. Author of an autobiography, *Staying Strong: 365 Days a Year* (2013), Demi is forthcoming about her struggles with bipolar disease, depression, drug abuse, eating disorders, and bullying. In *Simply Complicated* (2017), a YouTube documentary produced with Lovato's full collaboration, Demi reiterates her love for Valderrama, even years after their break-up. As per the playbook of neoliberal health issues, confessional mea culpa, and self-help marketing (Bailey 2011), Lovato has turned a difficult history with issues of eating disorder, substance abuse (Adderall, cocaine, and alcohol), and self-harm into two books, an activist role as advocate for issues of children and mental health and for the LGBTQ community, and a YouTube documentary. Her self-reported health maintenance includes massive doses of MMA and jujitsu. She appeared on the cover of *InStyle* magazine in April 2018, with a large photo spread and an interview heavy on discussions about her resilience and healthy workout regime. Nonetheless, through the release of the song "Sober" in June 2018, Demi revealed she had relapsed. On July 24, she was hospitalized following an overdose in Los Angeles. In August, after leaving the hospital, she entered a residential rehab facility, which she later temporarily left to seek mental health treatment with a doctor in Chicago. Demi remains open about her struggles with eating disorders and addictions, and she has received well wishes from many celebrities, including Selena Gomez, with whom she continues to be best friends. Francia Raisa's kidney donation to Gomez positions her as an even better best friend to Selena – or, as Francia always claims on Instagram, a sister. However, in terms of celebrity visibility, Selena and Demi remain a best-friend duo, especially as they simultaneously battle mental and physical health issues.

Ongoing entertainment careers for both actors include a range of activities in different media, not all necessarily owned by Disney. Demi Lovato played recurring character Danny in four episodes of *Glee* (2013–14) and a judge on the extreme-competition show *The X Factor* (2012–13), both on the Fox network. But her focus remains her singing career. Her debut album, *Don't Forget*, came out in September 2008, and she has since released five more, all of which have received RIAA gold status and placed in the top five of the US charts. Lovato goes on tour whenever she releases a new album, and has a loyal following of fans who call themselves "Lovatics." As her career has gained strength, her tours have expanded globally, to include Europe and South America. She was nominated for Best Pop Vocal Album for *Confident* at the 2017 Grammys, and she has received a considerable number of accolades, including an MTV

Video Music Award, 13 Teen Choice Awards, five People's Choice Awards, an ALMA Award, a Latin American Music Award, and a Grammy Award nomination (Wikipedia).

Additionally, both real-life mied Latinas participate in commodity activism (Hearn 2012), synergized with Disney properties. In particular, Gomez and Lovato participated, along with tween queen Miley Cyrus, in Disney's CSR initiative Friends for Change: Project Green, through which children were encouraged to take up environmentally friendly practices such as turning off the lights – as well as to register their emails with Disney, something Hearn decries as particularly troubling. Both Gomez and Lovato continue to have viable careers, to appear across a range of media and celebrity culture, and to background their Latinidad. Their most Latina/o activities include participating in a program to rescue dogs in Puerto Rico (Gomez) and a Get Out the Latino Vote drive (Lovato); in her *Simply Complicated* video, Demi admits that she joined the latter just so she could meet Valderrama.

Selena Gomez has parlayed her ambiguous Latina beauty into a profitable and popular after-Disney life that includes a spot on *Time* magazine's Firsts: What Does it Take to be the First? list (http://www.time.com/firsts).[29] Her section is titled "The Tastemaker," and her claim to fame – the reason she is included on the list alongside women like Hillary Clinton and Oprah Winfrey – is that she was "the first person to reach 100 million followers on Instagram." The article does not mention her Latinidad, ethnic roots, or anything other than her digital connection with her fans. As already mentioned, she is one of the executive producers of the immensely popular *13 Reasons Why*, which has been greenlighted for a second season. She regularly graces the covers of fashion magazines (*InStyle*, *Vogue*, *Cosmopolitan*, *Harper's Bazaar*, etc.), sometimes being called the "New Miley Cyrus."

Though both girls/young women/real-life Disney princesses have left behind some of their wholesomeness as they have moved through and beyond Disney, they have not abandoned their ambiguity and light Latinidad. This seems to be a lesson well learned. A postfeminist consumerist context – performance of whiteness, beauty, and consumerism, control and maintenance of the body – coupled with colorblind representation structures the inclusion of ethnicity within mainstream popular culture. For instance, Blue (2013, p. 664) articulates postfeminism to obsession with public visibility via greater attention to control of the body. Demi and Selena's ongoing career development bears out the performative, body-centered focus of postfeminism, and their engagement with philanthropy furthermore connects their self-branding to contemporary discourses of neoliberalism. Their struggles with mental and physical health track the cost of laboring as real-life Disney princesses – this is not a job for the faint of heart.

In sum, Miranda and Gabriella predate real-life Latinas Selena and Demi, who must live in the real postfeminist neoliberal world, act accordingly, and suffer the costs of their success. All four of these light Latinas, in turn, predate princesses Sofia and Elena in a continuous trifecta of contemporary subtle, ambiguous, and gendered Latinidad.

Sofia the First

In addition to fictional ambiguous Latinas Miranda and Gabriella, and actual ambiguous Latina celebrities Selena and Demi, Disney rounds out its gingerly Latinidad with Princesses Sofia and Elena of Avalor. Neither of the previous Latina sets have been vocally celebrated for their ethnicity, and certainly not by Disney. The last two Latinas discussed in this chapter, however, represent the more explicit ambivalence around issues of Latinidad from Disney. Arguably, they have the most contentious relation with Latinidad despite being the most recent ambiguous Latinas released to a national audience – one whose aware-ness of Latina/os is more salient, as well as continuously linked to highly divi-sive political rhetoric, as explicitly articulated by the 45th President of the United States. Sofia the First and Elena of Avalor coexist in an era of increased Latina/o presence, spending power, and political backlash. Though they are both fictional characters, they still had to cross over into mainstream presence, across the shaky bridge of animated Disney Latinidad.

Announced in December 2011 and introduced in November 2012, Sofia is a different type of Disney princess, in that she is a child rather than an adolescent – as all members of the princess pantheon are – and she appears on regularly scheduled television programming (on ABC/Disney). This move allows for two lucrative options. First, a regular show delivers regular audi-ences to advertisers with a broad range of synergistic options, rather than the less regular, occasional audience garnered by a film. Second, Sofia's age targets a younger demographic – 2- to 7-year-olds – that expands the princess brand and potentially hooks little girls at a younger age.[30] Narratively, Sofia becomes a princess by virtue of the king marrying her mother – therefore, she is a step-child to the king as well as a commoner. This tale resonates with contem-porary royal reality, wherein both Prince William of Britain and King Felipe IV of Spain are married to commoners – as are some of the Disney princess pantheon, such as Mulan and Belle. Sofia the First lives in Enchancia.[31] Her mother is named Miranda, just like one of the characters in the first set of Latinas discussed in this chapter, the ambiguously Latina best friend of Lizzy McGuire.

Sofia is voiced by the half-Greek Ariel Winter, of *Modern Family* fame (ABC, keeping it in the Disney family). In October 2012, she was identified as Disney's first Latina princess, when a blogger noted that her mother's skin was notice-ably darker than her own. After announcing that Miranda, Sofia's mother, would be voiced by Sara Ramirez, executive producer Jamie Mitchell asserted that Sofia was Latina (Rome, 2012). Immediately, the reaction to this news demonstrated the difficult and troubled waters of ethnic representation in the mainstream. In sum, both furious backlash and appreciative affirmation followed. The backlash predictably criticized Sofia's skin lightness, her blue eyes, and her light auburn hair (Sieczkowski 2012). For example:

> "If Disney were truly to finally step out and directly cater to the Latino community that has been crying out for decades for a Latina princess to represent our girls," said Ana Flores, blogger for Spanglishbaby, "She would be as Latina as Tiana is black or as Pocahontas is Indian-American."
>
> *(Rodriguez 2013)*

This interesting quote does not mention any particular specificity required of Sofia, but rather a conceptual authenticity that the blogger correctly ascribes to two previous Disney princesses. Both of those other princesses were explicitly tied to a particular ethnicity, yet both also generated plenty of backlash for their stereotypical racialization and white love interests. The marketing for the television princess Sofia was different than that for Tiana in *The Princess and the Frog*, whose storyline explicitly identifies her as African American. Set in early 19th-century New Orleans, *The Princess and the Frog* included well-known African American actors such as Oprah Winfrey and Terrence Howard voicing some of the main characters. Furthermore, the movie was explicitly billed and celebrated as starring Disney's first African American princess. To be sure, there was controversy with this representation. For instance, the inclusion of voodoo and the fact that Tiana falls in love with a Caucasian prince generated critique. Granted, Tiana was a princess in a full-length feature film, so the magnitude and character of the marketing campaign was bound to be different from that for a TV show. However, the explicit avowal of her ethnicity and the explicit disavowal of Sofia's is significant for understanding Disney's approach to representing and including Latinidad. This did not go unnoticed by the press. For example, Hairston (2016), when announcing the introduction of Elena in the context of Sofia's disavowal, noted Disney's backpedaling regarding its desire to make Sofia just a fairy princess, without specific ethnicity.

The fact that Sofia is voiced by a "white" actor also rankled some viewers (HLN in Sieczkowski 2012). Others felt Disney got it "just right" (Fox News in Sieczkowski 2012), as they did not want yet another stereotypical Latina who was brown and ate beans (NBC News in Sieczkowski 2012). The Fox News story asserts that Sofia was modeled after Queen Sofia of Spain, who also has light auburn hair and blue eyes, as does her granddaughter Princess Sofia. Maybe Disney's choice of Ariel Winter to voice her was partly informed by Queen Sofia's Greek provenance. This was a very confusing set of factors, as Disney could – and did – easily disavow Sofia's Latinidad, while audiences, and even a temporarily misinformed executive working on the series, could see elements of it.

Disney faced the quintessential fissure of utopian representation politics, which demands identifiability outside of stereotype and desires representation where it is lacking. The wide-ranging criticism and support of the character reiterate Julien and Mercer's admonition that the "burden of representation thus falls on the Other" (1988, p. 6). If Sofia was the first Latina in the Disney princess universe, different segments of the audience wanted her to embody so much that had been missing from the company.

In response to the mis-outing of Sofia's Latinidad and the unleashing of the "burden of under-representation" discourse arising in the press and other channels, Disney was quick to follow up with an affirmation of its commitment to diversity, as well as a clarification that quickly turned into disavowal or "backpedaling" (Llona 2015). The initial response that Disney does not like to call out specific ethnicity (Rodriguez 2013) transitioned into Nancy Kanter, Senior Vice President of Original Programming and General Manager of Disney Junior Worldwide, making the correction that Sofia is actually of mixed heritage, as fairy princesses tend to be, and her provenance was "inspired" by Spain. Her fictional country of Galdiz looks like and rhymes with the Andalusian city of Cadiz. Craig Gerber, co-executive producer of Sofia, added that whereas Sofia's mother's heritage was "inspired" by Spain, her father's was "inspired" by Scandinavia (Sieczkowski 2012), thus further inscribing Sofia within white-ness, as opposed to the brownness suggested by the original Latinidad referred to by Mitchell. By the time representatives of the National Hispanic Media Coalition (NHMC) met with Disney in September, 2013, they reported that Nancy Kanter:

> "... shared that Sofia the First is in fact not a Latina character and that the producer of the television program misspoke," NHMC president and CEO Alex Nogales said in a statement. "We accept the clarification and celebrate the good news that Disney Junior has an exciting project in early development that does have a Latina as the heroine of the show."
> *(Rodriguez 2013)*

One cannot blame Mitchell, the executive producer, for suggesting Sofia was Hispanic. First of all, her name, Sofia, could be Spanish, and the modifier "the First" seems to suggest the first Hispanic princess. Furthermore, her mother's character is voiced by Latina actor Sara Ramirez (Dr. Callie Torres in *Grey's Anatomy*, another ABC show), and Sofia's skin is a little darker than that of her step-siblings and other Disney princesses. Granted, these are not huge signifi-ers of Latinidad in general, but they fit right along with Disney's gingerly approach to the representation of Latina/os. As such, they are riddled with ambiguity. For example, Sofia is actually a Greek name, meaning "wisdom," and is widely used throughout the Mediterranean, including in Italy and France. That could make Sofia the First a Mediterranean-"inspired" princess. Yet, the ambiguous elements appear to be anchored by the choice of the actor voicing Sofia's mother. In relational terms, the mother plus the ambiguous ethnic elements set Sofia apart from previous Disney princesses and accord with the subtle Latinidad preferred by Disney and illustrated by the previous two sets of princesses discussed in this chapter. Disney's disavowal of Latina/o specificity – that is, Latina/o in relation to other ethnicities not particularity of Latinidad – was enacted through the frequent use of the adjective "inspired," which itself avoids any specificity and therefore any claims for authenticity with any country or ethnicity.

When Mitchell's initial assertion of Latinidad was immediately and forcefully followed by Disney disavowal, some of the press coverage justified Disney's reaction in relation to young audiences. Disney asserted that its goal was to have every little girl identify with Sofia. Sofia lives in a fictional place, and the cast of her show includes no easily identifiable actors other than Tim Gunn, of *Project Runway* fame. This actor's queer target audience does not necessarily include the pre-K crowd, and Sofia's indeterminate provenance might also not be noticed by pre-K audiences. This tactical move, suggesting that audiences are more likely to identify with an ambiguously ethnic and somewhat European girl than with a culturally specific national minority, such as a Latina, gave Disney some time to come up with a response to the ethnic outcry it inadvertently had activated in an audience containing outspoken individuals and organized Latina/o media critics. The outcome of this little spat apparently inspired and alerted Disney to the reality that there is such thing as a Hispanic audience and a demand for Latina/o characters. Copious data about Latina/os as a significant and growing portion of the population and the fact that Latina/os attend movies in disproportionate amounts was apparently not as persuasive, detectable, or acknowledged as the response to the incorrectly attributed ethnicity of Sofia the First. By the time Aimee Carrero was rolled out as the voice of Elena in *Elena of Avalor*, she outspokenly and openly traced her family's engagement with Disney back to her grandmother and explicitly and gleefully asserted Latinidad.

Elena of Avalor

Elena of Avalor is the story of Princess Elena, a teenager who has saved her enchanted, Latin American inspired kingdom from an evil sorceress and now must rule as Crown Princess until she is old enough to be queen. Elena is an empowered princess who is learning to lead the kingdom of Avalor with the help of her friends and family. She is a strong and compassionate leader whose independent and curious spirit shines in each adventure she goes on. Elena's Royal Scepter, the Scepter of Light, can channel the power within her in order to help her kingdom and her family.

(Girls Scouts/Disney Leadership Guide,
Becoming a Leader Will Be her Greatest Adventure, p. 1)

Following the denial and disavowal of Princess Sofia's Latinidad, Disney created a spin-off by setting Elena of Avalor free from an amulet, worn by Sofia, in which she was trapped. Sofia literally released Elena from centuries-long captivity – a pithy metaphor for subsumed Latinidad in US popular culture. Elena's kingdom, Avalor, includes the Spanish word "valor," which means courage, bravery, nerve, gallantry, worth, cost, and value, among many other related concepts. Elena is introduced to the public as a courageous, nervy princess in charge of her own island territory/nation. Totally expectedly, and given Elena's birth from the Sofia show, news coverage of the introduction of this Latina Disney princess inevitable referenced the avowal and disavowal of Sofia. For example:

> This time it seems to be for real – Disney is introducing its first Latina princess, Elena of Avalor, an olive-skinned beauty who will make her debut in a special episode of "Sofia the First," the Disney Junior hit TV show, and then will go on to have her very own spin-off. If the news sound vaguely familiar it's because a little over a year ago there was a lot of buzz when Sofia the First was mistakenly introduced as Hispanic. Despite the Spanish spelling of the name, it all turned out to be a misunderstanding, with President and CEO for the NHMC Alex Nogales playing a central role in clarifying the issue. This time around this "real" unambiguous Latina is introduced with the approval of the NHMC and the understanding that Sofia's Latina heritage was a "misunderstanding." In fact, Craig Gerber, Sofia's creator, also the creator for Elena, claims that the misunderstanding about Sofia's Latinidad alerted him to the fact that there was a demand and an audience for a Latina princess. Unlike Sofia who is a little girl, Elena at 16 matches the age of other Disney princesses (such as Ariel, Belle, and Cinderella). Unlike the other teen princesses, and like Sofia, Elena is introduced through a television show and becomes a television show. Whether she will transition into the big screen is seldom discussed and deferred into the future. When asked about this possibility, Nogales, president of the NHMC does not seem bothered by the Latina princess' location in the small screen: "The new series will start with one full-hour episode and then will continue developing as a series." Nogales said he is not bothered by the fact that Elena is not jumping to the big screen anytime soon … "You start somewhere," he said. "They are going to have a big long episode and then they will take it from there."
>
> *(Llona 2015)*

Some Latina/o critics identify this television move as a "shun," especially considering that in that very same year Disney was about to introduce *Moana*, a Polynesian princess to the big screen.[32]

(Hairston 2016)

Big or small screen, Elena is a Latina Disney princess. Despite her "olive"/slightly orange skin, her body bears the unmistakably elements of Disney adolescent princesses: her hair is virtually a third of her body size (Lacroix 2004), her eyes are large and almond-shaped, and her waist is tiny in comparison to her chest and hips (Götz 2008). She combines these generic princess traits with Latina dark skin, dark hair, red lipstick, and huge gold hoop earrings. Nancy Kanter managed to walk the tightrope between specificity and ambiguity in her comments about Elena:

In making the announcement on Thursday, Kanter said her creative team has delivered "a universal story with themes that authentically reflect the hopes and dreams of our diverse audience." The princess will be voiced by Aimee Carrero, of ABC Family's "Young & Hungry."

(Llona 2015)

Somehow, Elena must be universal, diverse, and authentic. Among other elements of continuity, notice that the voice talent remains within the Disney synergistic universe, once again drawing from ABC television. The flattening of difference, so common in Disney history vis-à-vis Latin Americans and US Latinidad, can be found throughout the young series. Elena is "Latina" or "Hispanic," but she is really Latin American – located outside the United States in an indeterminate island region. Islands are traditionally recurring locations for Latinas in US popular culture. Dora the Explorer, Princess Rosalinda/Demi Lovato, and now Elena all live in these offshore, semitropical, vaguely Hispanic locations. In addition to the usual body shape, the princess is composed of a blend of Latin American cultures, in the mainstream tradition of the flattening of difference. For instance, Elena's red dress was designed by Layana Aguilar, a former *Project Runway* participant of Brazilian descent who describes it as follows: "The feeling to it is very Peruvian, Inca-like" (Hairston 2016); the flowers embroidered on it are based off her Brazilian grandmother's wedding dress. The whole outfit represents a hybridity of South America to clothe Disney's first avowed US Latina princess. Also, the narrative is supposedly filled with Latin American elements. The first episode alone, Disney claimed, contained influences from Chile ("an elf-like shapeshifting creatures based on a Chilean *peuchen* myth") and Mexico ("a spiritual guide based on the beliefs from a Mayan tribe") (Wikipedia).

In that first episode, 16-year-old Elena strives to become the leader of her island territory by forming a royal advisory team. She rescues her sister from the *peuchen*, shapeshifters that can change from humans into animals. Apart from their Chilean origin,[33] these creatures also seem to reference the Midas myth, as everything they bite turns into gold. Pan-Latin American mythology follows the company line of "a story *inspired* by diverse Latin cultures and folklore" (Wagmeister 2016; Umstead 2018; The Futon Critic; emphasis my own), often quoted in pseudo stories about the show that obviously draw on a Disney press release, as they all use exactly the same words in discussing it. The fact that the story is "inspired," of course, gives Disney great license to draw on a range of sources and to invent its own, as it has always done with all of its feature-length movies and television shows. In this sense, *Elena of Avalor* is no different than any other Disney show in that it constructs a fantasy world inspired by an actual culture or location, with healthy doses of magic thrown in, to draw audiences to the story and therefore to any number of media and other products that the company can synergistically market through its narrative.

Press releases tout Elena as her own hero, scripted to pursue activities other than romance and to show exemplary leadership skills. Disney announced that there would be a musical number in every episode, and Elena's musical instrument is the guitar. The music in the show ranges from salsa to Spanish flamenco acoustic guitar. The inclusion of music in every episode harks both back to the musicality of Disney princess tradition – all of the feature-length animated princess films are musicals – and to the Latina spitfire trope, in that this princess dances and sings as she resolves problems of state. To be sure, all Disney princesses sing – but they do not all play an instrument and dance at the same time.

Treated as the "first princess of Hispanic descent" (Williams 2016), Elena is voiced by Aimee Carrero, a Latina actor of Puerto Rican and Dominican descent who is outspoken about her own Latinidad and that of Elena of Avalor in the many interviews synergistically arranged for her by Disney. Moreover, Carrero traces her own Disney fandom back two generations to her grandmother – thus simultaneously securing the fandom lineage among Latina/os and outing Latinidad as an explicit and purposeful element of Elena. Elena's grounding in Latinidad is both strong and tenuous. To begin with, the theme song pronounces the name "Elena" in an English manner – *Eleina*. The castle in which she resides resembles the Alhambra in Granada as well as the royal palace in Segovia, both in Spain. Most major characters have Spanish names: Elena Castillo Flores, Isabel the little sister, Abuelo/Francisco the grandfather, Armando the buffoonish attendant, and Abuela the grandmother, whose seldom-mentioned given name is Luisa. Elena is the latest in a long line of Disney characters who draw on the Disney archive of Latin American and Spanish stereotypes to deliver a composite unambivalent ambiguity.

Elena of Avalor, the show and the character, is, as expected, articulated to many ancillary ventures. Given that she was introduced as a natural leader, the partnership with the Girl Scouts of America seems, well, predetermined. After all, her slogan, present on many products and websites, is, "Becoming a Leader Will Be her Greatest Adventure." The Elena/Girl Scout guide is available in English and Spanish (*Leadership Guide/Guía de Liderazgo*), thus asserting not only the Girl Scouts but also Latina girls as target audiences. Girls are guided in grade-specific modules (pre-K, K-1, 2–3, and 4–5). As well, *Elena* was one of the few Latina/o mainstream productions nominated for a 2017 Emmy, for Outstanding Animated Program (Betancourt 2017). The 2017 season's list of nominees, like previous ones, consistently underrepresented Latina/o talent, so *Elena*'s nomination for a main category is all the more notable. As it turns out, though nominated for a number of awards, *Elena* did not win any.

Conclusion

All of this synergy, casting, and marketing speaks of the Disney playbook, at which the company succeeds fantastically. Yet, I am not solely interested in the representational elements of these princesses, as they fall squarely within Disney iconography, which itself falls centrally within US and Western mainstream representations of femininity in general and children's media in particular (Berger 1972; Götz 2008). Rather, I explore the deployment of Latinidad in relation to history and other ethnicities and the strategies Disney follows to present its first avowed Latina princess as an indication of the gingerly steps being taken by mainstream media industries regardless of demographic and spending data. If hard data, as embodied by demographic and spending numbers, drives media production, then, logically and rationally, representations could shift to include the Latina/o population growth (in size and diversity), and the accompanying shift in spending power. Making the argument that hard data (in terms of economic and demographic data) is not necessarily what drives media production and representation (not what the audience wants) takes us back to ideology and the power of racial and gender discourses that structure production and representation regardless of shifts in population demographics and therefore in spending preferences and habits. Even a major global media conglomerate with nearly unlimited resources, doubtlessly spent on research on a broad range of metrics, fears the expansion of representational parameters. Despite data documenting the growth of the brown population nationally and the prevalence of the brown population globally, Disney takes gingerly steps to the expansion of its ethnic representational register.

A long history of representation of Latin America as different, more colorful, and prone to music and dancing positions this region of the Americas as the geographical spitfire in relation to the rational North part of the continent. Additional elements of political instability and outright violence lurk just beyond the horizon of even G-rated Disney fare. This history of barely subterranean threat and disorder has contributed to the ability of mainstream media, including Disney, to conceptualize the inclusion of the US Latina/o into domestic narratives. As a content producer whose target audience is global in scope, Disney represents US culture to the rest of the world. Indeed, Disney itself, as a symbol, through the mouse ears, becomes a representation of the United States, period. Beginning with the mouse and successfully branching out to representations of normalized US morals, families, and personhood, Disney provides a consistent universe in which typecasting is essential for continuity of narratives, audiences, and cross-business licensing agreements. Introducing a new set of characters with relational attributes that do not take away from the moral high ground represented by whiteness yet expand tired stereotypes proves to be a difficult task. Such moves can generate more backlash than increased audience size – and, therefore, profit. Alteration of the tried and tested company playbook is not impossible, but only proceeds through cautious and nearly imperceptible measures.

Latinas in Disney constitute an ambiguous and nonthreatening presence. Much as the spitfire in cinema, television, and popular culture provides a humorous and unthreatening bridge to assuage fears of racial mixing and immigration (see Chapter 2), the ambiguous Latina represents a sign of the times. Through the characters of Miranda and Gabriella, the Latina surfaces at a moment of public acknowledgment of Latina/o population presence in the United States. Fear and desire mix in the popular imaginary to create a sexualized and hyperfertile figure. Disney has to sanitize this tendency, especially in its children- and tween-targeted fare, so its Latinas are ambiguous, assimilated, and pure. The Disney Latina across the lifespan of childhood – from pre-school through young adult – is also part and parcel of the construction and marketing of the tween category, targeting a gendered sliver of the audience with significant consumption power whose Disney fandom or engagement may have begun pre-birth and has to be nurtured through the life cycle. Miranda and Gabriella appeared at the cusp of Disney's expansion into global children's television, and following publication of the Census data documenting US Latina/o population growth. Selena and Demi put a human face to the continuing deployment of subtle Latinidad. Their grooming as subtle, postfeminist, neoliberal young celebrities draws on decades of Disney marketing strategies. Their ambivalent success stories lay bare the difficulty of living in the limelight as real-life Disney princesses. Lindsay Lohan and Hilary Duff,[34] both of whom were spun out of the Disney universe, serve as cautionary tales of delayed resilience: both are now back in show business, relatively healthy and productive. Not only have Selena and Demi attempted to turn their physical and mental health issues into neoliberal tales of resilience, but Disney must have negotiated lucrative enough contracts that they didn't depart from the company on bad terms. That tween and girl culture propelled the Disney Channel into high profitability guides this analysis about the inclusion of Latinidad and its subtlety and ambiguity – inclusivity cannot mess with profitability for a major global conglomerate. Sofia and Elena round out the still ambivalent pattern of Latina inclusion within the Disney universe. Whereas Sofia remains the non-Latina Latina, at least in relation to how some members of the audience interpret her, Elena unambiguously represents Latinidad, though within Latinidad she's of ambiguous origin. Moreover, she reiterates the eternal-foreigner trope, because as Latina as she is touted to be, she truly remains a Latin American.[35] Present in pre-school television, these last two princesses prime audiences to a light Latinidad that draws on stereotypical elements, including flattening of difference.

None of these six ambiguous Latinas is located in any identifiable ethnic or national-origin community, yet all represent Disneyfied Latinidad. Regardless of their gingerly approach to Latinidad, all six productions created profitable franchises, all of which continue to generate returns for Disney and its shareholders. These are economically successful ventures. There appear to be no plans to develop a more identifiable, specific, US-based, and browner Latina on the Disney horizon. Despite the success of *Coco* (2017), which drew audiences across the ethnic spectrum, including Latina/os, the gendered deployment of Latinidad within Disney remains subtle, ambiguous, foreign, light, and highly profitable.

Notes

1 "Disney claims to be the world's largest licensor of intellectual property and the world's largest publisher of children's books and magazines" (Wasko 2017, p. 16).
2 These numbers were rounded off to the nearest million.
3 Partly due to this movie role, Dwayne Johnson was named *People* magazine's "Sexiest Man Alive" for 2016.
4 Another promotional opportunity for *Moana* presented itself at the 2017 Oscars, since the title song, "How Far I'll Go," was nominated for an award. Dwayne Johnson participated off-site through virtual link, and Auli'i performed the song live at the ceremony.
5 Other than Vice-President-elect Mike Pence, who attended the *Hamilton* November 18, 2016 performance and was greeted by a personal message from the cast onstage after the end of the show, most people are unable to secure a ticket. Indeed, at the 2017 Oscars, Jimmy Kimmel walked up to Lin-Manuel Miranda, who was accompanied by his mother, and marveled at the ability to hang out with him, given that otherwise one has to pay "$10 000" for a ticket.
6 This was an unusual trio, as Princess Tiana received much less exposure than white and brown Disney princesses. The fact that Tiana occupied the center and foregrounded image on the can made it quite an unusual marketing ploy for a Disney campaign, which usually background Tiana or leave her out altogether.

7 For those who are not up on all things Dora, Diego is a spin-off show featuring a boy.

8 From anecdotal experience, I can attest that many children refuse to accept a nonsynergized Band Aid. If it doesn't have a character, they will not wear it. Conversely, if it has their favorite character, they will plaster a bunch on before a parent or guardian realizes a whole box has been used up, regardless of whether they have a minor injury or not. Of course, this latter use is precisely the type of consumption hoped for by marketers.

9 There are many more. Here, I just mention three to illustrate some of the most prominent children's and Disney media marketing strategies.

10 There is a large body of research on these issues, so I point to some of the references and broad themes as they inform this project.

11 Michael Real was on faculty at UCSD and San Diego State University during these years. Youth in Southern California, as Real details in the book, were frequent visitors to Disneyland, and participated in a ritual overnight in the park following high-school graduation – present author included.

12 Access to internal company deliberations about the strategy to reach out to and represent merging demographic categories is beyond the scope of this present research. Usually, unless there is a leak or we are sufficiently historically removed from the time of deliberations, this information is not made available to scholars.

13 The United States sought to secure the region as an ally in geopolitical formations, as well as to present a softer hand and better relations in dealing with Latin America, partly by representing Latin Americans as friendly and happy people in a hemispheric PR effort. These films had a double goal: to represent Latin Americans as friendly and happy and to show Latin Americans – who consumed mostly Hollywood films – that the United States was a friendly and benign neighbor. These efforts were partly funded by the Office of the Coordinator of Inter-American Affairs (OCIAA), established by the US government to "gain solidarity from Latin America for WWII." The OCIAA's Motion Picture division distributed free prints of its films to embassies and consulates across the region (Miller and Kraidy 2016). Production and distribution were partly managed by US government funds, with geopolitical aims. The films' narrative devices dovetailed these aims.

14 It is interesting that Disney selected Donald Duck instead of Mickey Mouse as its inter-American diplomat.

15 The choice of Uruguay as one of the four countries remains unusual. Seldom is Uruguay mentioned, let alone chosen as a representative Latin American country.

16 "Carioca" is the term used in Brazil to refer to people who live in Rio de Janeiro.

17 Wasko (2017) identifies the Eisner era as one in which "Team Disney" revived and reclassified classic Disney, with the retroactive creation of the "Princess" franchise.

18 The name of this category will eventually have to be supplanted, as all "modern" things have to be renamed when a new modernity takes place.

19 Much has been written about Disney princesses and the ideal of beauty – from the work at IZI to Haines and Delacroix.

20 To be sure, Disney also prefers mixed-race actors to represent African Americans and Asian Americans, but that history is beyond the scope of this chapter.

21 As audience and therefore marketing categories, "tweens" and "teens" are not universal constructs. Disney's globalizing thrust banks on the spread of these categories as more and more countries enter into and participate in global conglomerate capitalism. Huong (2015) details the discursive construction of the Vietnamese teen as that country entered into globalization after its difficult history of long-term war followed by withdrawal from the global economy and eventual return to the global community.

22 Brandes (2006) traces this holiday/religious celebration "to the colonial encounter ... between Europe and America," though the "impetus for change" comes in the mid-20th century after "intensification of contact between Mexico and the United States" (p. 13).

23 At present, Disney is filming *High School Musical 4* – so this profitable franchise has yet to end production.

24 Dating back to *Romeo and Juliet*, via *West Side Story* (1961).

25 This cannot be overstated. Every one of Sharpay's outfits has sequins. In the closing scene, she actually has sequins in her eyebrows, as part of her make-up.

26 One of my colleagues, a leading scholar in Girls Studies, emailed me many years after the third HSM and said: "Why didn't you tell me Gabriella was Latina?!?!"

27 The show barely made it to 2011. It was canceled on January 2, 2011.

28 Not wanting to include a full overview of the film, I nevertheless find it necessary to note that as part of the titular "protection program," a make-over process is absolutely essential.

29 The list includes Rita Moreno, Selena Williams, Issa Rae, and other women of color whose ethnicity is mentioned as part of their inclusion.

30 It is very difficult to find data about boy viewership of this show. The press releases comment on the girl viewership, but anecdotal evidence suggests that boys are very engaged by this character. Similar to *Dora the Explorer*, the audience cannot be reduced to just girls.

31 Disney locations usually have names that must be somewhere in Europe and are nowhere at all. For instance, in *The Princess Diaries* (2001) and *The Princess Diaries 2: Royal Engagement* (2004), Mia is a real-life princess from Genovia, which looks a bit like a cross between Monaco and Switzerland.

32 At a panel on Latina/o studies at the FLOW 2018 conference, held at the University of Texas at Austin, a couple of women in the audience came up to the panelists and complained that getting a Latina princess on the small screen felt like a "diss."

33 A brief and unscientific survey of Chileans revealed that none had ever heard of this myth. However, given that it is traced to the extreme south of the country, while those interviewed came from central Chile, this may be unsurprising.

34 Blue (2017) notes that part of Duff's inability to come to terms with Disney contractually was due to Disney's gendered approach to salaries and its underpayment of its new cash cow.

35 As such, she resembles Dora the Explorer (Harewood and Valdivia 2005).

4

Latina/o Media Utopias

The Ideal Place or No Place

"Media" and "Utopia" are somewhat like successor terms to state and ideology, but, shorn of their repressive, historically negative connotations, offer themselves instead as neutral categories, unmarked by prevailing regimes of power and domination.

(Rajagopal and Rao 2016, p. 5)

During a "post-racial" moment where race and ethnicity are no longer supposed to matter, the casting politics surrounding black Latina/o actors produce a triple-burden across gender, ethnic, and racial barriers that is increasingly difficult to navigate.

(Molina-Guzmán 2013b)

It is the contention here that it is impossible for a utopia to exist in an American societal context without the representation and equalization of racial difference. By extension, it is impossible for utopia to exist in that same context without the representation and equalization of class and gender difference.

(Flanagan 2009, p. 309)

What kinds of representations of Asian Americans would be more or less problematic, and what counts as "Asian American" to begin with in a world where individuals embody multiple and shifting identities?

(Lopez 2012, p. 4)

This chapter explores some of the major contours of the implicitly utopian elements of efforts by Latina/o communities at inclusion in and transformation of mainstream media, as well as some of the debates that accompany these efforts, regardless of outcomes. Debates about the politics of and approaches to the inclusion and presence of previously minoritized groups inevitably involve a utopian popular culture component. While politics of inclusion and

The Gender of Latinidad: Uses and Abuses of Hybridity, First Edition. Angharad N. Valdivia.
© 2020 John Wiley & Sons Ltd. Published 2020 by John Wiley & Sons Ltd.

utopia are not synonymous, their relationship or placement along a continuum of social change deserves discussion. The goal of an inclusive utopia, which might mean a change in the media system as we know it, undergirds a broad range of impulses, critiques, and movements. Implicit yet unarticulated utopias guide much of the research and activism about issues of discourse and representation, production and labor, and audience and interpretation in Communication/Media and Ethnic Studies in general, and Latina/o Media Studies in particular. The American Dream, globalization, inclusive media, media activism – none of these commonly invoked concepts are straightforward, yet all undergird utopian media impulses, and in particular Latina/o presence, inclusivity, participation, and transformation. At issue is the multiplicity of implicit utopian goals. For instance, is one implicit goal to have a presence – any kind of presence? Presence is fleeting and ever-changing, yet its indeterminacy should not prevent us from including it in our utopian impulses. In most cases, presence is hard-fought and not entirely settled, as there can always be slippage. Presence can be better than absence, but not always. Since present presence leaves much to be desired, its implicit improved futurity is part of its promise. Situating change in the future (Bennett 2010) might be the very definition of the utopian concept of media futures (see Gates 2013). So, what type of presence are we fighting or hoping for? A Latina/o media utopia at the very least would include presence in production, content, and audiences, as well as in scholarship and scholars. This only seems ambitious because it has proven so difficult to achieve minimal levels of inclusion.

The spectrum from reformist to radical utopianism includes explicit and implicit utopias across a complex terrain of hybrid Latinidad. Reformist utopias take the current system as given, unchangeable, or just, and envision an inclusion within its terms. Explicit utopias are visibly or audibly articulated and require organization, resources, and archiving. Implicit utopias, which guide much of the inclusionary efforts in media, rest at a barely subtextual level and are multiplicitous, as those holding them don't usually check with one another regarding uniformity, or even agreement. They imply a utopia where Latinidad has an enlarged media presence as a result of a meritocratic distributive system in which merit relates to artistic/aesthetic qualities rather than commercial ones. Inclusion in an existing media system differs from inclusion in a potentially transformed media system. Radical utopian media activism and scholarship would explicitly invoke an alternative media system imaginary. Meritocracy itself would be challenged (Littler 2018) as a myth that privileges particular subjectivities and groups at the expense of many others.

Are there explicit Latina/o media utopias that animate bodies of work? For mainstream media, there are libertarian and Habermasian media utopias, for instance, which can be found to reside in places like the media reform movement. Though theorizing an inclusive public sphere, these are often rightly criticized for imagining away difference, or, rather, assuming a level playing field. Radical Latina/o utopias would add to the reductive Libertatian/Habermasian/Fraserian imaginary while positing an imagination and future that, nonetheless, can still guide our present action. A starting point for the difficulties of advocating for a representational utopia is the diversity and hybridity within Latinidad. A unified utopian dream would be difficult enough from within a population that was more or less homogeneous. Latina/os are not homogeneous, but radically hybrid (Valdivia 2004b, 2005c). Through country of origin (recent or past), race and ethnicity, religion, political tendencies, sexual orientation, and so forth, they span the spectrum of possibilities. Furthermore, this spectrum geometrically expands when we consider hybridities. That is, Latina/os can be white or black, but also Afro-Latina/os, Blasian Latina/os, Catholic/Jewish, Argentinian/Boricua, and so on. As well, the institutionally allocated imaginary location within a multicultural vision is that Latina/os occupy the space in between normative whiteness and aberrant blackness. Thus, we as a population are supposed to provide a middle-of-the-road, acceptable, safe representation and presence of ethnicity in relation to the implicit paragon – whiteness – and against that which the mainstream refuses to assimilate – blackness. Somehow, demands for inclusion and visibility form part of a terrain of assuaging the identity crisis of a nation. It is no wonder that Latina/o representations are so fraught with symbolic landmines.

Dating back at least a century, underrepresented populations in the United States[1] have sought presence and change in their mainstream representation. As Antonio Gramsci (1929–35) noted, popular culture is a terrain of cultural struggle, and the struggle is never entirely settled. While he was not necessarily identifying ethnically minoritized populations as part of that struggle, nevertheless Gramsci's insights are applicable to contemporary cultural politics. Popular culture extends from mainstream movies, television, and music to digital culture – the combination of legacy and digital media. The contemporary terrain of culture is at once synergized and converged: we consume content on multiple platforms in a constant state of updating and renewal, and providers of content operate across a wide range of media. Increased presence promises to extend in a liquid sense across platforms (see Bauman 2000), yet its slippery existence also threatens to continue the displacement or outright exclusion of a large component of the population. Can we "Unthink Eurocentrism" (Shohat and Stam 1995) long enough to gain a sliver of dignified presence for the other? Gramsci, Bauman, and Shohat, while providing powerful critiques of contemporary exclusionary conditions, also hold out the possibility of better times, better arrangements, better existence – in sum, a utopia.

This chapter explores some of the heterogeneity of utopian impulses undergirding so much of Latina/o Media Studies research, and the impossibility of satisfaction given the multiplicity of impulses, strategies, and outcomes. In order to arrive at some of these possibilities, I explore the bimodal definition of "utopia," before presenting a selective overview of some of the Media Studies research that foregrounds "utopia" as a key word. A brief examination of two of the latest media productions that take up "utopia" as an explicit part of their title, *Detropia* and *Zootopia*, sheds light on some of the elements that guide the representation of utopia in contemporary media. Beyond representation, the inclusion of Latinidad and Latina/os in recent award ceremonies provides yet another glimpse into utopian inclusivity.

The rise of neoliberal policies, the deployment of postracial discourses in the United States, and the widespread adoption of postfeminism all have a great influence on contemporary representations of ethnic populations, and consequently on the social movements and political activism that seek to make a difference in these representations. Latina/o representations circulate and reiterate traditional narratives about gender, race, sexuality, and nation, which in turn trigger a range of recognizable audience responses and community reactions. The definition of "inclusion" and the terms under which these debates can be held inform a range of possibilities. The mainstream industry's reiterations of the "coming of age" of Latina/os in the media and the latest discovery of the Latina/o audience suggest both purposeful amnesia and a rehashing of a tired utopian cliché. Award shows prove to be another space in which to consider explicit and implicit utopias. Latina/o efforts to produce award shows within – yet, on the margins of – the mainstream speak of an achievement within difference. At the level of awards in mainstream award shows such as the Oscars, the obfuscation of presence and the displacing of the US Latina/o with Latin American talent once more render US Latina/os foreign within their own country. Finally, Latina/o Media Studies books explore the inclusion/exclusion/cooptation in the mainstream carried out in relation to previously mentioned overarching discourses that, in turn, release or exert a huge pressure to have sanitized, safe, and ambiguous representations in the mainstream.

Representation cannot be studied outside of production. Visibility is contested and produced. Utopian impulses have to go through those involved in the production of media content, who must contend with social expectations of media industries, their industry's economic profit imperatives, and audiences' implicit demands for the presence of identifiable people who go beyond stereotypes and of narratives that work toward social justice rather than toward reifying oppression. Producers and artists do not have full agency. Individual companies do not have full agency. Entire swaths of media producers do not have full agency. In concert with one another, in relation to historically established practices, and within a volatile global economy, all stakeholders at the production side must navigate a very turbulent mainstream. Audiences, publics, and populations engage with media in a broad range of ways. At the center of it all are the representations of depoliticized and consumable bodies (Molina-Guzmán 2010) that unite the producers with audiences and force questions such as: What will make them/us happy? When and under what circumstances will they/we feel that Latina/os in mainstream popular culture are included in a satisfactory manner, in a satisfying way? What will resolve the gender and racial discomfort of the mainstream (read, implicitly normative white audience) and the expectations of the Latina/o audience? Where is that fine line between offensive and demeaning stereotype and the whitening of culture or flattening of difference? Does representing Latina/o success automatically get us into a coopted space? What structural measures will satisfy the demands of Latina/o audiences, Latina/o artists, and Latina/o producers? What is the ideal for which we aim? Or, rather, what are some of the ideals we implicitly hold dear? Where do we aim to be? How do we want to be visible? We have to remember that mainstream access involves not only representations, but also Latina/o producers and actors who seek a space of employment and creation, as well as Latina/o audiences that want something different or better.

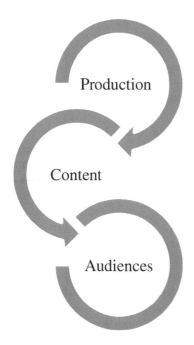

Production

Content

Audiences

Tension between a stereotype or easily recognizable racialized discourse and erasure or subtle presence places mainstream media producers in a difficult position. Which option within this difficult and nearly untenable spectrum should they generate given that audiences' responses, recognitions, and potential reactions work within a discourse of implicit utopias that wants both the obvious and the subtle? A dearth of explicit utopias makes this task even more difficult. If these producers are Latina/os (and there is a small chance that they are), the tension is at least doubled, for not only do they have to deal with the difficult spectrum of possibilities, but they also have to prove that they can function in the mainstream as producers who will heed the most important call – maximization of profit – and that they will not endanger this pursuit for the sake of ethnic – their ethnic – goals and representations (Rodriguez 1999). In other words, Latina/o producers function within restricted degrees of freedom, as institutional imperatives largely dictate the terms of their output.

The erasure and marginalization of Latina/os from mainstream life is a process of symbolic annihilation (Tuchman et al. 1978) and symbolic colonization (Molina-Guzmán 2010). The former finding takes the underrepresentation of women and minorities in the media to offer a more nuanced examination of additional elements of trivialization, sensationalization, and victimization. The latter expands on this classic finding and proposes an "ideological process that contributes to the manufacturing of ethnicity and race as a homogenized construct" (Molina Guzmán 2010, p. 9). As such, symbolic colonization explores the taming and domestication of Latinidad within mainstream US racial formations. While this is not the utopian goal, it is part of the process of aiming for the ideal place. The terrain of struggle contains impulses toward inclusion, marginalization, and domestication. Utopian efforts must follow the cartography of this terrain to reach beyond reformist inclusion into radical utopian transformation.

It bears repetition that for both symbolic annihilation and symbolic colonization, a minimal presence is required. The amassing of political capital must include the media's role in brokering power and shaping public opinion (Amaya 2013) – a process that requires presence in the mainstream. Many mainstream producers, who undeniably function within an industry that foregrounds the profit motive, nonetheless sometimes attempt to create representations that extend, extenuate, or rupture previous tendencies. Indeed, Molina-Guzmán (2010) offers "symbolic rupture" as the counterpart to her concept of symbolic colonization. But whereas Molina-Guzmán explored symbolic ruptures through digital spaces, Latina/o communities and audiences enact such ruptures throughout the multiplicitous and converged media terrain, expecting linear progress to address historical issues of exclusion and stereotyping, and contemporary gains to acknowledge their majority/minority status – especially since 2000. Linearity and progress are intertwined elements of utopian dreams, but they seldom move in the same direction simultaneously – that, in itself, is a utopic dream. Social change is composed of a mixture of forward, lateral, and backward movements, and internal contradictions abound – linear progress, a Comtian vestige, is seldom borne out by history.

Representation in the mainstream is not about a reflection of percentage in the population, but rather about the relative power held by different groups in our society. Power struggles seeking representation through visibility themselves represent a shift in population composition. Internally contradictory impulses – such as a positive energy toward inclusion interpreted as utopic progress, in tension with negative energy resisting change in inclusive representations experienced as displacement instead of expansion and enrichment – coexist in uneven power formations. Representational struggles involve issues of production – who produces the media, and how – and audiences – who consumes the media, under what conditions, and with what expectations. When considered in concert with each other, if these three mediated elements were found to be moving in the direction of inclusion, transformation, and social justice, this would be a road to utopia.

Whereas some would argue that inclusion in existing media systems is not utopian and is more a desire to follow the path of previous groups, like Jews or the Irish,[2] its constantly deferred accomplishment marks inclusion, at the very least, as a major roadblock on the way to utopia. Other ethno-racial groups also pursue utopian goals without clear agreement among themselves (e.g. Lopez 2012). Yet, before transformation, we must have inclusion – so, if it is not the ultimate goal, inclusion is at least a step along the path.

Other than inclusion through presence, there are many other factors that pave the way to utopian goals. Recognition in the form of box-office returns, audiences, sponsorship, and awards builds on and contributes to inclusion, presence, and transformation. Sustained and sustainable activism also forms the backbone of utopic dreams and destinations.[3] Redistribution of resources (ranging from acquisition of broadcasting licenses to net neutrality), diversification of the professoriate through inclusive and transformative strategies, and transformation of meritocratic metrics into an alternative ladder generating greater parity at collective levels in grant and production budgets (Littler 2018) all form part of a utopian strategy, which, in turn, redounds to other strategies previously mentioned in this chapter. Even academic research, in the sense that utopian efforts become a topic that is carried out in intersectional transformativity, is an important element in utopian strategies (Ahmed 2012; Ferguson 2012; Melamed 2011). In all of these strategies, the mainstream media functions as a spoke node connecting utopian impulses, possibly including them, reinventing the wheel, and ideally getting us to a better place. All of these ongoing projects contain uneven recent gains and losses, and leave room for improvement.

Beyond presence and inclusion, a range of divergent goals and approaches potentially splinter activists, yet shared visions of improvement unite them in an ongoing internally contradictory project. Research and academic work in the overlapping interdisciplinary projects of Media Studies, Gender Studies, Ethnic Studies, and Area Studies – in sum, any intersectional study of difference – have a twofold goal. First, situated in the academy, these areas of study promise to fill in gaps in previous research, develop enhanced theoretical approaches, and authorize methodologies that enable the investigation of populations, histories, and cultures whose record, for reasons inevitably traced to power differentials, has either been ignored, subsumed, destroyed, or denigrated. As a useful example of the ease of studying people of record versus those whose history has not merited recording, let us consider the following. It is one thing to study the mythical Thomas Jefferson, a statesman who lived and recorded his life with the knowledge that his experience would educate for posterity. It is entirely another to study Sally Hemings (Gordon-Reed 1997, 2008), whose proximity to Jefferson – the fact that she, a slave, bore six children for him – went largely underrecorded and undercirculated. Furthermore, as we begin to learn about Hemings and her family, our knowledge of Jefferson shifts, changes, and muddles, transforming the myth from nature into the messy terrain of culture (Barthes 1957). Jefferson, a founding father, was also a slave owner who engaged in sexual relations with a young slave.[4] The purity of the founding father mythology no longer can be sustained. Issues of race, class, and gender de-purify the Jeffersonian myth. Pursuing the intersectional study of difference not only de-purifies mythological constructs but also contributes to academic knowledge of a heterogeneous population and culture that has always been present, if unacknowledged, in a way that nearly always add complexity to previously homogenizing narratives. A theoretical, and equally important aspect of the study of media and intersectional difference aims to use this embodied, de-purified, and complex knowledge of history to create a utopian future of increased social justice, a transformed practice. Theory and history inform practice and utopia. The latter guides the former. The former informs the latter.

Utopia

Utopia as a concept has more than one meaning. Its Greek roots reveal that it either means no place or a good place. Whereas Plato's *Republic* (380 BCE) remains the original utopian proposal, there are many contemporary formulations. The *Republic* is really the model of a certain kind of normative utopian thought, where an imaginary perfect world is used to derive principles for the real one; this came to serve as an end point for a progressive history in Christian versions (Augustine).[5] Scholars also identify St. Thomas More as an important theorist of utopia, tracing back the bimodal definition to 1516 and "a Greek pun in Latin between 'ou topos', or no place, and 'eutopos', or good place" (Milner 2009, p. 827). Analogously, in addition to taking place in the space of dialogic debate, some of today's utopias are circulated in the terrain of popular culture and mainstream media.

Slightly more contemporarily, in *Ideology and Utopia* (1936), Mannheim treated utopia in relation to ideology as an entire category of thought that contrasts with utopia defined as a challenge and revolutionary change to the social order *structured* by ideology: "The concept of utopian thinking reflects the opposite discovery of the political struggle, namely that certain oppressed groups are intellectually so strongly interested in the destruction and transformation of a given condition of society that they unwittingly see only those elements in the situation which tend to negate it" (Mannheim 1936, p. 40). Mannheim defined ideology and utopia in terms of the "collective unconscious," in that utopia obscures the real conditions from the group that holds ideological power *and* from the utopian group seeking transformation. Neither group can see beyond its immediate critique and efforts to either hold on to or challenge power. In concordance with previously bimodal definitions of utopia, Mannheim argued that even if humans can envision an ideal/utopia, they are likely to fail, as their present will be processed through ideology. Mannheim's work was highly influential. Linking his conception of ideology to Marx, many of the scholars who positively reviewed him, such as Herbert Marcuse and Max Horkheimer, would go on to form the backbone of what is now known as the Frankfurt School. Scholars of the Frankfurt School proposed to join the aesthetic notion of culture with the economic concept of industry. They criticized the cultural industries as repetitive and predictable, and indeed criticized ideology and argued for a utopian transformation. As such, Mannheim opposed utopia to ideology, which was influential to critics of mainstream capitalist popular culture – the terrain within which Latina/os must try to survive and thrive, if they are to transform it. Mannheim also provided the tools to distinguish between research/activism that is inspired by a utopian imaginary and the kind that imagines only a fairer version of the existing reality.

Dictionaries draw on this complex history of the term and simplify their definitions. The Merriam-Webster online dictionary provides three meanings: an imaginary and indefinitely remote place; a place of ideal perfection especially in laws, government, and social conditions; and an impractical scheme for social improvement (http://www.merriam-webster.com/dictionary/utopia, retrieved September 29, 2017). Both the first and the third definitions suggest that there is no such place – that the utopic future is always deferred or, worse yet, "impractical." Wikipedia informs us that a desired society or a perfect place is common usage, but that dating back to its Greek origin, utopia also means no place.

One might be tempted to equate utopia's double meaning with the social-scientific "null hypothesis," in that it can never be proved. Nonetheless, just as social scientists search for some connection of effect between two or more variables despite the presumption of a null hypothesis, so the utopian elements of media activism and representational politics aim for an effect that will transcend or replace contemporary exclusion of racialized groups despite repeated failures and setbacks. An inclusive media utopia, as a good or perfect place, perhaps can never be reached, and thus our task transforms from trying to reach an ideal place into constantly striving toward a better one. Yet, even if these efforts will never get us to a perfect place, this does not stop us from trying to reach it, even if this is an "impractical" task – though that label is related to challenging existing power relations, an impractical situation for those who have power. In sum, utopia can be operationalized as a temporary situation with dynamically relational elements rather than a specific location or temporality. As such, the target evolves, in predictable and unpredictable ways, as befits hybrid Latinidad as a shifting and unstable category. Utopian goals remain moving targets, as cultural and political shifts have greatly influenced what is possible, what is envisioned, what is practical, and what is to be gotten beyond – what is our fantasy?

In a recent lecture at the University of Illinois, Vijay Prashad[6] suggested that anyone working in the progressive movement needs to work on fantasy – another way of stating Mannheim's need to see beyond ideology. Similarly, Rajagopal and Rao (2016) note that much of the critique and rejection of modernist projects rests on the perceived failure of grand utopian narratives. Rajagopal, much like Prashad, traces the end of modernist utopias to the post-Cold War period, when neoliberalism assumed its post as the newest grand narrative:

> the moment marked an end to mass utopias, that is, to the widespread belief in collective emancipation fostered by technologies of the modern state ... When historical explanation itself doesn't have a narrative anymore – and this is arguably the case after the Cold War, when nation-building is out of fashion and some kind of empire seems to be back, but without its earlier claims about the rights of its subjects, utopia may be all we have for the moment.
>
> *(Rajagopal and Rao 2016, pp. 2–3)*

Milner (2009) examines this fantastic Marxian perspective on utopia: "Utopias, Marx and Engels had themselves warned, were merely 'fantastic pictures of future society, painted at a time when the proletariat is still in a very undeveloped state and has but a fantastic conception of its own position'" (Marx and Engels 1967, p. 116, quoted in Milner 2009, p. 831). As all theorists of utopia have noted, the present cannot be the measure for the future, and as Prashad adds, the future has to be seen through a fantasy – in other words, as a utopia. The concept of the proletariat can, for the purposes of this chapter, be replaced by the "minoritized population," of which hybrid Latina/os compose but one group. Much in the same vein, Bennett (2010) proposes: "As a mode of critique, however, utopian discourses hold the potential for generating frames that combat the depressing realities of everyday life" (p. 459). Perhaps Oscar Wilde put it best: "A map of the world that does not include Utopia is not worth even glancing at, for it leaves out the one country at which Humanity is always land-ing. And when Humanity lands there, it looks out, and seeing a better country, sets sail" (in Bennett 2010, p. 472). Wilde reiterated utopia's double meaning as a place to strive for that can never be reached and a constant journey for improvement – or colonization by the empire, as the case was then. Wilde's utopia resulted in the dispossession of the Global South.

As just illustrated, everyone operates with implicit and explicit utopian goals (Levitas 2010, 2013). Part of the process of aiming for utopia is the effort to distance oneself from contemporary dystopian, undesirable, and hopefully sur-mountable problems of the present. For instance, Prashad's and Rajagopal's utopias might strive toward the eventual victory of socialism or communism, and they are set against present neoliberal agendas that subsume the voices, rights, and populations from the Global South. For Media Studies scholars, inclusionary and transformative practices in production, representation, and audience participation fall within the realm of the possible future and are set against long histories of exclusion, avoidance, colonization, and outright discrimination. We have to envision a future, a fantastic future, especially given so many recent retrenchments and some unexpected recent hopeful signals such as the #MeToo movement.[7]

Media utopias have to be global and transnational in nature. Even Oscar Wilde, who may have been queer but nonetheless was a product of Eurocentric expansionism, understood in the late 19th century that this was a global pro-ject. When Marx exhorted the "workers of the world" to unite in the *Communist Manifesto*, global expansion had been present in Western utopic impulses since at least the Columbian period in the 15th century. The ascension of capi-talism as a powerful economic system depended on uneven relations of exchange across a global terrain. Marx's utopian fantasy may have targeted the workers of the world, but his historical markers, like Wilde's, were rooted in European ideals. Marx's utopia inspired Prashad, who turns it upside down, transferring agency to the Global South. Geographic location and projection are but two of the moving variables within global utopias.

Temporally, possible progressive outcomes take us into a utopian future, and setbacks return us to dystopian pasts or keep us in a dystopian present.[8] At the outset, one of the tensions within utopian discourses is that there is a wide range of utopias in people's minds. While social movements usually cohere around an agreed-upon dystopian set of issues and people to overcome (such as dicta-tors or exploitative relationships such as slavery), the future is seldom discussed ahead of time, other than in terms of getting beyond these most evident obsta-cles. Indeed, history is full of examples of revolutions and overthrows of power that either lasted a short time (in a historical sense) or solidified into iterations quite different from their original impulse, precisely because the aftermath involved a plurality of visions, which could not coexist long after the heady moments, days, years, or decades of the initial overthrow of power.[9] We have Mao in China, Fidel Castro in Cuba, the Sandinistas in Nicaragua, Allende in Chile, and so on. Not just media industries, then, but political systems too find it expedient to settle for syncretic, singular options rather than continuously harnessing a multiplicitous hybrid state. Indeed, the unitary concept of the nation exists in opposition to multiplicity.

Media Studies scholars reiterate this tension of exuberant overthrow and divergent institutionalization within the definition of utopia. The myth of the technological sublime is but another term for utopian desires accompanying the adoption of each new mass-media technology. Within the field of Media and Communication Studies, utopic discourses form part of our history – indeed, of our identity. Every new communications technology, most of which are eventually recruited and transformed to deliver commercial media, has been greeted by both utopian and dystopian discourses (Mosco 2004). Every new medium as a content delivery system – AM and FM radio, VHF and UHF television, cable, the internet – has been touted with the promise of solving our social problems and of getting us closer to that utopian future. Conversely, new technologies and the widely expanding availability of content have fueled dystopic fears of disintegration, lack of cohesion, and technological malaise. As scholars have documented, these hopes and fears have been remarkably consistent across time and technology (e.g. Marvin 1988; Mosco 2004). Contemporary discourses about the promises and challenges of digital culture, especially in regards to minoritized populations, provide yet another continuous moment in this long history of the technological sublime (Valdivia forthcoming).

Media Studies and Utopia

A smattering of Media Studies research focusing on utopia demonstrates that utopian elements are ever-present within our field, especially as media technologies promise to erase barriers of time and space. Dating back to radio, that still-important global medium, Ouzounian (2007) remarks: "Concepts of nonplace or *utopia* are not foreign to radio discourses" (p. 130). Radio promised the utopian transcendence of physical space into a nonplace – thus neatly encompassing both elements of the definition of the concept. However, radio's institutionalization turned its critical and democratic utopian promise "into a tool for maintaining, not disrupting borders" (Ouzounian 2007). Turnbull (2010) reminds us that Richard Dyer (1977) famously classified entertainment as utopia, "offering us the vision of a better world" (p. 819). Marshall McLuhan, a foundational scholar in the field now known as Media Studies, has been praised and criticized for his utopian analysis of media technologies (Chandler 2012). McLuhan asserted that his analysis was not utopian, and scholars

(Mander 1978) found his analysis of television ignored many of its potentially dystopian elements. Chandler (2012) concludes that though optimistic, McLuhan cannot be faulted for being utopian.

Other scholars explore implicit claims to utopia made by mainstream media. For example, Flanagan (2009) proposes that Mayberry, the location of the *Andy Griffith Show* (1960–68), offered a "central claim to utopia" in its "communal harmony and redemption of the Other." Mayberry accords to the definition of utopia as an "ideal place that does not exist in reality." Flanagan (2009) concludes that "it must be self-reflexive, irreverent, and courageous to become and remain utopic in 1960s television land without succumbing to the perverse idea of a segregated utopia" (p. 309). Indeed, and harking back to Dyer, much of what is now known as "classic tv" provides a utopic universe according to Flanagan's analysis. Also true, "classic tv" was incredibly segregated, often representing a lily-white universe.

Inevitably, cyber-utopianism is but the most recent version of the reiteration of the myth of the technological sublime (e.g. Pace 2017). Just as radio promised transcendence over space, so digital communications technologies' promises of transcendence have to be weighed against the sheer volume of traffic and the hypercommercialization of the internet, which works against the realization of its democratic promise (Dean 2005; Everitt and Mills 2009). Moreover, traffic assumes access – something that virtually disenfranchises a segment of the population without resources or beyond the reach of digital signals from this latest utopian dream, by virtue of geographical location or income. Public libraries, one of the last remaining bastions of free and democratic access to information, continue to serve their purpose by providing free internet access. Traffic becomes a barrier issue, since great demand for internet generates processes limiting access. Libraries are forced to set time limits on internet use, in order to provide democratic access to large numbers of otherwise disenfranchised users (Becker et al. 2010).

Finally, more recent developments such as the dark web in general and the Silk Road in particular reveal unexpected contours of utopian impulses as they apply to the internet. Created as a utopian space, "contrary to its founder's vision of a libertarian utopia, the digital free market in contraband was plagued with fraudulent economic practices, underwritten by a market logic that exploited the site's unique infrastructure" (Pace 2017, p. 2), and was "subject to the most aggressive elements of capitalist exchange: blackmail, scam, coercion, and monopoly" (p. 6). Indeed, one of the extreme "aggressive elements" was murder, for which the Silk Road's founder, Ross William Ulbricht, was sentenced to jail. Its utopian promise, as envisioned by Ulbricht, quickly turned into a highly dystopic virtual location with life-and-death consequences.

Beyond particular genres and technologies of media offering utopian dreams, groups within the population cohere around utopian goals. Writing broadly about activism across a range of media, Lopez (2012) questions Asian American "strategies of activism [that] have implicitly aimed for assimilation into the mainstream – not to be othered – but maybe another tactic is necessary" (p. 37). Assimilation, as a syncretic practice, brings presence without cultural baggage/culture of origin but does not transform systems and thus is not the goal of most utopian strategies, though it may be a way station. Similarly, Bennett (2010) examines anxieties and possibilities generated by queer teens and the symbol of the rainbow flag, widely employed in discourses of social movements, as a utopian expression: "In its most basic form, utopian discourse seeks to transcend present political conditions and foretells a future free from social ills and cultural constraint. Like the rainbow flag, utopian visions yearn for a polis that celebrates harmony, equity, and thoughtful deliberation" (p. 456). Bennett adds: "Utopias, for example, create aspirations of purity impossible to fulfill, but the implementation of that desired perfection obliges a reiteration of group practices that renews identification for those seeking change" (p. 457). Assimilation, harmony, and equity are but three different strategies on the way to utopia used by activists working within and through the media. Aspirations for purity muddle these efforts, as, in a hybrid world, purity is impossible to fulfill.

Indeed, there are plenty of mediated utopias and dystopias for us to choose from. Scholars of the zombie genre and other contemporary monstrosities locate their popularity as an effort to represent contemporary dystopias in an audiovisual language that speaks to large audiences (Calafell 2015; Levina and Bui 2013; Fojas 2017). Even, or perhaps especially, documentarists with social justice goals seek to represent contemporary dystopias in the audiovisual language of realism as a way to nudge us to utopian activism. One such feature-length documentary is *Detropia* (2012), produced by Heidi Ewing, Rachel Grady, and Craig Atkinson. Aired on the film festival circuit, this documentary sought to give voice to some of the people who have stayed in Detroit – a city that, as the film attests, has lost 50% of its jobs and 25% of its population in the past decade. Fojas (2017) claims that in *Detropia*, "they imagine the city through different ideas about progress, futurity, and creative habitation to preserve the past and refuse the deleterious course of capitalist obsolescence and supercession" (p. 139). The play on words in the title takes Detroit and combines it ambiguously with either utopia or dystopia. The celebrated mobility of the US upper middle class, who can, for example, engage in global real-estate shopping such as that represented in *House Hunters International* (Celeste 2016), is available neither to the natives of those places where they buy, and who are displaced by them, nor to those at home who must remain in cities like Detroit because they do not have the resources to go elsewhere. Those left behind – quite literally by the productive industries, as well as by the welfare state as it morphs into a neoliberal one – have no capital to search for a second home in a Caribbean paradise, nor even the possibility of moving to a nearby location in the United States. Detroiters must fashion ways to survive in the new reality of their city. *Detropia* follows "several citizens trying to survive the D and make sense of what is happening" (http://detropiathefilm.com/synopsis). Fojas (2017) asserts that *Detropia* provides an "alternative imagery of the city beyond the regenerative tropes of capitalism" (p. 139). It represents those left behind as they assume agency over their future and the future of Detroit. *Detropia*'s utopia envisions a post-capitalist world. It is not a happy film – it provides a cautionary tale – but it is also set against the implicit utopia of what could once again be, albeit this time for a broader and more diverse group of people than those benefitting from Detroit's motor-vehicle heyday. In the difficult circumstances that many Detroit residents endure, the fantasy of the future remains a survival tactic.

Disney, Utopia, and the American Dream

The "American Dream" has remained one of the utopic concepts guiding the US popular imaginary and exported globally through mainstream media productions. As the most prolific producer of mainstream media, nearly all of it anchored within the Walt Disney sensibility of the marketing of utopia, it should not come as a surprise that Disney has also contributed to contemporary and explicit representations of utopia. Beyond constructing Celebration, an entire community on the implicit utopic model of Disneyland, Disney continuously rehashes its utopic dreams through its movies. In 2016, the company produced *Zootopia*, an Oscar-winning representation and reformulation of utopia that was much more widely circulated than *Detropia*. *Zootopia*, Disney's version of Plato's *Republic* by way of *Animal Farm* (Persall 2016), is set in a futuristic land populated by anthropomorphic animals. It invokes utopian ideals of a good place, a better place, and a just place. The unambiguous combination of the word "zoo" and the concept of "utopia" bring us the fictional location of Zootopia, where animals live in perfect harmony.[10] *Zootopia* introduces us to a world where urban and rural differences still exist, but where "anything is possible" within its major city. Judy Hopps, *Zootopia*'s protagonist, is a small bunny who dreams of moving to the big city and becoming a police officer. Though her parents, hundreds of siblings, and farm community do not quite believe this is possible, Hopps enters the police academy and, upon graduation, is assigned to work in Zootopia. She leaves Bunnyburrow and heads to the big city on a utopian rail ride that introduces us to the geographic and seasonal diversities in Zootopia, all of them environmentally clean and sustainable. The movie's animators and producers drew inspiration from the urban design of major global cities like New York City, San Francisco, Las Vegas, Paris, Shanghai, Hong Kong, and Brasília (Wikipedia), supposedly taking the best elements of each as they composed their fictional utopia.

The utopian premise of *Zootopia* is that in a city built by and for mammals, all animals live in harmony, despite their previous binary history as predators and prey, a radical anti-essentialist premise. Nonetheless, once Hopps arrives in Zootopia, she realizes positions of power are occupied by predators while prey fulfill secondary roles within an urban hierarchy populated by easily identifiable gendered, racialized, and classed animal characters. As a coherent thread throughout the movie, Shakira voices a Thomson gazelle pop star, singing "Try Everything," which functions as Hopps' motto and the ethos for the city of Zootopia. The refrain serves as both inspiration and cohesion, or, as Flanagan (2009) remarked of Mayberry, communal harmony and redemption of the Other, both narratively and in terms of many of the characters demonstrating fandom for the pop star and positive affect for the song:

> I won't give up, no I won't give in
> Till I reach the end
> And then I'll start again
> Though I'm on the lead
> I wanna try everything
> I wanna try even though I could fail

The lyrics contain the utopian elements of ongoing search for a better place, an endless process. *Zootopia* follows its spunky can-do heroine (Harris 2004) through her coming-of-age process, much like modern Disney princess movies. However, Hopps, neither a princess nor in the market for a prince, aims for professional goals, believes in justice and fair play, behaves ethically, and takes responsibility for her mistakes. For instance, when she hastily attributes a biologically essentialist reason to predators going savage, she recoils from the consequences of her mistake and leaves the police force. Hopps' dedication to truth and justice exposes a prey-supremacy scheme. Her belief in the goodness of others leads to her recruiting sly fox Nick Wilde to the police force and restoring Chief Bogo to power. Shakira's performance of "Try Everything" closes out the movie as all animals rejoice and dance together during a concert.

The movie, which as of June 2018 has generated more than a billion dollars in box-office receipts, won the 2016 Academy Award for Best Animated Feature as well as other awards including the Golden Globe and the Critics' Choice. Reviewed as a parable where trust and tolerance win out over distrust and prejudice, its implicit inclusionary politics at the levels of gender, race, and size were widely touted. Indeed, some reviews directly asked if *Zootopia* was a utopia. Furthermore, the utopian impulse was sometimes seen as a commentary (Hoffman 2016) on contemporary politics in the Trump era. To the question, "Is *Zootopia* a metaphor of utopia?", Nina Schreiber answered: "In some ways yes, but it is more contradictory to that since the movie tries to say how Zootopia isn't perfect" (http://www.quora.com/Is-Zootopia-a-metaphor-of-Utopia, retrieved

September 29, 2017, now removed). This answer locates the movie within both definitions of the word utopia. Jing Zhao concludes that Judy turns Zootopia, which despite its name runs according to stereotypes, into a utopia through her actions and belief in justice (https://thecadreupei.com/2016/03/18/zootopia-is-it-an-utopia, retrieved September 29, 2017).

It is fitting that Disney delivers an explicit reference to utopia, as Disney theme parks and its entire animated universe always allude to a place of perfection, which can only exist in the realm of the imaginary or in the fantastic spaces maintained through its hyperreal illusions. The utopian plot, location, and resolution of *Zootopia* squarely fit within the impulse to treat popular media as a representational site of activism to get us to a better place. The movie tackles gender and race stereotypes, glass ceilings, symbolic annihilation, pay disparities, workplace discrimination, and bullying in the wide swath of issues to be resolved on the way to utopia. Some reviewers argued that despite the disneyfication of utopian discourses, *Zootopia* represents a "subversive" effort (*Rolling Stone*) toward inclusivity and circulation of utopian representations. Nonetheless, Disney's fantasy of utopia, in which millions indulge repeatedly, does not apply at the level of production, where the major players – those authoring, producing, directing, and animating the movie – remain absolutely normative, nearly all of them white males. Little bunnies might be breaking through the glass ceiling in Zootopia, but not at Disney Studios. The utopian narrative was created by a workforce that remains resolutely lacking in diversity.

Even dystopian *Detropia* has an implicit utopian future beyond neoliberal capitalist ideologies. Representing a wide range of Detroit residents of color carving out a multiplicity of activities and professions, the documentary reminds viewers that Detroit, though in crisis, still survives and might even thrive again – perhaps in a future version of the success that Pittsburgh now represents. The documentary is a utopian intervention toward not just better media, but also a better future and more critical assessment of global restructuring and its effects on some cities. Production wise, *Detropia* represents a broader range of diversity than *Zootopia*, as we might expect from an alternative media production in relation to the most mainstream of mainstream, Disney. However, in both *Detropia* and *Zootopia*, Latina/os appear minimally. Shakira's vocal presence introduces Latin Americanness into a movie that strives to present a wide range of US ethnicities, reiterating the US Latina/o paradox.

Latina/o Media Utopias

Into the gap that exists within the black–white binary, and asserting presence and belonging in the United States, Latina/os seek to participate in an inclusive utopia. The late-1990s coming-of-age discourse implied that mainstream crossover, shedding specificity to enter into Anglo mainstream, was our utopian goal (Cepeda 2000). Counterintuitively, Ceisel (2011) illustrates the counter-crossover agency exercised by an artist like Juanes, who refused to sing in English precisely because he did not want to abide by the US-centric terms of crossover success.

Shakira (Cepeda 2010) and Selena (Parédez 2009) crossed over, the latter posthumously, into US mainstream popularity. In both cases, the utopian dream of crossover generated untold riches for the Latin American and Latina artists and their heirs, yet was greeted by a variety of responses from the Latina/o community, ranging from celebration to charges of selling out and cooptation. Shakira still basks in the global success partly facilitated by her US crossover, and Selena has become an important historical marker of the late-20th-century Latina/o boom, when the US mainstream once more rediscovered Latinidad, thus repeating the myth of discovery that it is the privilege of mainstream culture to perform, over and over. One might argue that Shakira has reached her utopia. She has firmly crossed over into global modernity as a floating signifier across a range of geographical terrains, and "Try Everything" anchors the utopian impulse of the previously discussed *Zootopia* just as "Waka Waka" in 2010 attempted to capture the utopian impulse of including Africa in the global imaginary as it hosted the World Cup. It is a bit less clear whether Shakira's global success is considered a utopian achievement by the Latina/o community. Crossover stardom represents a utopian instance of inclusion and assimilation, or of inclusion and transformation. Crossover, as Cepeda and Ceisel remind us, is premised on privileging the mainstream as the utopic destination. Though less frequent and lucrative, crossing over into subaltern media spheres deserves more study as it represents an utopic impulse to engage with the Global South.

These examples illustrate the ruptures and continuities that turn up in exploring the limits and possibilities of the inclusion of Latinas in contemporary mainstream popular culture. Latina/os have transitioned from absence into rhetorical inclusion, as well as into a set of groups organized to make inclusionary and transformative demands. Minimal visibility regardless of presence and contribution, the Latina/o paradox, continues despite growing spending power (Negrón-Muntaner et al. 2014; Negrón-Muntaner and Abbas 2016). The difficult question we need to ask ourselves as scholars of Latina/o Media Studies is, what form of representation and cultural inclusion would satisfy our utopian vision for inclusivity? Moreover, how do we balance, or rather combine, these demands with an acknowledgement of hybrid population flows, media forms, genres, and interpretive strategies? Stereotypes anger us, but subtle inclusion – potentially imperceptible – cannot be the answer. With the former, we argue that they fall within racist narratives or symbolically annihilate us. With the latter, we fear cooptation into white normativity or domestication into symbolic colonization. Is there an acceptable utopic location beyond this spectrum of outright stereotype and assimilationist incorporation into a transformative media system with accompanying representations? As an example, take the case of Sofía Vergara's Gloria Delgado-Pritchett in *Modern Family*. Her easily recognizable Latinidad, and the resulting success she has experienced as an actress in the contemporary terrain of popular culture, are highly criticized because of her reiteration of the trope of the spitfire and all that it implies (see Chapter 3). Selena Gomez, on the other hand, represented a barely Latina Alex in *Wizards of Waverly Place*, as did Vanessa Hudgens in *High School Musical* and Lalaine in *Lizzie McGuire*. These characters generated no negative outcry from Latina/o audiences, but this may partly be because they are barely perceptible as Latinas and therefore do not even register to audiences as such. We do not know if lack of recognition or preference for their light approach to blending in/assimilating accounts for the lack of controversy. The appearance of barely perceptible Latinas in children's/tween programs cannot be the only reason for a lack of backlash, as there has been a loud ongoing debate about *Dora the Explorer* and her Latinidad (Harewood and Valdivia 2005). Nonetheless, public children's television seems to be a safe space for racial inclusivity, as demonstrated by the many actors and celebrities of color that have appeared in *Sesame Street* and *The Electric Company*. Rita Moreno, one of the spitfires from Chapter 2, retreated to public children's television after being hopelessly typecast following her *West Side Story* Oscar. Indeed, even if contemporary barely-Latinas are recognized as such, the lack of antipathy or affect toward their performance and inclusion may well be the syncretic outcome desired by mainstream media industries – inclusivity without recognition, or at least without outcry. Such uncontested light-brown presence is a middle ground, for now, between absence or stereotyping and imperceptibility, but it is certainly not the utopian dream. Rejection of inclusion through whitening or middle-classing, as outlined by Dávila (2001), joins the battleground of Latina/o mainstream representation and arguably becomes one of the way stations on the route to utopia. One of the resulting questions about utopia is, "For whom?" One could argue that Shakira has reached her utopia, but Latina/os and Latinidad have certainly not equally reached their ideal place. If one of the elements of utopia is a collective transition, then Shakira's individual transit remains just that – an instance of individual success.

There are three main ways for US Latina/os to appear in Hollywood film and US mainstream television. They can be a minor side character, who is additionally highly stereotyped. This was the predominant way to appear until recently. With the advent of multicultural casts, they can be part of an ensemble cast that includes a predominance of whites and a sprinkling of ethnics. Such a cast might include just one Latina/o, as in *Desperate Housewives*, or a Latina/o and another ethnic, as in *Saved by the Bell*. Finally, and less commonly, they can be part of a mostly Latina/o cast, such as in PBS's *¿Que Pasa USA?* (1977–80), which remains a fond memory for Latina/os in Miami, as it was located in and based on the local Cuban-American community, which deemed the show respectful and accurate. Rojas (2013) asserts that "years after it ended, an entire generation of Cuban-Americans still remembers the series as the first one to accurately and humorously depict their lives." The show remains in syndication.

Shortly after *¿Que Pasa USA?*, perhaps based on its positive reception, ABC rolled out *Condo* (1983), a sitcom about two families: a downwardly mobile WASP family[11] and an upwardly mobile "Hispanic" one. Much of the humor derived from ethnic and religious jokes. It was the first time that mainstream US television had produced a show about a middle-class upwardly mobile Latina/o family, but decreasing ratings resulted in the show's cancelation after less than a full season. ABC responded the following year with *a.k.a. Pablo* (1984), produced by Norman Lear. Returning to a more familiar narrative of a struggling Mexican family, the show faced audience protests over its offensive stereotypes (for example, one of the six episodes that aired was titled "The Whole Enchilada"; April 3, 1984). Coupled with its low ratings, this contributed to its cancelation after little more than a month (Shamma 2001). ABC did not try to do another Latina/o ensemble show for nearly two decades, until 2002's *George Lopez*. It finally found its long-term Latina/o global hit with *Ugly Betty* (2006–10). This very brief overview of Latina/o-focused shows on ABC demonstrates the tricky road to Latina/o inclusion, which nevertheless includes a range of different approaches, from the hyperstereotypical through the revolutionary.

Constance Marie/Angie Lopez and Belita Moreno/Bennie represent two female roles in *George Lopez* (2002–07), providing two different types of Latinas in familiar gendered tropes: the abnegated wife and the aging and wonky mom.[12] Angie's domesticity exists in stark contradistinction to Bennie's rejection of the housewife role, her lack of parenting skills, and her labor in the public sphere. The Angie and Bennie characters reiterate gender tropes that represent women as either competent in the domestic sphere and absent from the public or as disruptive in the public sphere and incompetent in the domestic, a Latina/o version of Dow (1996). The Latina/o element in *George Lopez* is that Angie, Bennie, and most of the characters are solidly working class – in distinction to, for instance, those in *Murphy Brown* (1988–98), who were upper-middle class.[13] This is part of the pattern of Latina/o representation in US mainstream media: Latina/os have traditionally been represented as working-class characters. While *George Lopez* was utopic in that it contained a universe largely populated by Latina/os, with a Latino in a managerial position, a happy nuclear family at home, and the avoidance of most of the most noxious Latina/o stereotypes, it also drew on broader cultural gender tropes and kept Latinidad in the working class.

Netflix's *One Day at a Time* (2017–19), produced by Norman Lear, rebooted a 1970s liberal feminist show. Firmly situated within contemporary Latinidad, this second version of the show focuses on a single-parent Latina/o family, whose mother is a nurse and a Vet, whose daughter comes out, and whose grandmother, played by Rita Moreno, serves as historical memory and borders on comic relief.[14] Highly touted by Latina/o communities, it took massive social media campaigns to renew it to the third season. As of this writing, the show has not been renewed for a fourth, though rumors abound that it will be picked up by another distributor. Regardless of its ability to endure, the characters, as well as the writers, embodied a mature Latinidad, in that at the levels of production and representation, inclusivity prevailed. In turn, Latina/o audiences responded positively. Given Netflix's refusal to share ratings data even with its own show producers, it is impossible to tell the composition of the show's audience.

A more usual form of mainstream Latina/o appearance is through symbolic annihilation or by representing the Latina/o in an ensemble cast. Given that these characters function as representatives of their entire ethnicity, they more often than not flatten the diversity within Latinidad. For instance, Mario Lopez played the character A.C. Slater in NBC's *Saved by the Bell* (1989–93), which also included an African American female character. Slater's ethnicity was visibly clear yet not narratively explored in the series, until when in the spin-off *College Years* (1993–94), Mario's father revealed that he had changed his name from Sanchez to be able to get into a military academy (Rojas 2013). There are many instances of a sole Latina/o in an ensemble cast. For example, in *Desperate Housewives* (2004–12), Eva Longoria's sexpot/spitfire Gabrielle Solis appears as the token Latina/o in a larger cast. Longoria's starring role was simultaneously a huge coup in terms of inclusivity in primetime drama and a reiteration of the spitfire trope, a classic form of inclusion bordering on symbolic annihilation. As one of the protagonists, Longoria was not marginalized. Yet, she was the only person of color among the five main characters. Longoria remains one of the most branded Latinas in contemporary mainstream popular culture, and went on to produce the *Desperate Housewives* spin-off *Devious Maids*, which incorporated the domestic Latina trope and extended it through a complex diversity of characters (Báez 2015). *Saved by the Bell* and *Desperate Housewives* contributed to Latina/o presence in the mainstream, a core component of steps toward a utopian goal.

Dynamically hybrid narratives, characters, settings, and contributions seldom appear in mainstream entertainment because of a preference for more syncretic cultural constructions that are stable, domesticated, easily duplicated, and therefore recognizable to white mainstream audiences (Levine 2001). Much of the occasional presence of Latina/os evolves into syncretism, yet even these instances contain elements of the utopic. Desi Arnaz's Ricky Ricardo in CBS's *I Love Lucy* (1951–57) drew on many of the classic Latina/o tropes, including musical performance and accent and language malapropisms, to drive the laugh track of the hit comedy show (Pérez-Firmat 1994). To be fair, Lucy's hysterical housewife character represented a classic gendered role as well. Nonetheless, the show was groundbreaking in terms of its huge popularity despite the bi-ethnic protagonist couple being composed of a Latino and a white woman. Elements of Latinidad included music and other cultural aspects. Lucille Ball was a major productive force in a business that to this day is largely controlled by men, remaining a historical exception. Lucy and Desi owned the production company that produced the show, something that remains a fantasy for most Latina/os in mainstream television. One could argue that the show was quite hybrid, only eventually settling into domesticated syncretism in its spin-offs. Its presence in eternal syndication continues to function as a disruptive element, something that could be classified as a time-traveling mini-utopia. Ball and Arnaz were visionary in the production of this sitcom, which allows us to transition to that element of utopia.

Utopia and Production

Another component of a Latina/o media utopia has to be production and labor. Some Latina/os are involved in the production of mainstream cultural forms, but in very small percentages, as production of mainstream popular culture remains stubbornly entrenched within white male hands.[15] Implicitly – and this is not quite borne out by empirical evidence – many believe that if we increase representation at the production level then the resulting images, narratives, tropes, and so on will represent a wider and more ventilated Latinidad. However, an increase in, for instance, women in the profession of advertising has not necessarily resulted in less gendered ads or in a reduction of sexualization of women in advertising. Similarly, an increase of women in entry-level journalism positions has not changed highly gendered mainstream news coverage. What has changed are the prestige and real salaries of these professions, both of which have decreased as women have increased their presence within them – what is known as *pink collarization.*

Research on ethnicity in the media workforce yields similar findings. Drawing on Rodriguez (1999), we see similar outcomes for the inclusion of Latino journalists. Either they are segregated to ethnic news outlets or they are mistrusted as producers within mainstream (white) news. Nonetheless, at the very least, an increase of Latina/os in the production of media would mean an additional opportunity to labor in an area of the economy that has heretofore been largely inaccessible to them and to other marginalized groups. Granted, this increase would come precisely at the moment when highly paid positions in unionized contracts are shifting into the precarious "flexible" economy of piecemeal self-employment. Nonetheless, there is perhaps a critical-mass point, a tipping point, at which Latinos will be able to influence representation. While this is certainly a utopic goal, we are nowhere near it. We do not know even roughly what the percentage would have to be. At this point, increased employment either in these highly coveted jobs or within the flexible workforce, by itself, would be a great advance in terms of employment, role models, and, hopefully, changing narratives and representations. Given that media is part of a broader cultural milieu, utopic changes in production and representation would have to go hand in hand, would have to move past a critical point where the presence could go from tokenism and barely held positions to a level of power and stability that would allow for the changing of narratives, genres, and discriminatory production practices[16] – a transformative effect.

However, it is also the case that, dating back to the 1970s, all-Latina/o casts have appeared on US television, and movies about Latinidad have reached high levels of popularity (e.g. *West Side Story*, 1961). From *I Love Lucy* through *George Lopez*, *Ugly Betty*, *Devious Maids*, and *One Day at a Time* on television, and with *Frida*, *Spy Kids*, *Stand Up and Deliver*, and so on in film, the production of mainstream Latinidad includes Latina/os. *George Lopez* was co-created and co-produced by George Lopez based on his stand-up comedy act. Desi Arnaz and Lucille Ball created Desilu Productions to produce *I Love Lucy* within the union rules of television production at the time. Salma Hayek largely shifted her energies toward production through her Ventanarosa company to increase the presence and variety of Latin Americanness and Latinidad in mainstream popular culture, including and especially her own. Director and writer Robert Rodriguez produced a number of films wherein Latina/o actors, characters, and themes range from the subtle to the prominent, including *El Mariachi* (1992), *Desperado* (1995), *Spy Kids 1*, *2*, *3*, and *4* (2001, 2002, 2003, 2011), and *Curandero* (2005). Presence in production is part of the road toward utopia. Mainstream narratives and production practices foreground the stability of the system. Transformative impulses face resistance at the institutional, organizational, and individual levels of analysis. Nonetheless, incremental gains, which are never fully secured, have to be recorded, celebrated, and protected on the way to that fantastical place that is the utopia.

Award Shows as Embodiment of Utopia

In presence and erasure, Latina/os stand in for the imagined nation. They track the interstices and struggles of the contemporary identity crisis that faces the United States, which formerly thought of itself as homogenous or binary (i.e. black and white) in composition. One indicator of valued presence is the annual television and film award season, whose celebrations are broadcast through award ceremonies. This section begins with an overview of award ceremonies, then explores the value of ethnic ceremonies in relation to mainstream "generic" ones, and ends by looking at the subsumed presence of Latinidad within mainstream ceremonies.

Award ceremony research ranges from generic events to ethnic ceremonies. Watson and Anand (2006) assert that award ceremonies serve as arbiters of commerce and canon. González and Heuman (2003) explain that the Latino Grammys and the American Latino Media Arts (ALMA) Awards have been able to achieve three important rhetorical goals: to participate in or perform Latino identity in order to preserve it; to mediate Latino identities to the non-Latino audience; and to call into question mainstream practices that exclude Latinos and perpetuate negative stereotypes about Latinos (p. 49). Ethnic award ceremonies, created as a response to exclusion within mainstream award ceremonies, represent an insertion of minority culture into the mainstream, especially where they are broadcast at prime time on major networks following heavy advertising. However, praise for these award shows can also be accompanied by fears of segregation. If there were inclusion at the Oscars and the Grammys then Latina/os would not need the ALMA Awards or the Latin Grammys. Yet, as we saw in 2015, mainstream academies and their award ceremonies seldom nominate or award people of color and narratives about race.

The discourse of unity and difference within ethnic award shows embodies intrinsically contradictory push-and-pull tendencies. Though these shows celebrate culture, they inevitably involve political issues, due to the diversity and hybridity within ethnic categories in general and Latinidad in particular. Popular culture is a terrain of struggle. Thus, the utopic space of transformative inclusion can easily become a dystopic space of exclusion, controversy, and in-group fighting. The ALMA Awards and Latin Grammys represent two similar efforts to create an alternative utopian space. The ALMA Awards, sponsored by the National Council of La Raza (NCLR), recognize actors and media underrepresented in mainstream media and awards shows. ALMA is an acronym, but "alma" also means soul in Spanish. Since 1987, when they were called the Bravo Awards, the ALMA Awards have strived to create a utopic space, a place where Latina/o media producers and artists are recognized. With a few interruptions, and some network changes (from Univision, to ABC, to NBC), until 2015 the ALMA Awards constituted an event for Latina/o artists and producers, despite the somewhat meager audiences and grosses of some of the awarded films. On October 2015, ALMA announced it would "reassess" its future, and went on a 3-year hiatus. In 2018, Fuse, a satellite music channel, in concert with UnidosUS, the revised name for the NCLR, bought the rights to the show (Pedersen 2018), broadcasting the ALMAs on Fuse telecast and music cast in November 2018. Thus, economic issues also affect the regularity and location of award shows.

The Latin Grammys (hosted by The Latin Academy of Recording Arts and Sciences, LARAS) have carved out a space to highlight "Latin" music, since generic Grammy Awards given to English-language music artists ignore "Latin" talent, in any language. While both the ALMA and the Latin Grammy awards sought to include and foreground Latinidad, the former represented English-language Latina/o media productions and artists while the latter represents Spanish music within a bilingual prime-time televised show. Both foreground mainstream artists in order to hook and appeal to the mainstream audience – not just Latina/os – just as the advertisers who sponsor these shows run the gamut of products, from "ethnic" to mainstream.

Latina/o award ceremonies showcase as hosts such stars as Eugenio Derbez, a Mexican actor with numerous roles on Mexican television, occasional roles in US films, and a couple of crossover attempts. In addition to *Instructions Not Included* (2013) and *How to be a Latin Lover* (2017), Derbez's movie credits in the United States include *Girl in Progress* (2012) – distributed by Lionsgate – wherein he plays the character of Mission Impossible, and Adam Sandler's *Jack and Jill* (2011), wherein he plays both Felipe and Felipe's Grandmother, two highly stereotypical (as most are in Sandler movies) Mexican roles. *Girl in Progress*, despite a dismal showing at the box office – it grossed less than half its $5 million production budget – won the Favorite Movie Award at the 2012 ALMA Awards. Derbez also directed and hosted the ALMA Awards in 2010, and participated in this show until its last iteration. His presence in motion picture and recorded music US Latina/o award ceremonies underscores the flattening of difference between US Latina/o and Latin American media and artists enacted by such shows, which supposedly seek to create a utopian space for US Latina/os. Does Derbez appeal to the Mexican and Mexican American part of the audience that might recognize him? Are there no US Latina/o actors who could also be foregrounded in these shows?

Unsurprisingly, the inherent tensions in these award ceremonies have bubbled over several times. Martínez (2006), for example, explored tensions generated by the Latin Grammys being designed as market-friendly, pan-ethnic, and depoliticized, hailing artists and audiences through their country of origin. The 2000 broadcast was revolutionary in that it was the first time a bilingual Spanish-English show was broadcast on prime-time network television, showcasing popular music in Spanish. Martínez (2006) details the tensions with Cuban music, which could not be named as such, given that the producers of the show included the anti-Castro Emilio Estefan, who was also honored as "Person of the Year," and the show was filmed in Miami, where anti-Castro forces hold a considerable amount of political and cultural power. Casillas (2014) further explores the controversy over what constitutes "Latin music" and the reliance on recent crossover artists of the "Latin boom," which excluded Mexican and Mexican American music and artists despite the sales of Mexican genres greatly overshadowing those of tropical Latin ones. Foregrounded tropical music at the Latin Grammys was more palatable to mainstream non-Latina/o audiences. The Mexican musicians' boycott of the 2000 ceremonies was reversed in the 2002 ceremony, when an award was given to ranchera star Vincente Fernandez. The Latin Grammys continue to be plagued by controversy in terms of the diversity of Latin music, the political debates about Cuban music, the participation of Cuban artists, and the reception of such artists by the Cuban American music industry. All of this caused the venue to be changed from Miami to Los Angeles. Despite the desire to create a utopic space of celebration and inclusion, diversity in genres, national origins, and politics generates controversy and conflict within Latinidad in "Latin" award ceremonies. Nonetheless, these award shows do provide a space for "Latin" music celebration. A case in point is the 2017 Song of the Year award at the (mainstream) Grammys, which went to Bruno Mars for "That's What I Like" even though Luis Fonsi and Daddy Yankee's "Despacito" was a far greater hit nationally and globally. As a utopian intervention, "Despacito" won best song at the Latin Grammys, thereby underscoring the inherent tension in ethnic award shows: as a crossover, "Despacito"'s award was relegated to the ethnic award show despite its undeniable and quantifiable mainstream success.

Two other components of the awards system deserve mention: sponsors and the method of selection. Both give us an insight into the operationalization of the utopic ethnic award space.[17] The latest Latin Grammys were sponsored by Buchanan (liquors), Bulova (watches), L'Oréal, McDonald's, Nissan, Walmart, and Colgate. Mastercard is singled out as a "Latin American: sponsor." The 2015 ALMA Awards were sponsored – in different capacities – by MSNBC, mun2, Telemundo, NBC/Comcast, Target, Chevrolet, Child Hunger Ends Here, McDonald's (whose slogan for the Spanish-speaking population is "Me Encanta"), Prudential, State Farm, Wells Fargo, Anheuser Busch, Southwest Airlines, Bank of America, El Rey Network, FedEx, Google, and Northern Trust. In addition, the ALMAs were sponsored by the NCLR, and further supported by the National Association of Latino Independent Producers (NALIP) and the Hispanic Heritage Foundation. The sponsorship map is broad and includes major corporations and media industries in large sectors of the national and transnational economy. The utopic space carved out to recognize Latina/o talent and productions could not exist outside of the mainstream economy comprising global conglomerates. Beer, fast food, soft drinks, mega cheap stores, make-up, and cut-rate airlines predictably appear. Minoritized populations, including Latina/os, are often the targets of inferior goods.[18] As a sign of economic ascendance, the list also includes telecommunications, transportation services, banking, insurance, and investment firms – all outside of the universe of minoritized advertising until quite recently. More expectedly, the presence of broadcasting networks that either target the Latina/o population or host the awards ceremony serves as cross-promotion. Largely missing from the list are Latina/o-owned businesses and moguls – other than El Rey Network, reiterating something many Latina/o scholars, including Dávila (2008), have been saying for years: that it really behooves companies that market primarily to Latina/os such as Goya, Old El Paso, and so on to contribute to Latina/o cultural production and diversity. The sponsorship pattern shows that mainstream economic interests find that it is worth investing in Latina/o awards shows – a gain toward utopia. Yet, as the history of media suggests, sponsors have a bit to say about the content that they support, and this partly explains the fact that both shows skew to the center in terms of politics, class, and culture. This tendency in return seeks to tame hybrid cultural output to make it palatable to the mainstream, the syncretic. Pride has to be broadcast in a subtle and self-conscious way so as to not alienate the mainstream audience and sponsors.

Finally, in terms of the production of these events, the process whereby an artist or media product is included in the shows is also indicative of the nature and character of the utopian space of award ceremonies. The Latin Grammys post their process in Spanish, which I will quote in full in both Spanish and English:[19]

El Proceso de Votación Para Los Latin Grammy

Este proceso comienza con miembros de La Academia Latina y compañías disqueras inscribiendo productos, los cuales son luego revisados para confirmar su elegibilidad y ubicados en las categorías apropiadas. Los miembros votantes de La Academia Latina, todos los cuales trabajan en alguno de los diferentes aspectos creativos y técnicos de una grabación, participan entonces en (1) el proceso de nominación que determina los cinco finalistas (10 finalistas en el caso de las Categorías Generales) y (2) en el voto final que determina los ganadores del Latin GRAMMY

(https://www.latingrammy.com/es/proceso-del-latin-grammy,
retrieved November 29, 2014)

The Voting Process for the Latin Grammys

This process begins with members of La Academia Latina and record companies registering products, which are then reviewed to confirm eligibility and placed in the appropriate categories. The voting members of the Academia Latina, all of whom work in one of the different creative and technical aspects of musical recording, then participate in (i) the nomination process that determines the five finalists (10 finalists in the case of General Categories) and (ii) in the final vote that determines the winners of the Latin Grammys.

This process foregrounds the decisions made by the Academia Latina, headquartered in Miami and composed of music professionals from the United States and 30 other countries with Spanish- and Portuguese-speaking communities. The Academia Latina members select the nominations on the basis of artistic achievement rather than sales. It is important to note that this academy is transnational and likely to have more non-US members than US ones, thus reiterating another element notable in the findings of Latina/o Media

Studies scholars: the US Latina/o is a marginalized minority in the production and assessment of US Latina/o media – not a utopic situation.

Shortly before its cancelation, the ALMA Awards changed its submission and selection process:

> This year, the NCLR ALMA Awards production will not have an external submission process due to a short planning window. Individuals and English-language programs and projects included in video packages and music performances and acts will be determined by the producers of the show. Special award recipients and tributes will be selected by the NCLR ALMA Awards staff in consultation with the network and show producers. Recipients will be considered for outstanding achievements in the entertainment industry and sports; commercial US box office ranking, English-language Nielsen ratings and Billboard chart accomplishments, media/social media prominence and/or the impact of the program, project, role, or performance; and, service and commitment to national and international social causes and philanthropy between July 7, 2013 to September 15, 2014
>
> *(http://www.almaawards.com/rules-eligibility, retrieved November 29, 2014)*

In other words, the selection process went totally in-house, as part of the production of the ceremony rather than a measure of popularity or quality. The equivalent for the Oscars would be the production team deciding who was nominated and selected in consultation with ABC, the network broadcasting the ceremony, and the staff of the Academy Awards – rather than artists, members of the Academy, and so on. This process was far less representative and democratic than even the Grammys process, which likely overrepresents Latin Americans in relation to US Latina/os. In hindsight, this was a last-gasp effort to craft a show that could draw both audiences and sponsors. It may have been the final nail in the coffin of a utopic effort whose future remains uncertain.

One utopic reason for the end of ethnic award shows would be that the mainstream has been so transformed that these ameliorative spaces are no longer necessary. That clearly remains the future. At the level of nominations and acknowledged representation, mainstream award shows remain noninclusive of difference, nearly erasing US Latina/os. In the 2015 generic[20] award season, Gina Rodriguez won the Golden Globe Award for Best Actress in a Television Comedy for her work on the CW's *Jane the Virgin*. Yet, mainstream award seasons continue to be marred by controversy about ethnic exclusion. Rodriguez was the only Latina so honored in the 2015 Golden Globes. In a tearful but brief acceptance speech, she accepted the award for "represent[ing] a culture that wants to see themselves as heroes." This sentence bore the full weight of the burden of underrepresentation and minimal inclusion in a 2015 mainstream that appeared to snap back to normative whiteness with a vengeance. The 2015 Oscars nominations were also widely criticized for the exclusion of nominations of themes and people of color. The only major winner of diverse background was Alejandro González Iñárritu, of Mexican citizenship, who won Best Picture and Best Original Screenplay for the movie *Birdman*. Touted as a Latino winner, he is Mexican, and thus Latin American. *Selma*, a movie foregrounding African American agency, was one of eight films nominated for best picture, but lost to *Birdman*. So, at the level of nominations, racial inclusivity loses out to whiteness in the final decision. Nominations and awardees largely remained within the realms of whiteness and masculinity, and Iñárritu's inclusion follows the pattern of including international players rather than internal minorities, echoing indigenous Latina/os' eternal foreigner status. In addition to being highly gender-segregated – nearly no women join the ranks of Best Director and other major award categories – the US media industry continues to prefer Latin American talent, both acting and producing, to US Latinos (Dávila 2001). Iñárritu set a recent version of this pattern and preference at the Oscars, winning two years in a row, followed by Guillermo del Toro and Alfonso Cuarón.

The 2016 Oscars not only did not reverse the exclusionary pattern foregrounded the previous year, but reiterated and exacerbated it. As a result, activist April Reign created the hashtag #OscarsSoWhite, which became a rallying cry for those addressing Hollywood resistance to inclusivity. In 2016, Iñárritu won yet another Oscar as Best Director for *The Revenant*, but other than him, the awards and most of the nominees were not inclusive of a diversity of producers, themes, or actors.

By the 2017 Oscars, public outcry resulted in a slightly changed membership, partly spurred by Cheryl Boone Isaacs, the Academy's first African American female president and the only person of color on the 51-member board of governors. All of the major acting categories contained at least one actor of color, and all but one of the main categories included at least one diverse entry. Among the many diverse winners were *Moonlight*[21] for Best Picture (the first film with an all-black cast to win this award), Mahershala Ali for Best Supporting Actor (the first Muslim actor to win an Oscar), Viola Davis for Best Supporting Actress, *Moonlight* for Best Adapted Screenplay, *Zootopia* for Best Animated Feature, and *O.J.: Made in America*, about O.J. Simpson, for Best Documentary Feature. That last documentary category included the James Baldwin biopic, *I am Not Your Negro*, an unapologetic indictment of racial politics in the United States with epistolary focus on Malcom X, Martin Luther King Jr., and Medgar Evens. After this notable burst of mostly African American inclusivity and diversity, observers wondered if the 2017 Oscars were an anomaly or a step toward a utopic future. It did not bode well that the incoming president of the Academy of Motion Picture Arts and Sciences as of August 3017, John Bailey, was a white normative male. In the wake of his election, questions about the implications of replacing an African American woman with a white male were brushed aside with comments such as:

> But the board may feel it has nothing to prove. A black woman has served as Academy president for four years, Barry Jenkins' "Moonlight" was this year's best-picture Oscar winner (three years after Steve McQueen's "12 Years a Slave"), and the Academy has received a lot of attention for its moves to increase diversity throughout the membership and on the board
>
> *(Tapley 2017)*

It might be entirely too soon to feel like there is "nothing to prove," but the 2017 awards show felt utopic to many who had lived through the previous two years' drought of inclusion and, frankly, a history of exclusionary policies in Hollywood in general and within and through the Academy in particular.

For the 2018 Oscars, of nine movies nominated for Best Picture, one, *Get Out*, explored racial themes and one, *Call Me By Your Name*, explored sexuality. *The Shape of Water*, directed by Guillermo del Toro, was the latest in what is now an established pattern of Mexican directors being included in and winning the important award category of Best Director in addition to Best Picture. *The Shape of Water* and *Coco*, which won Best Animated Feature, included Latin American themes and a focus on the Mexican holiday/religious celebration Día de los Muertos. In addition, the Chilean film *Una Mujer Fantástica*, about a trans main character, won Best Foreign Film; this led to the first time in the history of the Oscars that a trans person accepted an award.

The 2019 Oscars ceremony literally located African Americans as supporting actors, with Regina King winning Best Supporting Actress for *If Beale Street Could Talk* (2018) and Mahershala Ali winning Best Supporting Actor, a second time, for *Green Book* (2018). Latina/os were conspicuously absent in this event. *Roma* (2018), which won both Best Director and Best Foreign Film, failed to win Best Film; that award went to white-savior narrative *Green Book* (2018), which beat out racially, sexually, and gender-inclusive movies.

From a utopian media perspective, steps taken toward inclusivity and a transformed pool of nominees included expansion of the voting members of the Academy and an inclusion of people and themes of color in the nominees. The former influenced the latter. Part of the criticism of the nominating process had been focused on the advanced age of many of the voting members. Supposedly, lowering the average age of members, in addition to expanding their number – by a record 693 in 2016, 46% of whom were women and 41% people of color – yielded a wider field of nominations. Membership of the Academy is a closely guarded secret, though a 2012 *Los Angeles Times* study suggested it is 94% white and 77% male. From a Latina/o Media Studies perspective, there is no way of knowing whether the increase in membership included any Latina/os. One imagines a minimal presence in the Academy, given that winners and nominees for Oscars are automatically invited to membership. In terms of Oscars won, there really has been no increase in the presence of US producer Latinidad, unless one considers Mexicans Iñárritu, del Toro, and Cuarón as representative. As previously mentioned, within US Latina/o Studies, scholars find that mainstream media is much more likely to foreground Latin American talent and include Latin American media producers than US Latina/os. Within Media Studies, we know that in Hollywood film, historical exclusion of women as producers remains an issue, with numbers barely budging across the past several decades. As such, Iñárritu, del Toro, and Cuarón represent the latest example of this pattern – dominant-culture Mexican men producing successful crossover films.

Before declaring recent Oscar seasons indicative of erasure, symbolic annihilation, or colonization of Latinidad, we might want to consider the implicit or unrecognized Latinidad within Oscar-winning films. *Moonlight* illustrates the inescapably mixed race within African Americans and Latina/os. Latinidad in *The Shape of Water* and the highly stereotypical Mexicanidad of *Coco* round out Latina/o Oscar narrative presence. Written and directed by Barry Jenkins, *Moonlight* is a coming-of-age film set in Miami, Florida. While not much has been made of this location in reviews, the fact is that Miami is a city inescapably traversed by Latin American, Caribbean, and, therefore, Latina/o population flows. In fact, 67.4% of the population of Miami is "Hispanic," 19.8% black, and 11.3% white. The specific location of the movie is Liberty Square within the Liberty City neighborhood. Serving as a community for African Americans in the era of segregation, Liberty City and Liberty Square remain working class and mostly African American, but also Latina/o. Recent efforts to redevelop this area have yet to bear fruit. In sum, Miami is inescapably Latina/o and Liberty City/Square has Latina/o populations. Notice that we have to go into an implicit subtext to find Latinidad in this film.

Foregrounding themes of black masculinity and sexual identity, the movie begins with Juan, a Cuban American drug dealer, helping Chiron, who is being bullied by a gang of boys. Juan's girlfriend, Teresa, takes Chiron in for the night. Teresa and Juan are English-dominant Afro-Latina/os, representing a middle class whose income derives from drug dealing as members of the racialized underclass. Juan reminisces about his youth with his grandmother, in Cuba. The movie ends with Kevin serving Chiron rice and black beans – a classic Cuban dish. The camera zooms in on Kevin slicing the lime, molding the rice, and chopping the cilantro – all ingredients and preparation anchoring the authenticity of the iconic dish. Some of the characters' Spanish names – Juan and Teresa, without an h – combined with their Cuban roots and ending with the classic Cuban food subsume a Latinidad inevitably present in Miami, a location without ethnic purity that nonetheless is discussed in binary black and white terms in most reviews of this film. The implicit presence of Latinidad subsumes actual Latina/os and historical traces, and erases the ongoing coexistence of Latina/os and African Americans, as well as the existence of Afro-Latina/os.

Black Panther (2018), whose massively popular release in February 2018 rippled through the Oscars ceremony with the presence of its mostly African American and African cast in attendance, similarly manages to represent Oakland, California as a space of working-class black purity. The hybridity present on the ground of major cities, most evidently through their mixed-race populations, seems to be too much for Hollywood to try to represent. A settled and familiar white and black binary is favored.

In *The Shape of Water* (2017), the presence of Latin American-ness includes shades of magical realism, a feminized genre attributed to Latin America. The water creature, whose capture, torture, and deliverance form the basis for the movie, and around which normative masculinity literally rots, hails from the Amazon and some premodern tribe whose existence locates the Latin American region firmly within tradition. As a background to some of the action, the film includes an occasional clip of Desi Arnaz in *I Love Lucy* or of Carmen Miranda singing a song. The protagonist Elisa Esposito/Sally Hawkins plays a mute orphan whose last name, Esposito, used to be assigned to Latina/o orphans abandoned by their parents. Of ambiguous dark hair and brown eyes, Elisa cannot speak, so her presence and provenance remain a mystery despite minor details given by her workmate. The movie's resolution, in which Elisa joins the creature in amphibian rapture, suggests that the hybrid couple will somehow escape and swim their way back to the Amazon, beyond the Cold War politics in which they have inadvertently found themselves. Whereas the film depicts highly stereotypical African American working-class and white middle-class characters, as with *Moonlight*, we are left to surmise and read the presence of Latinidad between the lines.

Coco received massive amounts of prerelease publicity as an authentic representation of Latinidad. Located in Mexico, the narrative takes place on Día de los Muertos, in a mythical premodern Mexican village. Magic and high tech coexist in this hybrid tale. Miguel, the protagonist, accidentally crosses over into the Land of the Dead and needs his great-grandfather to return to the Land of the Living. Surveillance computer technology regulates traffic on the night of the Day of the Dead in coexistence with Miguel's family living in a premodern Mexican town. The movie debuted in Mexico the weekend before the Day of the Dead holiday and was a big hit both there and in the United States. Despite assertions as to its authenticity, the representation of Mexico was very traditional in terms of location, family structure, and gender roles. Disney's nod to Latinidad included a mariachi band playing the opening music and consultation with "Latin" experts. The movie is set in Mexico, so it is not a representation of US Latinidad, but rather of Latin America/Mexico. *Coco's* success is more an indication of the amazing ability that the Walt Disney Company has to market a syncretic, luminous, and domesticated difference than a utopic moment of authenticity and transformative inclusivity.

In all of these instances of presence in recent Oscar awards and seasons, Latinidad appears through absence or through displacement, and that seems to be the place of Latina/os in contemporary academy awards. One can look between the lines for Latina/os. Or, one has to accept Mexicanidad: at the level of production, as in the case of the all-male Director Awards; at the level of content, as in *Coco*; or at the level of audiences, as in the Mexican segment of US Latina/os, who make up a disproportionate share of the US movie audience. If the Oscars represent one aspect of utopian media aspirations, there is a long road to travel to reach that utopic space for Latina/os in the media.

Plus ça change…

Part of the problem with utopian media hopes is the loss of memory and myth of discovery that ahistoricize contemporary productions, as if some new achievement were happening. To be sure, commercial media relies on recycling for programming: "a new show like no other" usually refers to yet another form of a popular genre, sometimes even a copy of a recently successful show. Similarly, advertising practically relies on presenting products as if they were new. As well, mainstream media presents stars as "discovered," taken out of their ordinary lives and promoted to the national and global stage by virtue of their "it" talent, as if they hadn't been groomed and constructed according to industrial imperatives (Blue 2017, p. 25). And, as previously mentioned, new media technologies step right into the myth of the technologically sublime, each new medium being represented as the savior and solver of all social ills; each introduced as if the previous medium did not present the same promise and bear out a similar deviation from utopian possibilities. So, it is not surprising that we encounter Latina/o booms every few years – the discovery of the hotness of Latinidad being something that hopefully generates more profits every time our culture is rediscovered and marketed as the new "it" thing. Desi Arnaz, Rita Romero, Charo, Ricky Martin, Jennifer Lopez, Sofía Vergara – each ushered in a realization of the hotness of Latinidad and generated profits for mainstream media industries. Utopian dreams strive for presence, visibility, stardom, influence, and transformation against a backdrop of mainstream media history that abounds with occasional discoveries of Latina/o hotness. What does not change is that Latina/o culture is hot and, as a result, racialized and othered in relation to the white coolness of mainstream culture. What also does not change is that Latina/os are part of the US population and have been since the creation of the republic, yet we continue to be ignored, subsumed, or displaced. As well, it is undeniable that Latina/o absolute and proportional numbers are growing. The growing numbers in the population are not pure but represent a mixed race, mixed country of origin, and complicated hybridity that mainstream popular culture is either unable or unwilling to consider.

Much of the "new" talent, as well as foregrounded narratives – Día de los Muertos and magical realism – buttressing the latest wave of the myth of discovery continues to be Latin American, not US Latina/o. Granted, there is a great deal of overlap between the two groups, but they are not synonymous with each other.

Beyond award shows, we can examine how the myth of discovery routinely plays out through the more or less recent example of the release of *Instructions Not Included/No se aceptan devoluciones* (2013), starring the previously mentioned Mexican actor and personality frequent foregrounded in the ALMA Awards, Eugenio Derbez, whom *Variety* identified in 2014 as the most influential Hispanic male in the entertainment industry (Wikipedia). On September 24, 2013, *Variety* delivered a classic "myth of discovery" story:

> It seems Lionsgate and Pantelion have finally found the instructions for how to target widespread Hispanic audiences. The movie transitions from Acapulco, Mexico to Los Angeles in a tale of a US mom dropping off a baby with its unsuspecting Mexican daddy. The narrative was not creative, a mash up of *Kramer vs. Kramer* (1979) with *Chasing Papi* (2003), nor were the performances outstanding. But what stood out was the stale assertion that Pantelion, which calls itself "the first major Latino Hollywood studio" (Bilge 2013) had figured out that targeting Hispanics through family friendly fare was a successful strategy given Latina/os' tendency to attend films as a family rather than individually or in couples. This old tale has been rehashed in relation to ethnic audiences for decades.
>
> *(Dávila 2001)*

Variety points out the verifiable statistic (Negrón-Muntaner et al. 2014; Negrón-Muntaner and Abbas 2016) that "Latino audiences – the most enthusiastic movie going demo in the country, representing **22% of frequent moviegoers with only 16%** of the US population – turn out in outsized proportions for animated films and studio pics … But many previous attempts to directly target the massive audience with Spanish-language films or using Latino talent have stumbled, perhaps because the modestly-budgeted efforts looked too much like art films and lacked family appeal" (Dávila 2001). It is unclear which "art films" the article refers to, as there have been very few movies targeting US Latina/os, and the relative scarcity of art films in the United States makes it quite unlikely that one of these was actually produced to target Latina/os. The article adds that in terms of marketing, Pantelion "didn't rely just on Univision" but "also bought outdoor media and radio that would hit family and women demographics" Dávila (2001). *Instructions* grossed $99 million worldwide and was only recently replaced by *Coco* as the highest-grossing film in Mexico. Hoping to repeat the feat, Pantelion released *How to be a Latin*

Lover in 2017, also starring Eugenio Derbez, as well as Salma Hayek, Kristen Bell, Rob Lowe, and Raquel Welch. While not as profitable as *Instructions, Latin Lover* did deliver a $61 million box office, against a $10 production budget.

One might be tempted to file these two Derbez films in the temporary utopia category. The company line is they targeted Latina/o audiences through culturally sensitive marketing, in the process cementing Derbez's standing as a bankable Latino actor. Yet, the *Variety* coverage and the process whereby Pantelion recruited Latina/o audiences reiterate most of the elements of the myth of discovery and flattening of difference that Latina/o communities and Latina/o Studies scholars have been documenting for decades. First, the tired narrative of "Latina/os will go to 'family' and animated films" repeats stereotypical assumptions about Latina/os that do not appear to be borne out by research, taking us right back to early pages of *Latinos Inc.* (Dávila 2001), wherein advertising executives assign the onus of "family-centrism" to all communities of color – flattening any difference within and between ethnicities through this othering move. In sum, all Latina/os and ethnics are alike. Second, the claim to "outsized proportions" of family and animated film viewership infantilizes the Latina/o community and needs to be critically examined. For example, Negrón-Muntaner and Abbas (2016) find that Latina/o audiences are eager fans of action-adventure, and that ignoring this demographic can derail the success of a profitable franchise such as *The Fast and the Furious.* Third, the article conflates Latina/os with Spanish speakers, when data suggests that nearly 80% of Latina/o households are majority English-speaking (Pew Foundation 2014). How can the audience and therefore profit be maximized if companies are only appealing to 21% of the demographic? Fourth, singling out Univision as the locus of Latina/o audiences reiterates the misguided notion that Latina/os are Spanish-dominant, as Univision broadcasts primarily in Spanish and the non-Spanish speaking Latina/o audience is not likely to be watching it regularly.[22] Fifth, the article performs the traditional versus modern move (Lerner 1958) that has been so prevalent in the history of modern communications. Latina/os are stuck in tradition and in Mexico, unable to make the move into modernity and cross over into the US mainstream. *Coco* (2017) echoes this move as it situates the narrative in a Mexican village barely touched by modernity, even as digital identification is required to cross back and forth from the Land of the Dead. US modernity is where the mainstream resides; tradition is what happens in Mexico. The crossover has to be regulated upon entrance to the bridge, a metaphor for the Mexican–US border, whose increasing biometrization requires everyone to be registered and to submit to surveillance. Traditional narratives are laid at the feet of the implicitly traditional Mexican American audience. Crossover into the mainstream/modernity is part of the road to the implicit dream, the utopian move. The narrative is a crossover success, yet the Mexican tropes within it remain stuck in premodernity. The demographic target audience of "family" is code for women and children, who, in addition, are reached through billboards and radio – old-school media that implies a traditional, working-class, and static lifestyle instead of a modern and mobile digital existence for a feminized US Latina/o population, preventing its inclusion into the mainstream audience. Sixth, missing from this entire discussion and from demographic-based targeting of the Latina/o audience are Latino men as a component of the US population and as part of the audience. What do Latino men watch? Why are they discounted or ignored? Seventh, and finally, US Latina/o actors and audiences are conflated with Latin American and Mexican actors and audiences. *Instructions* was produced in Mexico with a Mexican cast. Eugenio Derbez, the lead actor, is a Mexican actor touted on IMDb as "unquestionably one of Mexico's best-known stars, the most recognized actor among the Spanish-speaking population in the United States" (http://www.imdb.com/name/nm0220240/?ref_=tt_cl_t3). *Instruction* and *Latin Lover* were far more successful in Mexico than in the United States: Derbez is a household name in Mexico, but in the United States, both movies had to compete against bigger budgets, stars, and marketing, and thus were not as successful. Within the United States, singling out this actor and these movies serves to extend language issues in stereotypes of US Latina/os – namely, the assignment of Spanish-only language skills to the US Latina/o population; a move that, among other things, contributes to US Latina/os' eternal-foreigner status, as their supposed adherence to Spanish makes them unassimilable. After all of these caveats, *Instructions* does not bear out the utopian sheen attributed to it by its own marketing machine.

After *Instructions*, *Latin Lover* included a group of well-known US actors, as well as, arguably, one of the foremost contemporary crossover Latina stars, Salma Hayek. The crossover energy generated by *Instructions* was used to rehash the Latin lover stereotype, quite likely the most enduring trope about Latin American, Latino, and garden-variety Mediterranean men in US popular culture. While generating box-office returns exceeding its productions costs, *Latin Lover* was widely panned. The celebrated production, marketing, and audience of *Instructions Not Included*, while touted as a utopian outcome of Hollywood savvy in collusion with "Latin" talent, bringing together Lionsgate and Univision to form Pantelion Films, turned out to reiterate minoritizing tropes and not be very utopian after all. Despite centuries of Latina/o presence in the United States and decades of activism about Hollywood film and visibility in the film industry, the mainstream does not appear to heed any instructions that might help it make and market a film about, by, and for Latina/os, and remains resolutely resistant to any transformative utopian changes. The result of this much-touted yet entirely stereotypical effort – which did not aim to reach the mainstream but self-consciously stayed within marginalized spaces for a marginalized audience – was a profitable $ 44.5 million US intake and nearly $100 million global intake for a film that cost $5 million to produce. The self-congratulatory industry press – employing an us-versus-them language – celebrated Hollywood mainstream savvy in reaching the Latina/o other. US Latina/o communities didn't praise the films, though revenue per screens targeting US Hispanic moviegoers was way above average. One can only wonder at the economic and audience potential of a film that took into consideration some of our seven caveats for its marketing and reception in the United States. If they were to be included in the utopian representational, production, and audience terrains, the results would surely yield better profits for the US film industry. Despite the capitalist drive to maximize profit, racialized narratives and representations work against the profit motive and contribute to ongoing marginalization. Ideological blinders are costly for all involved. The playbook for targeting films to Latina/os is not inscrutable, unless tired stereotypes continue to guide production and marketing. As small a step as this is, it largely remains to be taken. Being able to see past ideology – as Mannheim warned – so as to envision an ideal – which would also generate more profits – is indeed a utopian desire. Here's hoping for this highly realistic utopian move.

Where To?

> Celebration is the latest version of the American Dream, a town built in 1996 in the swamp of central Florida by the master of make believe The Disney Company. Once again Disney had its thumb on the pulse of the American public: to return to community, to a neighborhood. Celebration is a beautiful, pristine and crisp town with pre-1940s architecture that takes you back to a safer, more comforting place where neighbors greeted neighbors. Almost ten years later it is the home of 8000 residents. The film shows six couples in search of utopia. It was Disney that attracted them to Celebration. They all remember their first time to Disney World, a magical and care-free place. When they heard that Disney was building a town which went back to the past instead of the future they packed their belongings and felt like modern day pioneers. "Celebration" is a documentary about people in search of a better life and a better place to live. Yet behind the beautiful facades and white picket fences is a real place with real people and real problems. When press got bad and Disney realized it couldn't control a town like a theme park they sold the town to Lexin Capital, an investment company from New York. Some people leave Celebration, disillusioned, but still in search for something new, somewhere different, a new promise. **After all, the search for utopia, is a great American tradition**.
>
> *(https://www.imdb.com/title/tt1282028/*
> *plotsummary?ref_=tt_ov_pl, emphasis mine)*

After reformist and implicit utopias, we need to ask ourselves if there is such a thing as a Latina/o utopia? In *Modernidad, Identidad, y Utopia en America*

Latina (*Modernity, Identity, and Utopia in Latin America*), Quijano (1990) built on the genealogy of Mannheim and Horkheimer to consider the utopian promise of modernity rather than its ideological deployment as control and dispossession in the name of progress. Modernity as an ideal, a utopia, could be applied to the utopian possibility of a better future for Peru, at a difficult time in that nation's history. Quijano (1990) identifies communitarianism and solidarity as forces that sustain the marginalized populations in Latin America. "All utopia is, after all, a project of reconstruction of the historical sense of a society" (p. 65, quoted in Martí 1993, p. 234). Externally produced utopic versions of history, such as the juxtaposition of tradition and the utopia of modernity, or the assignment of tradition to Latin America in relation to the modernity of the United States, with all the attendant baggage of colonialism and imperialism, do not arrive as deliverable utopias but rather as outright discriminatory and oppressive regimes. The fantastical imagination of utopia, as both Prashad and Rajagopal indicated earlier, has to reach beyond the current conditions, has to turn previous utopias upside down (as in the case where Prashad imagined the revolution from the Global South instead of from the belly of the Global North), and has to slough through what is on the way to what could be.

Celebration, originally a Disney town, sought to provide a radical utopia, where people could live a 24/7 Disney life. Alas, everyday matters could not be fully controlled, and therefore the town had to be sold. Ironically, as Disney is in the business of selling utopias, it sold off its utopic town at the moment that its utopic elements could not be guaranteed. One of the many reasons that the radical utopia that Celebration was supposed to be fell short of the ideal was that this utopia was eerily lacking in racial diversity. Very few African Americans bought or rented the original properties, and most who did left within a short time (Ross 1999). Utopia, "the great American tradition," retains huge tinges of racial exclusivity. One nearly articulated reason why some of the residents bought into the community was its racial homogeneity, buttressed by its economic wealth. Utopian Disney towns can only exist in the magical world of Disney representation and in its highly controlled theme parks, leased islands, cruises, and so on. These temporary experiences provide temporary utopian flights. Racial homogeneity excludes many, including Latina/os, and Celebration was not created to increase diversity. A constructed and planned utopia, Celebration could deliver on its promise only to those included in its vision. Research on the ethnic, racial, and class make-up of the workers in relation to the owners might yield more of a diverse presence.

Academia

As a field or specialization develops a history, tendencies, controversies, and subspecializations, scholars begin to write on the accumulated scholarship and its vision – or, from the perspective of this chapter, the implicit utopia. They take the efforts of minoritized scholars to be included in theory and practice as a site of analysis (Ahmed 2012). Aptly named *Represent and Destroy* (2011), Melamed's magisterial research explores the neoliberal cooptation of difference through the deployment of multiculturalism and depoliticization of demands for material and structural transformation. Similarly, in *The Reorder of Things* (2012), Ferguson examines the incorporation of minoritized subjects in the academy (pp. 189 and 191), partly as a process of management of race professionals. Latina/o media scholars are newcomers to the politics of redistribution in the US academy. Often, we are institutionally pitted against previous minoritized subjects for a share of the same shrinking piece of the funding pie. Utopic moves are tricky in the academic terrain, as gains for one ethnic group can generate a process of resistance by other groups. Given the utter hybridity of Latinidad, it has been difficult to preserve multiplicity while growing resources in a period of retreat from public education funding. Nonetheless – and the fact that this area of studies is growing and thriving is itself a bit of a utopic slice – there are a growing number of scholars whose productive endeavors contribute to field-wide assessments.

Latina/o media scholars critically examine cultural politics up to the contemporary moment – the decade after the 2000 Census announcement of Latina/o majority minority and the Latina/o boom resulting from Selena's crossover (Parédez 2009). Today, Latina/o communication and media studies have been anthologized in at least three books (Cepeda and Casillas 2017; Valdivia 2008, 2010), and Cepeda (2015) has published an entire article in *Feminist Media Studies* on the lessons and promises of Latina Feminist Media Studies. Dovetailing previous discussions in this chapter, two books have been written against the backdrop of an implicit yet unreached utopia: Amaya (2013) and Molina-Guzmán (2010). Highly dystopian presents yield conceptual frameworks toward a better future within Latina/o Media Studies. Hector Amaya and Isabel Molina-Guzmán take book-length, sweeping assessments of the state of the art of Latina/os and media scholarship. As with previous sites of intervention, their scholarship reveals the tensions inherent in proposing perspectives on a nascent and growing field, which, in turn, represents the recently acknowledged presence of US Latina/os. Both authors provide rigorous, sometimes heart-wrenching analyses, yet both strive to end on an upbeat note.

For instance, Amaya (2013), drawing heavily on Foucault, proposes the concept of citizenship excess, which he defines as "citizenship is inherently a process of uneven political capital accumulation and that the unevenness follows ethno-racial line" (p. 2). Furthermore, it "is also a media theory that explains how media structures participate in the pushing down and pushing away of Latina/os" (p. 3). Chapters include analyses of the Hutto Residential Center in Texas, especially its practice of detaining and jailing children, and coverage of soldiers killed in action in Iraq. This is not a book about upbeat topics. Yet, Amaya concludes his rather bleak collection of case studies by noting that

"These are the birthing pains of a new United States transformed by the Latino trans-nation" (p. 230). Birthing pains are no joke, yet somehow this ending speaks to a desire for a utopia that is still very far in the future.

Molina-Guzmán (2010) proposes the concepts of symbolic colonization and symbolic rupture, which function as push-and-pull forces of homogenization and disruption, respectively. Similar to Amaya, she includes an obligatory chapter on *Ugly Betty* ("'Ugly' America Dreams the American Dream").[23] She balances a tension throughout the book, wherein she considers the lived experience of Latina/os against mainstream representation of spectacular Latinas. Each case study, on Elián, J.Lo, Frida, *Ugly Betty*, and Latina domestic labor, treats issues such as immigration and the production of authenticity in relation to mainstream media visibility. Yet, as with Amaya, Molina-Guzmán concludes "on a less skeptical note" (p. 180). Her utopian possibility comes through the possibilities afforded by ethnic ambiguity, multiple audience readings, and the appreciation of "hundreds of students" (p. 181) for the small disruptive moments of Latinidad in the mainstream.

Beyond the trenchant analyses and hopeful endings provided by these scholars, their book covers represent another window into a vision of contemporary Latinidad. As Hegde (2011) reminds us, Foucault admonishes that visibility captures and circulates. The covers reveal part of the terrain of struggle. Amaya's is a photograph of a cell in the Hutto Residential Center. The empty narrow cell, painted in residential shades of green and gray, with a cement floor, contains a sink, a toilet, a crib, and a bare-bones metal bunk bed with stuffed animals on the bottom bunk and what seems like some small toys on the top. A jacket hung on the wall signals to the presence of an adult. It appears there is a narrow sunny window on the other side of the bed. This is a photograph of desolation, framed by black edges. Molina-Guzmán's cover is slightly more colorful and includes a human being, though the bulk of the iage is occupied by a blue-into-purple background. On the back, we are told this is a photograph of Jennifer Lopez performing at the American Music Awards in 2001. This in itself is a disruptive moment, as most Latina/o music performers seldom get access to the non-ethnic music awards. Lopez, in classic Latina big gold hoops, appears to be wearing a sailor-themed outfit: low-cut sailor button pants ad a cropped red-and-white top that leaves her toned midriff bare. She is not centered, but rather appears to the left of the image, lapping on to the back of the book. She literally slides out of the left side of the cover. As these images imply, the books are highly critical of the commodified Latinidad foregrounded in mainstream popular culture. Indeed, the covers provide stark and sobering reminders that there is so much more to be done; that even Jennifer Lopez's success is dangerous (as is the overdrawn signification of her body); and that inclusion in the "American Dream" should not be our goal, as the dream itself is racialized and inclusion comes at the cost of loss of heritage and the bodies of the majority of Latina/os who continue to be excluded.

The empty cell on Amaya's cover is a disturbing and implicit representation of exclusion even in one of the locations where Latina/os, including children, are overrepresented: in jails and detention centers.[24] The fact is that both covers represent a lonely and homogenized presence for Latinidad. They suggest that the utopian drive is far from accomplished, that presence for a few comes at the expense of the majority, and that even those who achieve presence do so under marginalized terms.

Where does the Latina/o media utopia lie? Certainly in the future! Where does it belong? Partly in the mainstream! But then, this futurism is part of the definition of utopia – an ideal place always deferred, never reached: no place. This is not to say that gains have not been made, but that these are part of the implicit utopian road. Symbolic colonization and symbolic rupture of Latina/o ethnicized and racialized bodies (Molina-Guzmán 2010; Chenyek 2018) are ongoing processes, whose achievements inevitably fall behind the newly formulated ideal goals. Presence, even if minimal, becomes a goal in the face of absence and a way-stop on the path to transformative inclusion. The many types of representational inclusion, from minimal presence through symbolic annihilation, and from colonization through multiculturalism and parity, turn into ameliorative strategies once we reach them and can see past our ideological fixation with the present to the ideal of what can be: that place that Wilde identified as the better country for which humanity is always setting sail.

Implicit utopian strategies, such as the attempt for inclusion in mainstream award shows or the creation of alternative spaces in ethnic award organizations or an ethnic offshoot of a mainstream award show, yield at least temporary increased visibility. It is unclear, however, whether this move transforms the mainstream media or absolves it from radical inclusivity at its core. Representations anchored to academic explorations of Latina/os and the media reveal the fissures in the utopian dreams within the scholarly community. Criticisms of Latina/os as middle class, suggesting gentrification, coexist with criticisms locating Latina/os as working class, always locating this group as socioeconomically marginal. Simultaneously, recent attempts to represent racially inclusive utopias, such as *Black Panther*, and the utopic Oscar win of *Moonlight* are accomplished through the twin process of foregrounding blackness and erasing Latina/o presence, or at the very best subsuming it. Industry claims of production, representation, and audience inclusivity largely depend on the reiteration of the myth of discovery, the flattening of difference between all Latina/os and between US Latina/os and Latin Americans, and the erasure of the US Latina/o in deference to the production and representation of Latin Americans. In search for increased US Latina/o audiences, the labor and bodies of US Latina/os are backgrounded in relation to Latin American talent. The promises of utopia from industry demonstrate the pitfalls of relying on top-down transformation.

As with residual culture, it is difficult to categorize the difference between transformative utopian measures and assimilationist ones without hindsight. And maybe this is part of the search for utopia. What now seems a utopian goal, once reached, turns out to be but an assimilationist step on the way to an eventual utopia. In the conclusion to their classic *Memory and Modernity*, Rowe and Schelling (1991) note that "Gratuitous, wasteful destruction should be distinguished from the other destruction which permits transformation" (p. 233). Yet, the transformation has to be guided with goals, not chosen at random. In Media Studies, we are understandably focused on how media is produced, for whom, and by whom. Part of our utopic path has aimed for inclusion of identity and recognition, often achieved through visibility. We have learned that visibility – a goal that should not be abandoned and which has not nearly been reached – is not enough. It is just another step on the road. While I have not spent much time discussing issues of authenticity, it is a measure deployed to demarcate the difference between in-group and out-group status. Authenticity is difficult, if not impossible to sustain, given that hybridity is nearly inescapable. Nonetheless, it is a tool, much like – or perhaps synonymous with – strategic essentialism, which serves to unify identity categories and protect cultures from appropriation and outright cultural and intellectual property theft. Authenticity can be harnessed toward a syncretic deployment of Latinidad, as Salma Hayek has done both in her construction of self as an authentic Latina and in her development of a line of beauty products sold via authentic materials and formulas. This move generated profits for CVS and Hayek, and positioned her as more authentic than other mainstream Latinas, especially Jennifer Lopez. It may have been a temporary utopic moment for Hayek and CVS, during the profitable years.[25]

But there is a long way ahead – or, rather, we keep heading to that place we can never reach. In his inaugural speech to the Center for Communication, Difference, and Equity (CCDE) at the University of Washington, Herman Gray asked us to redirect our focus, concluding with the notion that "we need to think about media and race in a way that includes explicit concerns at different scales about security, risk, vulnerability, danger, accountability rather than those limited to conventional concerns of identity, parody, visibility, and authenticity." This statement, observation, and call to action could only be made after we'd already traveled the long road of identity, visibility, and authenticity. New fields of security and surveillance – as well as the contemporary situation wherein we see so many of our hard-won gains being rolled back – redirect our attention to the ongoing dangers and vulnerability disproportionately borne by racialized segments of the population. Especially within the administration of the 45th President of the United States, racialized populations face growing violence and violated civil rights. Latina/os were singled out when 45 announced his candidacy and remain the target of much invective coming from his administration. This invective takes material form as entire segments of government, as well as efforts to change immigration laws and practices, single out Latina/os. A utopic media practice has to include transformation through accountability, reduce vulnerability through bearing witness, and transfer some of the risk from the most vulnerable to the mainstream media, which, despite some of the attacks being made to its viability, should continue its democratic and social justice tasks.

On the long road to utopia for Latina/os and the media, one of the options is to embrace our radical hybridity. This would move us to a place where we could recognize our heterogenous histories without flattening our differences, yet acknowledging that we are beyond purity. Recognizing our hybridity would open up the possibility for acknowledging our connections with all other ethnic groups, through history, blood, and culture. This would aim to decenter whiteness as another hybrid possibility in relation to Latina/o and other hybridities. In terms of media, the mainstream would become the hybridstream. It would be more complex to produce material drawing on, representing, and reaching unstable and unfixed identities and ethnic categories. Flexible and complex media moves us beyond identity and authenticity toward an understanding of something that we have already begun to acknowledge. It would require a politics of complexity that would generate alliances within and without Latinidad toward a media future that seems unreachable. Surely, we've devoted enough time to the separate-but-not-equal approach, which daily becomes more difficult to sustain. We've entered the stage of ambiguous representation as a strategy of subtle and imperceptible inclusion. We have yet to produce or demand the hybrid, though anthropologists and literature scholars have been documenting its presence for many decades. I do not want to forget the racist and colonialist history of hybridity that, though absolutely misguided, was a precursor to the acknowledgment of the inevitable mixture of populations. Hybridity is not the ultimate goal, but its acknowledgment does move us further along the path to that ideal place. We have to remain vigilant to ensure hybridity does not become yet another tactic to flatten difference in the name of profit (this book has demonstrated that as an always available option). We have to remain vigilant that light Latinidad does not continue to be used as an excuse to displace Afro-Latina/os, and black bodies in general. Aiming for a hybrid utopia will keep us busy, so that once we get close to it, we can set sail for the next destination.

Acknowledgment

I want to thank John Nerone for his invaluable reading, suggestions, and reorganization of this chapter. I ventured into utopia without proper philosophical training, and John gently guided me. Morten Stinus Kristensen and Diana

Leon-Boys provided expert research assistance. A much less developed version of this chapter appears as "Implicit Utopias and Ambiguous Ethnics: Latinidad and the Representational Promised Land" (2017), in I. Casillas and M. E. Cepeda (Eds.), *Routledge Companion to Latina/o Media Studies*. I was invited to present at a Latina/o Film Conference at the University of Indiana by John Nieto Phillips, where I originally began my exploration of Latina/o media utopias.

Notes

1 The specificity to the United States must be mentioned. While it is a fact that nearly all countries have histories of majority and minority populations and resulting representational issues, these vary according to context. The category Latina/o is transnational, yet we cannot generalize from the United States to other countries' experience.

2 I owe this observation to John Nerone, who links – and rightly so – this debate about Latinidad to previous debates over the inclusion of other "browned" segments of the US population.

3 Activism, as a separate strategy, is beyond the scope of this chapter. It deserves its own book.

4 Sally was three-fourths European, but nonetheless a slave according to US laws, which categorized freedom status according to the status of the mother.

5 Once more, this part is nearly verbatim from suggestive comments made by John Nerone.

6 "The Russian Revolution as a Mirror for Third World Movements." Lecture presented by the Center for Advanced Study.

7 There is no time to discuss this at this moment, but #MeToo has foregrounded whiteness, even as scholars and activists continue to note that bodies of color have also been sexually assaulted and continue to be silenced.

8 As of mid-November 2017, many people were posting on Facebook and Twitter that the United States had become a dystopia, especially in relation to routine mass murders, which show no sign of slowing down.

9 I began writing this chapter in October 2017 – 100 years after the Bolshevik Revolution in Russia, also called the October Revolution, which ushered in the socialist state of the Soviet Union/USSR, lasting from 1922 to 1991. I benefitted from the University of Illinois' many events commemorating this anniversary. Being a member of a great Research 1 institution inevitably enriches one's research.

10 The movie's name in the United Kingdom is *Zootropolis* and in Germany is *Zoomania* (Hoffman 2016), both naming changes distancing the film from its utopian discourse implications, perhaps in a nod to national differences about internal racial politics.

11 The hit CBS medical comedy-drama *M*A*S*H*, in which McLean Stevenson played one of the major supporting roles, had its final season in 1983. As that show ended, the major television networks and Hollywood studios sought to profit off the fame of its protagonists. *Condo* was one result.

12 Historically, Hollywood and US mainstream television have not necessarily cast Latina/o actors in Latina/o roles, nor matched the ethnicity of actors with the ethnicity of roles. Latina/o media scholars usually mention Natalie Wood, who played the character of Maria in *West Side Story* (1961). More recently, Asian American activists complained about Emma Stone being cast in the lead role in *Aloha* (2015), given that Stone is not Asian American. More often than not, Hollywood and US mainstream media tend to cast white actors to play all roles, even if blackface is necessary (see Chapter 3).

13 *Murphy Brown*'s heyday predated the appearance of *George Lopez* by over a decade.

14 Moreno, in her many discussions at Notre Dame University in February 2019, often asserted that she dialogued with writers to avoid becoming the comic relief for the series. She added that she had been asking for a narrative arc for her character because being cast as the sexy old lady inevitable leads to comic relief outside of a more fleshed-out personal story.

15 See Molina-Guzmán's research on showrunners and *Modern Family*.

16 Recent events such as Harvey Weinstein's fall and the #MeToo movement reveal how little change there has been in discriminatory production practices for the most privileged of minoritized subjects, white women. Things are worse for others.

17 Data on both of these elements is readily available through the ALMA Wikipedia entry and the Latin Grammys website (www.latingrammy.com).

18 I use this term in the economic sense: not as a judgment call on the quality or status of these products, but rather to mean the types of goods whose sale increases as income decreases or the economy falters.

19 The fact that the name of the show – The Latin Grammys – is in English and the process and much of the website is in Spanish speaks to the language tensions inherent in these award ceremonies.

20 I use the word "generic" to signify that these award shows are the mainstream versions, which foreground mostly US white music, as opposed to "Latin" or "urban" (which usually translates into African American and, less often, Latina/o musical artists and genres).

21 After a bizarre ending to the televised award show, when presenters Warren Beatty and Faye Dunaway mistakenly gave the award to *La La Land*, the Oscar was presented to the incredulous cast of *Moonlight*.

22 Exceptions include events such as the World Cup, which attracted huge audiences – English and Spanish, Latina/o and non Latina/o – as Univision provided much better coverage than US networks, including ESPN.

23 Amaya's is titled, "Labor and the Legal Structuring of Media Industries in the Case of *Ugly Betty*."

24 This eerie cover is all the more jarring in 2018, when the current administration appears to support a policy of separating children from parents in immigration situations and when stories about thousands of children in detention draw criticism from global bodies such as the United Nations.

25 I do not want to judge or deny the fact that many women who used the products identified with their authentic Latinidad and liked the results of using a particular shampoo or make-up foundation. The Nuance line resonated with many female users.

References

Ahmed, S. (2012). *On Being Included: Racism and Diversity in Institutional Life.* Durham: Duke University Press.

Aguayo, A. (2017, June). Plenary II: representation. RBMS 2017 (Rare Books and Manuscript Section conference – a division of the American Library Association).

Albarrán, A. (2009). *The Handbook of Spanish Language Media.* New York: Routledge.

Althusser, L. (1971). Ideology and ideological state apparatuses (notes towards an investigation). In: *Lenin and Philosophy and Other Essays* (ed. L. Althusser), 121–173. New York: Monthly Review.

Amaya, H. (2013). *Citizenship Excess: Latina/os, Media, and the Nation.* New York: New York University Press.

Aparicio, F.R. and Chávez-Silverman, S. (eds.) (1997). *Tropicalizations: Transcultural Representations of Latinidad.* Hanover: University Press of New England.

Báez, J.M. (2007). Towards a Latinidad feminista: the multiplicities of Latinidad and feminism in contemporary cinema. *Journal of Popular Communication* 5 (2): 109–128.

Báez, J.M. (2015). Television for all women?: Watching Lifetime's *Devious Maids.* In: *Cupcakes, Pinterest, Ladyporn: Feminized Popular Culture in the Early 21st Century* (ed. E. Levine), 51–70. Urbana: University of Illinois Press.

Báez, J.M. (2018). *In Search of Belonging: Latinas, Media, and Citizenship.* Champaign: University of Illinois Press.

Báez, J.M. and Avilés-Santiago, M.G. (2016). Spanish-language television. In: *Oxford Bibliographies in Cinema and Media Studies* (ed. K. Gabbard). New York: Oxford University Press.

Bailey, C. (2011). Coming out as homophobic: Isaiah Washington and the *Grey's Anatomy* scandal. *Communication and Critical/Cultural Studies* 8 (1): 1–21.

Banet-Weiser, S. and Mukherjee, R. (2012). *Commodity Activism: Cultural Resistance in Neoliberal Times.* New York: New York University Press.

The Gender of Latinidad: Uses and Abuses of Hybridity, First Edition. Angharad N. Valdivia.
© 2020 John Wiley & Sons Ltd. Published 2020 by John Wiley & Sons Ltd.

Barrera, M. (2002). Hottentot 2000: Jennifer Lopez and her butt. In: *Sexualities in History: A Reader* (eds. K.M. Phillips and B. Reay), 407–417. New York: Routledge.

Barthes, R. (1957). *Mythologies.* Paris, France: Les Lettres Nouvelles.

Bauman, Z. (2000). *Liquid Modernity.* Malden: Blackwell.

BBC News. (2016, September 22). Disney pulls "brownface" Moana costume. Retrieved June 10, 2019 from http://www.bbc.com/news/world-asia-37437316

Becker, S., Crandall, M.D., Fisher, K.E., Kinney, B., Landry, C., & Rocha, A. (2010). Opportunity for all: how the American public benefits from internet access at US libraries. Retrieved June 10, 2019 from https://eric.ed.gov/?id=ED510740

Beltrán, M.C. (2004). Más macha: the new Latina action hero. In: *Action and Adventure Cinema* (ed. Y. Tasker), 186–200. London, UK: Routledge.

Beltrán, M.C. (2005). The new Hollywood racelessness: only the fast, furious (and multi-racial) will survive. *Cinema Journal 44* (2): 50–67.

Beltrán, M.C. (2008a). Mixed race in Latinowood: Latino stardom and ethnic ambiguity in the era of dark angels. In: *Mixed Race Hollywood: Multiraciality in Film and Media Culture* (eds. M. Beltrán and C. Fojas). New York: New York University Press.

Beltrán, M.C. (2008b). When Dolores del Rio became Latina: Latina/o stardom in Hollywood's transition to sound. In: *Latina/o Communication Studies Today* (ed. A.N. Valdivia), 27–50. New York: Peter Lang.

Beltrán, M.C. (2009). *Latina/o Stars in US Eyes: The Making and Meaning of Film and TV Stardom.* Urbana: University of Illinois Press.

Beltrán, M.C. (2013). SNL's "Fauxbama" debate: facing off over millennial (mixed-)racial impersonation. In: *Saturday Night Live and American TV* (eds. N. Marx, M. Sienkiewicz and R. Becker), 191–210. Bloomington: Indiana University Press.

Bennett, J.A. (2010). Queer teenagers and the mediation of utopian catastrophe. *Critical Studies In Media Communication 27* (5): 455–476.

Berg, C.R. (2011). *Latino Images in Film: Stereotypes, Subversion, Resistance.* Austin: University of Texas Press.

Berg, M. (2016, September 16). How a business-first mentality earned Sofia Vergara $43 million this year. Retrieved June 10, 2019 from https://www.forbes.com/sites/maddieberg/2016/09/14/how-a-business-first-mentality-earned-sofia-vergara-43-million-this-year/#775c6cfd460c

Berger, J. (1972). *Ways of Seeing.* London, UK: Penguin.

Betancourt, M. (2017, July 13). These are the Latinos nominated for a 2017 Emmy Award. Retrieved June 10, 2019 from http://remezcla.com/lists/film/latino-2017-emmy-award-nominees

Bhaba, H.K. (1994). *The Location of Culture.* New York: Routledge.

Bilge, E. (2013, September 9). Your box office explained: *Instructions Not Included* and the power of the Latino moviegoer. Retrieved June 10, 2019 from https://www.vulture.com/2013/09/box-office-explained-instructions-not-included.html

Birkinbine, B.J., Gómez, R., and Wasko, J. (eds.) (2017). *Global Media Giants*. New York: Routledge.

Bitette, N. (2016, November 15). Kelly Osbourne defends racist Latino remarks in new memoir. Retrieved June 10, 2019 from http://www.nydailynews.com/entertainment/gossip/kelly-osbourne-defends-racist-latino-remarks-new-memoir-article-1.2874244

Blue, M.G. (2013). The best of both worlds? *Feminist Media Studies* 13 (4): 660–675.

Blue, M.G. (2017). *Girlhood on Disney Channel: Branding, Celebrity and Femininity*. New York: Routledge.

Born, P. & Brookman, F. (2015, December 30). Salma Hayek remakes her cosmetics line. Retrieved June 10, 2019 from http://wwd.com/beauty-industry-news/color-cosmetics/salma-hayek-cosmetics-line-cvs-10303324

Box Office Mojo. (2016, March 30). Moana. Retrieved June 10, 2019 from http://www.boxofficemojo.com/movies/?id=disney1116.htm

Bradshaw, P. (2016, December 1). Moana review – Disney's amiable Polynesian adventure. Retrieved June 10, 2019 from https://www.theguardian.com/film/2016/dec/01/moana-review-disney-polynesian-adventure

Brandes, S.H. (2006). *Skulls to the Living, Bread to the Dead: The Day of the Dead in Mexico and Beyond*. Malden: Blackwell.

Brown, L. (2018, March 30). The *perfect* Cover Girl™. Retrieved June 10, 2019 from https://www.instyle.com/news/jessica-alba-july-cover

Bulut, E., Mejia, R., and McCarthy, C. (2014). Governance through philitainment: playing the benevolent subject. *Communication and Critical-Cultural Studies* 11 (4): 342–361.

Calafell, B.M. (2008). Mentoring and love: an open letter. *Cultural Studies ↔ Critical Methodologies* 7 (4): 425–441.

Calafell, B. (2015). *Monstrosity, Race, and Performance in Contemporary Culture*. New York: Peter Lang.

Cardoso, F.H. and Faletto, E. (1979). *Dependency and development in Latin America*. Berkeley: University of California Press.

Casillas, D.I. (2005). Latin Grammys. In: *Encyclopedia of Latinas and Latinos in the United States* (eds. S. Oboler and D. Gonzalez), 477–478. New York: Oxford University Press.

Casillas, D.I. (2014). *Sounds of Belonging: A Cultural History of Spanish-Language Radio in the United States, 1922–2004*. New York: New York University Press.

Casillas, D.I., Ferrada, J.S., and Hinojos, S.V. (2018). The accent on *Modern Family*: listening to representations of the Latina vocal body. *Aztlan: A Journal of Chicano Studies* 43 (1): 61–87.

Casserly, M. (2012, October 24). Sofia Vergara's rich little secret: a multi million media empire. Retrieved June 10, 2019 from https://www.forbes.com/sites/meghancasserly/2012/07/18/sofia-vergaras-rich-little-secret-a-multi-million-media-empire/#2f3b77fb5f3d

Castañeda, M. (2012). Feeling good while buying goods: promoting commodity activism to Latina consumers. In: *Commodity Activism* (eds. R. Mukherjee and S. Banet-Weiser), 273–291. New York: New York University Press.

Ceisel, C. (2011). El rock star perfecto?: Theorizing Juanes and new directions in crossover celebrity. *Communication Theory 21* (4): 413–435.

Celeste, M. (2016). Entertaining mobility: the racialized and gendered nation in *House Hunters International*. *Feminist Media Studies 16* (3): 527–542.

Cepeda, M.E. (2000). Mucho loco for Ricky Martin; or the politics of chronology, crossover, and language within the Latin(o) music "boom." *Popular Music and Society 24* (3): 55–71.

Cepeda, M.E. (2001). Columbus effects: the politics of crossover and chronology within the Latin(o) music "boom." *Discourse 23* (1): 242–267.

Cepeda, M.E. (2003a). Mucho loco for Ricky Martin, or: the politics of chronology, crossover and language within the Latin(o) music "boom." In: *Global Pop, Local Talk* (eds. M.T. Carroll and H. Berger), 113–129. Jackson: University of Mississippi Press.

Cepeda, M.E. (2003b). Shakira as the idealized, transnational citizen: a case study of Colombianidad in transition. *Latino Studies 1*: 211–232.

Cepeda, M.E. (2010). *Musical Imagi/Nation: US Colombians and the Latin(o) Music "Boom"*. New York: New York University Press.

Cepeda, M.E. (2015). Beyond "filling in the gap": the state and status of Latina/o feminist media studies. *Feminist Media Studies 16* (2): 344–360.

Cepeda, M.E. (2018). Putting a "good face on the nation": beauty, memes, and the gendered rebranding of global Colombianidad. *WSQ: Women's Studies Quarterly 46* (1–2): 121–138.

Cepeda, M.E. and Casillas, D.I. (eds.) (2017). *The Routledge Companion to Latina/o Media*. New York: Routledge.

Chakravartty, P., Kuo, R., Grubbs, V., and McIlwain, C. (2018). #Communication SoWhite. *Journal of Communication 68* (2): 254–266.

Chandler, C. (2012). Marshall arts: an inventory of common criticisms of McLuhan's media studies. *Explorations in Media Ecology 10* (3/4): 279–293.

Chavez, C. (2015). *Reinventing the Latino Television Viewer: Language, Ideology, and Practice*. Lanham: Lexington Books.

Chavez, C. and Kiley, A. (2016). Starlets, subscribers and beneficiaries: Disney, Latino children and television labor. *International Journal of Communication 10*: 21.

Chenyek, R.K. (2018). Mediating alterity: transitive Indianness in US non-normative medicine [doctoral dissertation]. Retrieved June 10, 2019 from https://www.ideals. illinois.edu/handle/2142/101793

Chiu, M. & Marx, L. (2018, October 29). Selena Gomez back in treatment. Retrieved June 10, 2019 from https://www.pressreader.com/usa/ people-usa/20181029/281779925141180

Collon, A. (2016, October 21). Live with Kelly and Michael interview Sofia Vergara latest [video file]. Retrieved June 10, 2019 from http://www.youtube.com/ watch?v=_61AWdWeBFw

Contreras Porras, I.C. (2017). "Sofía Vergara made me do it": on beauty, costeñismo and transnational Colombian identity. In: *The Routledge*

Companion to Latina/o Media (eds. M.E. Cepeda and D.I. Casillas), 306–319. New York: Routledge.

Corinthios, A. (2015, August 4). Kelly Osbourne racist scandal: apologizes for comments about Latinos on The View. Retrieved June 10, 2019 from http://people.com/tv/kelly-osbourne-racist-scandal-apologizes-for-comments-about-latinos-on-the-view/

CSA Staff. (2011, November 3). CVS Caremark profits driven by pharmacy benefit management performance. Retrieved June 10, 2019 from http://www.chainstoreage.com/article/cvs-caremark-profits-driven-pharmacy-benefit-management-performance

DaCosta, K.M. (2007). *Making Multiracials: State, Family, and Market in the Redrawing of the Color Line*. Palo Alto: Stanford University Press.

Davies, J. (2017, March 23). Charo talks "Dancing with the Stars" performance. Retrieved June 10, 2019 from http://abc7chicago.com/1815452

Dávila, A. (2001). *Latinos, Inc.: The Marketing and Making of a People*. Berkeley and Los Angeles: University of California Press.

Dávila, A. (2008). *Latino Spin: Public Image and the Whitewashing if Race*. New York: New York University Press.

Dean, J. (2005). Communicative capitalism: circulation and the foreclosure of politics. *Cultural Politics 1* (1): 51–74.

Del Rio, E. (2017). Authenticity, articulation, appropriation: the cultural logic of Latinidad. In: *The Routledge Companion to Latina/o Media* (eds. M.E. Cepeda and D.I. Casillas), 9–21. New York: Routledge.

Diaz, T. (2018, March 14). Rosie Perez says Hollywood wanted her to be "completely white-washed." Retrieved June 10, 2019 from http://people.com/chica/rosie-perez-talks-racism-in-hollywood

Dockterman, E. (2014, October 22). Sofia Vergara on taking risks as an actor: "it's not like we're doing brain surgery." Retrieved June 10, 2019 from http://time.com/3531603/sofia-vergara-interview-thyroid-cancer

Dorfman, A. and Mattelart, A. (1971). *How to Read Donald Duck: Imperialist Ideology in the Disney Comic*. New York: IG Editions.

Dow, B. (1996). *Prime Time Feminism: Television, Media Culture, and Women's Movement Since 1970*. Philadelphia: University of Pennsylvania Press.

Dyer, R. (1977). *Entertainment and Utopia*. London, UK: Routledge.

England, D., Descartes, L., and Collier-Meek, M. (2011). Gender role portrayal and the Disney princesses. *Sex Roles 64* (7/8): 555–567.

Enloe, C. (1989). *Bananas, Beaches, and Bases: Making Feminist Sense of International Politics*. Berkeley: University of California.

Everitt, D. and Mills, S. (2009). Cultural anxiety 2.0. *Media, Culture & Society 31* (5): 749–768.

Ferber, L. (2011, April 7). Exclusive interview: Charo – bringing sexy back. Retrieved July 6, 2017 from http://lgbtweekly.com/2011/04/07/bringing-sexy-back

Ferguson, R. (2012). *The Reorder of Things: The University and its Pedagogies of Minority Difference*. Minneapolis: University of Minnesota Press.

Fernandez L'Hoeste, H. (2017). What's in an accent? Gender and cultural stereotypes in the work of Sofia Vergara. In: *The Routledge Companion to Latina/o Media* (eds. M.E. Cepeda and D.I. Casillas), 223–240. New York: Routledge.

Flanagan, J. (2009). Deconstructing Mayberry: utopia and racial diversity in the Andy Griffith Show. *Continuum: Journal of Media & Cultural Studies 23* (3): 307–319.

Flores, A. & Lopez, M.H. (2018, January 11). Among US Latinos, the internet now rivals television as a source for news. Retrieved June 10, 2019 from http://www.pewresearch.org/fact-tank/2018/01/11/among-u-s-latinos-the-internet-now-rivals-television-as-a-source-for-news

Fojas, C. (2017). *Zombies, Migrants, and Queers: Race and Crisis Capitalism in Pop Culture*. Champaign: University of Illinois Pres.

Fregoso, R.L. (1993). *The Bronze Screen: Chicano and Chicano Film Culture*. Minneapolis: University of Minnesota Press.

Fregoso, R.L. (1995). Homegirls, cholas, and pachucas in cinema: taking over the public sphere. *California History 74* (3): 316–327.

Fregoso, R.L. (2007). Lupe Vélez: Queen of the B's. In: *From Bananas to Buttocks: The Latina Body in Popular Film and Culture* (ed. M. Mendible). Austin: University of Texas Press.

Fusco, C. (1995). *English is Broken Here: Notes on Cultural Fusion in the Americas*. New York: New Press.

García Canclini, N. (1995). *Hybrid Cultures: Strategies for Entering and Leaving Modernity*. Minneapolis: University of Minnesota Press.

García Canclini, N. (2003). From national capital to global capital: urban change in Mexico City. In: *Globalization* (ed. A. Appadurai). Durham: Duke University Press.

Gates, K. (2013). Media studies futures, past and present. In: *The International Encyclopedia of Media Studies*, vol. *VI* (ed. A.N. Valdivia), 13–39. Oxford, UK: Blackwell Publishing.

Giles, J. and Middleton, T. (2008). *Studying Culture: A Practical Introduction*. Malden: Blackwell Publishing.

Gil-Montero, M. (1989). *Brazilian Bombshell: The Biography of Carmen Miranda*. New York: Dutton Adult.

Gilstrap, P. & Gilstrap, P. (2007, April 9). MGM, Hayek team for Ventanazul. Retrieved June 10, 2019 from http://variety.com/2007/film/markets-festivals/mgm-hayek-team-for-ventanazul-1117962733/

Girl Scouts and Disney. (2017). *Elena of Avalor Leadership Guide* [brochure]. Retrieved June 10, 2019 from http://cdnvideo.dolimg.com/cdn_assets/3dfa69f593c2b26b0e5e0d317a4ae42fa05ba178.pdf

Goldstein, J. (2017, July 10). "Beatriz at Dinner" puts a Trumpian mogul and an immigrant at the same table. Retrieved June 10, 2019 from https://thinkprogress.org/beatriz-dinner-movie-c78afeac8735

González, A. and Heuman, A.N. (2003). The Latin Grammys and the ALMAs: awards programs, cultural epideictic, and intercultural pedagogy. *Journal of Latinos and Education 2* (1): 47–57.

Gordon-Reed, A. (1997). *Thomas Jefferson and Sally Hemings: An American Controversy*. Charlottesville: University Press of Virginia.

Gordon-Reed, A. (2008). *The Hemingses of Monticello: An American Family*. New York: W.W. Norton & Co.

Götz, M. (2008). Girls and boys and television. Retrieved June 10, 2019 from http://www.br-online.de/jugend/izi/english/publication/televizion/21_2008_E/21_2008_E.htm

Gramsci, A. (1929–35). *Prison Notebooks*, trans. Buttigieg, J.A. [1992]. New York: Columbia University Press.

Gray, H. (2013). Race, media, and the cultivation of concern. *Communication and Critical Cultural Studies 10* (2–3): 253–258.

Griffin, S. (2000). You've never had a friend like me: target marketing Disney to a gay community. In: *Tinker Belles and Evil Queens: The Walt Disney Company from the Inside Out* (ed. S. Griffin), 182–214. New York: New York University Press.

Gutiérrez, F. (2012). More than 200 years of Latino media in the United States. Retrieved June 10, 2019 from https://www.nps.gov/articles/latinothemestudymedia.htm

Hairston, T. (2016, June 10). Everything you need to know about Disney's first Latina princess, Elena of Avalor. Retrieved June 10, 2019 from http://fusion.net/story/312629/disney-first-latina-princess-elena-of-valor

Hall, S. (1972). *Encoding and Decoding in the Television Discourse*. Birmingham, UK: University of Birmingham Centre for Cultural Studies.

Halter, M. (2000). *Shopping for Identity: The Marketing of Ethnicity*. New York: Schocken Books.

Harewood, S.J. and Valdivia, A.N. (2005). Exploring Dora: re-embodied Latinidad on the web. In: *Girl Wide Web: Girls, the Internet, and the Negotiation of Identity* (ed. S.R. Mazzarella). New York: Peter Lang.

Harris, A. (2004). *All About the Girl: Culture, Power and Identity*. New York and London, UK: Routledge.

Hearn, A. (2012). Brand me "Activist". In: *Commodity Activism* (eds. R. Mukherjee and S. Banet-Weiser), 23–38. New York: New York University Press.

Hegde, R. (2011). *Circuits of Visibility: Gender and Transnational Media Cultures (Critical Cultural Communication)*. New York: New York University Press.

Hill, L. (2018, April 2). "One Day at a Time" offers star Rita Moreno new insight into immigration. Retrieved June 10, 2019 from http://www.latimes.com/entertainment/envelope/emmys/la-et-st-rita-moreno-one-day-at-a-time-emmys-20180402-story.html

Hoffman, J. (2016, March 3). Zootopia review – Disney's furry fable gets its claws out for the bigots. Retrieved June 10, 2019 from http://www.theguardian.com/film/2016/mar/03/zootopia-zootropolis-zoomania-review-disney

Huong, N. (2015). Globalization, consumerism, and the emergence of teens in contemporary Vietnam. *Journal of Social History 49* (1): 4–19.

Hurtado, A. (2017). Sex, service, and scenery: Latina sexualities in the pages of *Vogue*. In: *The Routledge Companion to Latina/o Media* (eds. M.E. Cepeda and D.I. Casillas), 320–337. New York: Routledge.

Jhally, S. (2006). *The Spectacle of Accumulation: Essays in Culture, Media, & Politics*. New York: Peter Lang.

Jhally, S. and Lewis, J. (1992). *Enlightened Racism: The Cosby Show, Audiences, and the Myth of the American Dream*. Boulder: West View Press.

Joseph, R. (2010). "Tyra Banks is fat": reading (post-)racism and (post-)feminism in the new millennium. *Critical Studies in Media Communication 26* (3): 237–254.

Joseph, R. (2013). *Transcending Blackness: From the New Millennium Mulatta to the Exeptional Multiracial*. Durham: Duke University Press.

Julien, I. and Mercer, K. (1988). De Margin and De Centre. *Screen 29* (4): 2–11.

Kennedy, M. (2018). "Come on, [...] let's go find your inner princess": (post-)feminist generationalism in tween fairy tales. *Feminist Media Studies 18* (3): 424–439.

Kido Lopez, L. (2016). *Asian American Media Activism: Fighting for Cultural Citizenship*. New York: New York University Press.

Kim, S.H. and Lee, K.S. (2001). Korea: Disney in Korean mass culture. In: *Dazzled By Disney? The Global Disney Audiences Project* (eds. J. Wasko, M. Philips and E.R. Meehan). London, UK: Leicester University Press.

King, L. (2016, May 4). Charo on Jane the Virgin and Latinos in Hollywood [video file]. Retrieved June 10, 2019 from https://www.youtube.com/watch?v=xcYGzIhNEww

King, L. (2016, May 12). Charo clarifies Sofia Vergara insult: "I talk without I think" [video file]. Retrieved June 10, 2019 from http://www.ora.tv/larrykingnow/2016/5/2/charo-clarifies-sofia-vergara-insult-i-talk-without-i-think

King, L. (2016, May 14). Why Charo kept a pet bull at her Beverly Hills compound [video file]. Retrieved June 10, 2019 from https://www.youtube.com/watch?v=IZYBjzsyl4c

Kozma, A. (2017). Stephanie Rothman does not exist: narrating a lost history of women in film. *Camera Obscura 32* (1): 179–186.

Kraidy, M. (1999). The global, the local, and the hybrid: a native ethnography of glocalization. *Critical Studies in Mass Communication 16* (4): 456–476.

Kraidy, M. (2002). Hybridity in cultural globalization. *Communication Theory 12* (3): 316–339.

Kraidy, M. (2005). *Hybridity or the Cultural Logic of Globalization*. Philadelphia: Temple University Press.

Kraidy, M. (2006). Hybridity and cultural globalization. *Communication Theory 12* (3): 316–339.

Kraniauskas, J. (2000a). Hybridity in a transnational frame: Latin-Americanist and postcolonial perspectives on cultural studies. *Nepantla: Views from the South 1* (1): 111–137.

Kraniauskas, J. (2000b). Hybridity in a transnational frame. Latin Americanist and post-colonial perspectives on cultural studies. In: *Hybridity and Its Discontents: Politics, Science, Culture* (eds. A. Brah and A. Coombes). London, UK: Routledge.

Kuns, K. (2016, September 2). Surprise! Latinos for Trump founder is a real estate scammer. Retrieved June 10, 2019 from http://crooksandliars.com/2016/09/surprise-latinos-trump-founder-real-estate

Labanyi, J. (2000). *Gender and Modernization in the Spanish Realist Novel.* Oxford, UK: Oxford University Press.

Lacroix, C. (2004). Images of animated others: the Orientalization of Disney's cartoon heroines from The Little Mermaid to The Hunchback of Notre Dame. *Popular Communication 2* (4): 213–229.

Latorre, G. (2008). Icons of love and devotion: Alma López's art. *Feminist Studies 43* (1/2) (Spring/Summer 2008): 131–136. 146–150.

Leon-Boys, D. (forthcoming). Bienvenida a Disney Princess Elena: exploring race, age, and gender in Disney's *Elena of Avalor* [unpublished doctoral dissertation].

Lerner, D. (1958). *The Passing of Traditional Society: Modernizing the Middle East.* Glencoe: The Free Press.

Levina, M. and Bui, D.T. (eds.) (2013). *Monster Culture in the 21st Century: A Reader.* New York: Bloomsbury Academic Press.

Levine, E. (2001). Constructing a market, constructing an ethnicity: U.S. Spanish language media and the formation of a Latina/o identity. *Studies in Latin American Popular Culture 20*: 33–50.

Levine, E. (2005). Fractured fairytales and fragmented markets: Disney's *Weddings of a Lifetime* and the cultural politics of media conglomeration. *Television & New Media 6* (1): 71–88.

Levine, E. (2015). *Cupcakes, Pinterest, Ladyporn: Feminized Popular Culture in the Early 21st Century.* Urbana: University of Illinois Press.

Levitas, R. (2010). *The Concept of Utopia.* New York: Peter Lang.

Levitas, R. (2013). *Utopia as Method: The Imaginary Reconstitution of Society.* New York: Palgrave MacMillan.

Lipsitz, G. (1998). *The Possessive Investment in Whiteness: How White People Benefit from Identity Politics.* Philadelphia: Temple University Press.

Littler, J. (2018). *Against Meritocracy: Culture, Power, and the Myths of Mobility.* New York: Routledge.

Llona, C.M. (2015, January 29). After controversy, Disney introduces its first Latina princess: Elena of Avalor. Retrieved June 10, 2019 from https://www.foxnews.com/entertainment/after-controversy-disney-introduces-its-first-latina-princess-elena-of-avalor

Lopez, A. (2012). *Hollywood, Nuestra America, y Los Latinos.* Havana, Cuba: Ediciones Union.

López, A.M. (1991). Are all Latins from Manhattan? Hollywood, ethnography, and cultural colonialism. In: *Unspeakable Images: Ethnicity and the American Cinema* (ed. L.D. Friedman), 404–424. Urbana: University of Illinois.

Lowe, L. (1991). Heterogeneity, hybridity, and multiplicity: marking Asian American difference. *Diaspora: A Journal in Transnational Studies 1* (1): 24–44.

Lowe, L. (1996). *Immigrant Acts*. Durham: Duke University Press.

Lugo, A. (2000). Theorizing border inspections. *Cultural Dynamics 12* (3): 353–373.

Lustyik, K. (2013). Disney's high school musical: music makes the world go "round". *Interactions: Studies in Communication & Culture 4* (3): 239–253.

MacDonald, F. (2016). *Girlhood and Tween Girl Culture*. New York: Palgrave Macmillan.

Mander, J. (1978). *Four Arguments for the Elimination of Television*. New York: William Morrow.

Mannheim, K. (1936). *Ideology and Utopia*. London, UK: Routledge.

Manoucheka, C. (2016). Entertaining mobility: the racialized and gendered nation in *House Hunters International*. *Feminist Media Studies 16* (3): 527–542.

Martí, O.R. (1993). Review of *Modernidad, Identidad y Utopía en América Latina* by Anibal Quijano. *Utopian Studies 4* (2): 232–236.

Martin, L. (2008, September 18). Rita Moreno overcame Hispanic stereotypes to achieve stardom. Retrieved June 10, 2019 from https://www. latinamericanstudies.org/puertorico/rita-moreno.htm

Martínez, K.Z. (2006). American idols with Caribbean Soul: Cubanidad and the Latin Grammys. *Latino Studies 4* (4): 381–400.

Marvin, C. (1988). *When Old Technologies Were New: Thinking about Electric Communication in the Late Nineteenth Century*. New York: Oxford University Press.

Marx, K. and Engels, F. (1967). *The Communist Manifesto*. London, UK: Penguin.

Mayer, V. (2013). Making media production visible. In: *International Encyclopedia of Media Studies*, vol. *II* (eds. V. Mayer and A.N. Valdivia), 13–40. Hoboken: Wiley-Blackwell.

Mayer, V., Press, A., Verhoeven, D., and Sterne, J. (2018). How do we intervene in the stubborn persistence of patriarchy in communication scholarship? In: *Interventions: Communication Theory and Practice* (eds. D.T. Scott and A. Shaw). New York: Peter Lang.

McAllister, M.P. (2007). "Girls with a passion for fashion": the Bratz brand as integrated spectacular consumption. *Journal of Children and Media 1* (3): 224–258.

McDonald, S.N. (2015, May 11). How Sofia Vergara picked up Carmen Miranda's legacy – and ran with it. Retrieved June 10, 2019 from http://wapo.st/1cI2Sg7

McGladrey, M.L. (2014). Becoming tween bodies: what preadolescent girls in the US say about beauty, the "just-right ideal," and the "Disney girls". *Journal of Children and Media 8* (4): 353–370.

McRobbie, A. (2016). *Be Creative: Making a Living in the New Culture Industries*. Cambridge, UK: Polity Press.

Meehan, E.R. (2005). Transindustrialism and synergy: structural supports for decreasing diversity in commercial culture. *International Journal of Media and Cultural Politics 1* (1): 123–126.

Melamed, J. (2011). *Represent and Destroy: Rationalizing Violence in the New Racial Capitalism*. Minneapolis: University of Minnesota Press.

Mendible, M. (ed.) (2007a). *From Bananas to Buttocks: The Latina Body in Popular Film and Culture*. Austin: University of Texas Press.

Mendible, M. (2007b). Introduction. Embodying Latinidad: an overview. In: *From Bananas to Buttocks: The Latina Body in Popular Film and Culture*. Austin: University of Texas Press.

Mercer, K. (1990). Black art and the burden of representation. *Third Text 4* (10): 61–78.

Miller, M. (2017, April 18). Meet Sofia Vergara's flamenco dancer from *The Emoji Movie*: "People are always saying I look like her!" Retrieved June 10, 2019 from http://people.com/movies/sofia-vergara-emoji-movie-flamenco-dancer-character-first-look

Miller, T. and Kraidy, M.M. (2016). *Global Media Studies*. Cambridge, UK: Polity Press.

Milner, A. (2009). Changing the climate: the politics of dystopia. *Continuum: Journal of Media and Cultural Studies 23* (6): 827–838.

Miyashiro, A. (2016) Moana syllabus. Retrieved June 10, 2019 from https://moanasyllabus.wordpress.com

Molina-Guzmán, I. (2005). Gendering Latinidad through the Elián News Discourse about Cuban women. *Latino Studies 3* (2): 179–204.

Molina-Guzmán, I. (2010). *Dangerous Curves: Latina Bodies and the Media*. New York: New York University Press.

Molina-Guzmán, I. (2012a). Modern Family's Latina spitfire in the era of white resentment. Retrieved June 10, 2019 from http://www.flowjournal.org/2012/11/modern-family%E2%80%99s-latina-spitfire

Molina-Guzmán, I. (2012b). Salma Hayek's celebrity activism: constructing race, ethnicity, and gender as mainstream global commodities. In: *Commodity Activism: Cultural Resistance in Neoliberal Times* (eds. R. Mukherjee and S. Banet-Weiser), 134–153. New York: New York University Press.

Molina-Guzmán, I. (2013a). Commodifying black Latinidad in US film and television. *Popular Communication 11* (3): 211–226.

Molina-Guzmán, I. (2013b). Zoë Saldana: the complicated politics of casting a black Latina. Retrieved June 10, 2019 from https://www.flowjournal.org/2013/01/zoe-saldana-the-complicated-politics-of-casting-a-black-latina

Molina-Guzmán, I. (2014). "Latina wisdom" in "postrace" recession media. In: *Gendering the Recession: Media and Culture in an Age of Austerity* (eds. D. Negra and Y. Tasker), 58–80. Durham: Duke University Press.

Molina-Guzmán, I. (2016). #OscarsSoWhite: how Stuart Hall explains why nothing is changing in Hollywood and everything is changing. *Critical Studies in Media Communication 33* (5): 438–454.

Molina-Guzmán, I. (2018). *Latinas and Latinos on TV: Colorblind Comedy in the Post-Racial Network Era*. Tucson: The University of Arizona Press.

Molina-Guzmán, I. and Valdivia, A.N. (2004). Brain, brow, and booty: Latina iconicity in US popular culture. *The Communication Review 7* (2): 205–221.

Molina y Vedia, S. (2001). Disney in Mexico: observations on integrating global culture objects into everyday life. In: *Dazzled By Disney? The Global Disney Audiences Project* (eds. J. Wasko, M. Philips and E.R. Meehan). London, UK: Leicester University Press.

Moorti, S. (2017). Brown girls who don't need saving: social media and the role of "possessive investment" in *The Mindy Project* and *The Good Wife*. In: *Television for Women: New Directions* (eds. R. Moseley, H. Wheatley and H. Wood), 90–109. New York: Routledge.

Moreman, S.T. (2008). Hybrid performativity, South and North of the border: entre la teoría y la materialidad de hibridación. In: *Latina/o Communication Studies Today* (ed. A.N. Valdivia), 91–111. New York: Peter Lang.

Moreno, C. (2013, October 3). Charo rejects Sofia Vergara comparison with graphic response. Retrieved June 10, 2019 from http://www.huffingtonpost.com/2013/10/03/charo-sofia-vergara_n_4039495.html

Moreno, R. (n.d.). Rita Moreno, actress: Rita Moreno on immigrating to the US breaking into Hollywood and defying stereotypes [video file]. Retrieved June 10, 2019 from https://www.makers.com/profiles/591f27c5a8c7c4265c6428cc

Morley, D. (2006). Globalization and cultural imperialism reconsidered: old questions in new guises. In: *Media and Cultural Theory* (eds. J. Curran and D. Morley). New York: Routledge.

Mosco, V. (2004). *The Digital Sublime: Myth, Power, and Cyberspace*. Boston: MIT Press.

Mukherjee, R. (2006). *The Racial Order of Things: Cultural Imaginaries of the Post Soul Era*. Minneapolis: University of Minnesota Press.

Mukherjee, R. (2014). Rhyme and reason: "post-race" and the politics of colorblind racism. In: *The Colorblind Screen: Race and Television in Contemporary America* (eds. S.E. Turner and S. Nilsen), 39–56. New York: New York University Press.

Murphy, P.D. and Kraidy, M.M. (2003). International communication, ethnography, and the challenge of globalization. *Communication Theory 13*: 304–323.

Murrian, S.R. (2017, June 5). *Beatriz at Dinner* screenwriter reveals his inspiration and how Trump's election helped the movie. Retrieved June 10, 2019 from https://parade.com/575305/samuelmurrian/beatriz-at-dinner-screenwriter-reveals-his-inspiration-and-how-trumps-election-helped-the-movie

Naficy, H. (1993). *The Making of Exile Cultures: Iranian Television in Los Angeles*. Minneapolis: University of Minnesota Press.

Negra, D. (2001). *Off White Hollywood: American Culture and Ethnic Female Stardom*. London, UK: Routledge.

Negra, D. and Tasker, Y. (2014). Gender and recessionary culture. In: *Gendering the Recession: Media and Culture in an Age of Austerity* (eds. D. Negra and Y. Tasker), 1–30. Durham: Duke University Press.

Negrón-Muntaner, F. (1997). Jennifer's butt. *Aztlán 22* (2): 182–195.

Negrón-Muntaner, F. (2004). *Boricua Pop: Puerto Ricans and the Latinization of American Culture*. New York: New York University Press.

Negrón-Muntaner, F. (2017). What to do with all this beauty: the political economy of Latina stardom in the twenty-first century. In: *The Routledge Companion to Latina/o Media* (eds. M.E. Cepeda and D.I. Casillas), 287–305. Abingdon, UK: Routledge.

Negrón-Muntaner, F. & Abbas, C. (2016). The Latino disconnect: Latinos in the age of media mergers. Retrieved June 10, 2019 from http://media.wix.com/ugd/73fa65_76876cf755864193a610131c0954daa1.pdf

Negrón-Muntaner, F. Abbas, C., Figueroa, L., & Robson, S. (2014). The Latino media gap: a report on the state of Latinos in US media. Retrieved June 10, 2019 from https://www.scribd.com/document/230135450/Latino-Media-Gap-Report-by-Frances-Negron-Muntaner-with-Chelsea-Abbas-Luis-Figueroa-and-Samuel-Robson

Nelson, J. (2017, January 24). Sofia Vergara opens up about marriage, Latina stereotypes, motherhood and dating. Retrieved June 10, 2019 from from http://people.com/tv/sofia-vergara-talks-stereotypes-motherhood-dating-marriage-joe-manganiello

Nguyen, H. (2018, April 4). How to save a show: from "Community" and "One Day at a Time" to "Timeless" and beyond. Retrieved June 10, 2019 from http://www.indiewire.com/2018/04/tv-shows-renwed-community-timeless-one-day-at-a-time-1201948940

Nishime, L. (2005). The Mulatto cyborg: imagining a multiracial future. *Cinema Journal 44* (2): 34–49.

Nishime, L. (2014). *Undercover Asian: Multiracial Asian Americans in Visual Culture*. Urbana: University of Illinois Press.

Noriega, C.A. (1992a). *Chicanos and Film: Representation and Resistance*. Minneapolis: University of Minnesota Press.

Noriega, C.A. (ed.) (1992b). *Chicanos and Film: Essays on Chicano Representation and Resistance*. Minneapolis: University of Minnesota Press.

O'Connor, A. (1991). The emergence of cultural studies in Latin America. *Mass Communication 8* (1): 60–73.

O'Malley, K. (2018, March 9). Selena Gomez "could have died" following kidney transplant, says BFF Francia Raisa. Retrieved June 10, 2019 from https://www.elle.com/uk/life-and-culture/culture/news/a42223/selena-gomez-complications-death-kidney-transplant-francia-raisa

Orr, C. (2016, November 23). *Moana* is a big, beautiful Disney smash. Retrieved June 10, 2019 from https://www.theatlantic.com/entertainment/archive/2016/11/moana-a-big-beautiful-disney-smash/508568

Ouellette, L. (2012). Citizen brand: ABC and the do good turn on television. In: *Commodity Activism* (eds. R. Mukherjee and S. Banet-Weiser), 57–75. New York: New York University Press.

ourmarvellousworld. (2011, September 24). Sofia Vergara (Letterman) [video file]. Retrieved June 10, 2019 from https://www.youtube.com/watch?v=AjrWwIAjuOw

Ouzounian, G. (2007). Contemporary radio art and spatial politics: the critical radio utopias of Anna Friz. *Radio Journal 5* (2/3): 129–142.

Pace, J. (2017). Exchange relations in the dark web. *Critical Studies in Media Communication 34* (1): 1–13.

Parédez, D. (2002). Remembering Selena, re-membering Latinidad. *Theatre Journal 54*: 63–84.

Parédez, D. (2009). *Selenidad: Selena, Latinos, and the Performance of Memory*. Durham: Duke University Press.

Paz, O. (1959). *El laberinto de la soledad*. Mexico City, Mexico: Fondo de Cultura Económica.

Pedersen, E. (2018, August 27). ALMA Awards revived & reimagined as Fuse Media inks media partnership with UnidosUS. Retrieved June 10, 2019 from https://deadline.com/2018/08/alma-awards-revived-reimagined-as-fuse-media-inks-media-partnership-with-unidosus-1202452786

Peña Ovalle, P. (2010). *Dance and the Hollywood Latina: Race, Sex and Stardom*. New Brunswick: Rutgers University Press.

People Staff. (1995, July 17). Charo. Retrieved June 10, 2019 from http://people.com/archive/charo-vol-44-no-3

Pérez-Firmat, G. (1994). *Life on the Hyphen: The Cuban-American Way*. Austin: University of Texas Press.

Persall, S. (March 3, 2016). Review: Disney's "Zootopia" is packed with cute critters – and conflicting mature themes. Retrieved June 10, 2019 from https://www.tampabay.com/incoming/review-disneys-zootopia-is-packed-with-cute-critters-8212-and-conflicting/2267805

Pew Foundation. (2014). Facts on US Latinos, 2015: statistical portrait of Hispanics in the United States. Retrieved June 10, 2019 from http://www.pewhispanic.org/2014/04/29/statistical-portrait-of-hispanics-in-the-united-states-2012/#language-spoken-at-home-and-english-speaking-ability-by-age-race-and-ethnicity-2012

Phillips, E. (2001). The global Disney audiences project: Disney across cultures. In: *Dazzled By Disney? The Global Disney Audiences Project* (eds. J. Wasko, M. Philips and E.R. Meehan). London, UK: Leicester University Press.

Phoenix Marketing International. (2016). Predicting the impact of celebrity endorsement: how effective are celebrity endorsements in pharmaceutical marketing? [poster presentation]. Phoenix M3 Global Research.

Projansky, S. (2014). *Spectacular Girls: Media Fascination and Celebrity Culture*. New York: New York University Press.

Projansky, S. and Valdivia, A.N. (2006). Feminism and/in mass media. In: *The SAGE Handbook of Gender and Communication* (eds. B.J. Dow and J.T. Wood). Thousand Oaks: Sage.

Puente, H. (2011). *The Promotion and Distribution of US Latino Films*. New York: Peter Lang.

Quijano, A. (1990). *Modernidad, Identidad, y Utopia en America Latina*. Quito, Peru: Editorial El Conejo.

Rajagopal, A. and Rao, A. (2016). *Media and Utopia: History, Imagination and Technology*. New York: Routledge.

Ramirez-Berg, C. (2002). *Latino Images in Film: Stereotypes, Subversion, and Resistance*. Austin: University of Texas.

Real, M. (1977). *Mass mediated culture: case studies in contemporary communications and culture*. Englewood Cliffs: Prentice-Hall.

Retis, J. (2014). Latino Diasporas and the Media. Interdisciplinary Approaches to Understand Transnationalism and Communications in Global Cities. In: *International Companion to Media Studies. Methods in Media Studies Volume*, F. Darling-Wolf (Ed.), A.N. Valdivia (General Editor). New York: Wiley-Blackwell.

Reyes, G. (2015, June 26). Charo and her adopted bull Manolo [video file]. Retrieved June 10, 2019 from https://www.youtube.com/watch?v=1X39Fyl0esA

Robehmed, N. (2015, October 28). Elizabeth Taylor's earnings: $20 million in 2015. Retrieved June 10, 2019 from https://www.forbes.com/sites/natalierobehmed/2015/10/28/elizabeth-taylors-earnings-20-million-in-2015

Roberts, S. (1993). "The Lady in the Tutti-Frutti Hat": Carmen Miranda, a spectacle of ethnicity. *Cinema Journal 32* (3): 3–23.

Robinson, K.H. (2005). Queerying gender: heteronormativity in early childhood education. *Australian Journal of Early Childhood 30* (2): 19–28.

Rodriguez, A. (1999). *Making Latino News: Race, Language, Class*. Thousand Oaks: Sage.

Rodriguez, C.Y. (2013, September 9). Disney producer "misspoke": "First Latina princess" isn't Latina. Retrieved June 10, 2019 from http://www.cnn.com/2012/10/25/showbiz/disney-sofia-not-latina

Rodriguez, R.T. (2017). X marks the spot. *Cultural Dynamics 29* (3): 202–213.

Rodriguez-Estrada, A.I. (2006). Lupe Velez (1908–1944). In: *Latinas in the United States: A Historical Encyclopedia* (eds. V. Ruíz and V. Sánchez Korrol), 793. Bloomington: Indiana University Press.

Rojas, I. (2013, March 23). 9 sitcoms that helped put Latinos on the map. Retrieved June 10, 2019 from http://abcnews.go.com/ABC_Univision/sitcoms-put-latinos-map/story?id=18785088#

Roman, Z. and McAllister, M.P. (2012). The brand and the bold: synergy and sidekicks in licensed-based children's television. *Global Media Journal 12* (20): 1–15.

Ross, A. (1999). *The Celebration Chronicles: Life, Liberty, and the Pursuit of Property Value in Disney's New Town*. New York: Ballantine Books.

Rowe, W. and Schelling, V. (1991). *Memory and Modernity: Popular Culture in Latin America*. London, UK: Verso.

Ruiz, M.V. (2002). Border narratives, HIV/AIDS, and Latina/o health in the United States: a cultural analysis. *Feminist Media Studies 2* (1): 81–96.

Ruíz, V. and Sánchez Korrol, V. (2006). *Latinas in the United States: A Historical Encyclopedia*. Bloomington: Indiana University Press.

Schiller, H.I. (1992). Not just the post-imperialist era. *Critical Studies in Mass Communication 8* (1): 13–28.

Scott, A.O. (2016, November 22). Review: "Moana," brave princess on a voyage with a chicken. Retrieved June 10, 2019 from https://www.nytimes.com/2016/11/22/movies/moana-review.html?referrer=google_kp

Scott, K. (2018, March 9). Selena Gomez's kidney transplant almost killed her, says donor friend. Retrieved June 10, 2019 from https://globalnews.ca/news/4072867/selena-gomezs-kidney-transplant-almost-killed-her

Seiter, E. (1995). *Sold Separately: Children and Parents in Consumer Culture*. New Brunswick: Rutgers University Press.

Shamma, T. (2001, October 11). From Ricky Ricardo to Dora: Latinos on television. Retrieved June 10, 2019 from https://www.npr.org/2011/10/11/141054903/from-ricky-ricardo-to-dora-latinos-on-television

Shaw, D. (2010). Transforming the national body: Salma Hayek and Frida. *Quarterly Review of Film and Video 27* (4): 299–313.

Shields Dobson, A. and Kanai, A. (2018). From "can-do" girls to insecure and angry: affective dissonances in young women's post-recessional media. *Feminist Media Studies* https://doi.org/10.1080/14680777.2018.1546206.

Shohat, E. (1991). Gender and culture of empire: toward a feminist ethnography of the cinema. *Quarterly Review of Film and Video 13* (1–3): 45–84.

Shohat, E. and Stam, R. (1995). *Unthinking Eurocentrism: Multiculturalism and the Media*. New York: Routledge.

Shome, R. (2016). When postcolonial studies meets media studies. *Critical Studies in Media Communication 33* (3): 245–263.

Shome, R. and Hegde, R.S. (2002a). Culture, communication, and the challenge of globalization. *Critical Studies in Media Communication 19* (2): 172–189.

Shome, R. and Hegde, R.S. (2002b). Postcolonial approaches to communication: charting the terrain, engaging the intersections. *Communication Theory 12* (3): 249–270.

Shuggart, H.A. (2007). Crossing over: hybridity and hegemony in the popular media. *Communication and Critical/Cultural Studies 4* (2): 115–141.

Sieczkowski, C. (2012, October 23). Princess Sofia is not Latina, says Disney. Retrieved June 10, 2019 from http://www.huffingtonpost.com/2012/10/23/disney-princess-sofia-not-latina_n_2005288.html

Silva, K. (2016). *Brown Threat: Identification in the Security State*. Minneapolis: University of Minnesota Press.

Smythe, D. (1977). Communications: blindspot of Western Marxism. *Canadian Journal of Political and Social Theory 1* (3): 1–27.

Sommer, D. (1991). *Foundational Fictions: The National Romances of Latin America*. Berkeley: University of California Press.

Spangler, T. (2017, January 19). Sofia Vergara, Luis Balaguer and Emiliano Calemzuk launch Latino digital media startup Raze. Retrieved June 10, 2019 from http://variety.com/2017/digital/news/sofia-vergara-raze-luis-balaguer-emiliano-calemzuk-1201962625

Susman, G. (2015, May 11). Why was Reese Witherspoon's "Hot Pursuit" so chilly at the box office? Retrieved June 10, 2019 from https://www.moviefone.com/2015/05/11/reese-witherspoon-hot-pursuit-box-office

Tapley, K. (2017, August 8). John Bailey elected president of the Motion Picture Academy. Retrieved June 10, 2019 from http://variety.com/2017/film/news/academy-elects-new-president-1202516814

Tasker, Y. (2011). *Enchanted* (2007) by postfeminism: gender, irony, and the romantic comedy. In: *Feminism at the Movies: Understanding Gender in Contemporary Popular Cinema* (eds. H. Radner and R. Stringer). New York: Routledge.

Tasker, Y. and Negra, D. (2007). Introduction: feminist politics and postfeminist culture. In: *Interrogating Postfeminism: Gender and the Politics of Popular Culture* (eds. D. Negra and Y. Tasker), 1–26. Durham: Duke University Press.

Taylor, P., Lopez, M.H., Martínez, J., & Velasco, G. (2012, April 3). When labels don't fit: Hispanics and their views of identity. Retrieved June 10, 2019 from http://www.pewhispanic.org/2012/04/04/when-labels-dont-fit-hispanics-and-their-views-of-identity

Thussu, D.K. (2006). Contra-flow in global media. *Media Asia 33* (3–4): 123–129.

Toomey, A. & Malkin, M. (2015, August 11). Rosie Perez did not quit The View early over Kelly Osbourne's controversial Latina comments: get the details. Retrieved June 10, 2019 from http://www.eonline.com/news/685299/rosie-perez-did-not-quit-the-view-early-over-kelly-osbourne-s-controversial-latino-comments-get-the-details

Toussaint, T. (2015, August 11). EXCLUSIVE: "Kiss my a**!" Rosie Perez QUITS The View early in heated spat with ABC execs after being forced to apologize over her anger at Kelly Osbourne's racist Latino remark. Retrieved June 10, 2019 from http://www.dailymail.co.uk/news/article-3192848/Kiss-Rosie-Perez-QUITS-View-early-heated-spat-ABC-execs-forced-apologize-anger-Kelly-Osbourne-s-racist-Latino-remark.html#ixzz4nKMUszVa

Trionfo, B. (2015, January 31). Family Nuance, by Salma Hayek. Retrieved June 10, 2019 from https://www.vanityfair.com/style/2011/09/family-nuance-by-salma-hayek

Trope, A. (2012). Mother Angelina: Hollywood philanthropy personified. In: *Commodity Activism: Cultural Resistance in Neoliberal Times* (eds. R. Mukherjee and S. Banet-Weiser), 154–173. New York: New York University Press.

Trujillo-Pagan, N. (2006). Carmen Miranda. In: *Latinas in the United States: A Historical Encyclopedia* (eds. V. Ruíz and V. Sánchez Korrol), 478–479. Bloomington: Indiana University Press.

Trujillo-Pagan, N. (2018). Crossed out by LatinX: gender neutrality and genderblind sexism. *Latino Studies 16* (3): 396–406.

Tuchman, G., Daniels, K.A., and Benet, J. (eds.) (1978). *Hearth and Home: Images of Women in the Mass Media*. New York: Oxford University Press.

Turnbull, S. (2010). Crime as entertainment: the case of the TV crime drama. *Continuum: Journal Of Media and Cultural Studies 24* (6): 819–827.

TV News Desk. (2016, November 28). Disney's ELENA AND THE SECRET OF AVALOR simulcast is 2016's no. 1 cable TV show in key demo. Retrieved June 10, 2019 from https://www.broadwayworld.com/bwwtv/article/Disneys-ELENA-AND-THE-SECRET-OF-AVALOR-Simulcast-is-2016s-No-1-Cable-TV-Show-in-Key-Demo-20161128

Umstead, R.T. (2018, March 28 [updated]). Disney Junior to intro Latina princess in "Sofia"; network to launch "Elena of Avalor" series in 2016. Retrieved June 10, 2019 from https://www.multichannel.com/news/disney-junior-introduce-latina-princess-sofia-first-387430

Valdivia, A.N. (1996). Rosie goes to Hollywood: the politics of representation. *Pedagogy/Cultural Studies 18* (2): 122–141.

Valdivia, A.N. (1998). Stereotype or transgression? Rosie Perez in Hollywood film. *The Sociological Quarterly 39* (3): 393–408.

Valdivia, A.N. (2000). *A Latina in the Land of Hollywood and Other Essays on Media Culture*. Tucson: University of Arizona Press.

Valdivia, A.N. (2004a). Latina/o communication and media studies today: an introduction. *The Communication Review 7*: 107–112.

Valdivia, A.N. (2004b). Latinas as radical hybrid: transnationally gendered traces in mainstream media. *Global Media Journal 3* (4).

Valdivia, A.N. (2005a). Film producers. In: *Oxford Encyclopedia on US Latinas and Latinos* (eds. S. Oboler and D. Gonzales). New York: Oxford University Press.

Valdivia, A.N. (2005b). Geographies of Latinidad: constructing identity in the face of radical hybridity. In: *Race, Identity, and Representation* (eds. W. Critchlow, G. Dimitriadis, N. Dolby and C. McCarthy). New York: Routledge.

Valdivia, A.N. (2005c). The location of the Spanish in Latinidad: examples from contemporary US popular culture. *Letras Femeninas 31* (1): 60–78.

Valdivia, A.N. (2008). *Latina/o Communication Studies Today*. New York: Peter Lang.

Valdivia, A.N. (2009a). *Latina/o Media Studies*. Cambridge, UK: Polity Press.

Valdivia, A.N. (2009b). Mixed race on Disney Channel: from Johnnie Tsunami to the Cheetah Girls. In: *Mixed Race Hollywood: Multiraciality in Film and Media Culture* (eds. M. Beltrán and C. Fojas). New York: New York University Press.

Valdivia, A.N. (2010). *Latina/os and the Media*. Cambridge, UK: Polity.

Valdivia, A.N. (2011). This tween bridge over my Latina girl back: the US mainstream negotiates ethnicity. In: *Mediated Girlhoods New Explorations of Girl's Media Culture*, vol. *10*, 93–109. New York: Peter Lang.

Valdivia, A.N. (2013). Amnesia and the myth of discovery: lessons from transnational and women of color communication scholars. *Critical/Cultural Studies in Communication 10* (2): 329–332.

Valdivia, A.N. (2015). Latina/os, media studies, and interdisciplinary implications. In: *Silent Discourses and Contents in the Spanish Teacher Education* (eds. F. Zolin-Vesz and L. Mendonça de Lima). Goiânia, Brazil: Editorial Universidade Federal de Goiás.

Valdivia, A.N. (2016). Implicit utopias and ambiguous ethnics: Latinidad and the representational promised land. In: *Routledge Companion to Latina/o Media Studies* (eds. I. Casillas and M.E. Cepeda). New York: Taylor & Francis.

Valdivia, A.N. (2017). Othering. In: *Keywords for Media Studies* (eds. L. Ouelette and J. Gary). New York: New York University Press.

Valdivia, A.N. (2018). Latina media studies. *Feminist Media Histories 4* (2): 101–106.

Valdivia, A.N. (Forthcoming). Digital utopias, Latina/o mediated realities. In: *Latin American Digital Studies* (eds. J.C. Rodriguez and H.D. Fernandez L'Hoeste). Gainesville: University Press of Florida.

Valdivia, A.N. and Curry, R. (1996). Xuxa at the Borders of Global TV: The Institutionalization and Marginalization of Brazil's Blonde Ambition. *Camera Obscura 13:2* (38): 29–59.

Vidal-Ortiz, S. (2016). Sofía Vergara: on media representations of Latinidad. In: *Race and Contention in Twenty First Century US Media* (eds. J.A. Smith and B.K. Thakore), 85–99. New York: Routledge.

Vidal-Ortiz, S. and Martínez, J. (2018). Latinx thoughts: Latinidad with an X. *Latino Studies 16* (3): 384–395.

Vora, S. (2013, November 20). Not your grandmother's skin care? Retrieved June 10, 2019 from https://www.nytimes.com/2013/11/21/fashion/New-beauty-lines-including-family-secrets-gain-popularity.html

Wagmeister, E. (2016, August 11). "Elena of Avalor" renewed for season 2 on Disney. Retrieved June 10, 2019 from from http://tvbythenumbers.zap2it.com/more-tv-news/elena-of-avalor-renewed-for-season-2-on-disney/

Washington, M. (2017a). Black/Asian hybridities: multiracial Asian Americans on *The Voice*. In: *The Routledge Companion to Asian American Media* (eds. V. Pham and L.K. Lopez). London, UK: Routledge.

Washington, M.S. (2017b). *Blasian Invasion: Racial Mixing in the Celebrity Industrial Complex*. Jackson: University Press of Mississippi.

Wasko, J. (2001). *Understanding Disney: The Manufacture of Fantasy*. Cambridge, UK: Polity.

Wasko, J. (2017). The Walt Disney Company. In: *Global Media Giants* (eds. B.J. Birkinbine, R. Gómez and J. Wasko). New York: Routledge.

Wasko, J. and Meehan, E.R. (2001). Dazzled by Disney? Ambiguity in ubiquity. In: *Dazzled By Disney? The Global Disney Audiences Project* (eds. J. Wasko, M. Philips and E.R. Meehan). London, UK: Leicester University Press.

Wasko, J., Phillips, M., and Meehan, E.R. (eds.) (2001). *Dazzled by Disney? The Global Disney Audiences Project*. London, UK: Leicester University Press.

Watson, M.R. and Anand, N. (2006). Award ceremony as an arbiter of commerce and canon in the popular music industry. *Popular Music 25* (1): 41–56.

Whitten, S. (2018, February 28). McDonald's reunites with Disney on Happy Meals after more than a decade apart. Retrieved June 10, 2019 from https://www.cnbc.com/2018/02/27/mcdonalds-serves-disney-branded-happy-meals-after-more-than-a-decade.html

Williams, A. (2016, July 20). 10 things you should know about Disney's newest princess, "Elena of Avalor." Retrieved June 10, 2019 from http://abcnews.go.com/Entertainment/10-things-disneys-newest-princess-elea-avalor/story?id=40716449

Wilson, J.A. (2012). Cosmopolitan stars, interactive audience labor, and the digital economy of global care. *Television and New Media 15* (2): 104–120.

Yamaguchi, A. (2015, July 20). Keynote speaker Herman Gray talks "precarious diversity." Retrieved June 10, 2019 from http://www.com.washington.edu/2015/06/keynote-speaker-herman-gray-talks-precarious-diversity/

Young, R. (1995). *Colonial Desire: Hybridity in Theory, Culture, and Race*. London, UK: Routledge.

Index

The Gender of Latinidad: Uses and Abuses of Hybridity, First Edition. Angharad N. Valdivia.
© 2020 John Wiley & Sons Ltd. Published 2020 by John Wiley & Sons Ltd.